How We Learn

In today's knowledge- and information-led society, concepts of lifelong learning have become crucial to both the formation of policy and practice and the individual experience of learning.

How We Learn deals with the fundamental issues of the processes of learning, critically assessing different types of learning and obstacles to learning. It also takes up a broad range of other important questions in relation to learning, such as learning and the body, modern research into learning and brain functions, self-perception, motivation, competence development, intelligence, learning style, learning in relation to gender, life age, teaching, school-based learning, net-based learning, workplace learning and educational politics.

This vital textbook provides a comprehensive introduction to both traditional learning theory and the newest international research into learning processes, while at the same time being an innovative contribution to a new and more holistic understanding of learning.

How We Learn examines all the key factors that help to create an holistic understanding of what learning actually is and how and why learning and non-learning take place. It is also a refreshing and thought-provoking piece of scholarly work incorporating new research material, new understandings and new points of view.

Knud Illeris is Professor of Lifelong Learning at the Learning Lab Denmark, the Danish University of Education.

How We Learn

Learning and non-learning in school and beyond

Knud Illeris

 Routledge
Taylor & Francis Group

LONDON AND NEW YORK

First published 1999 in Danish as Læring
by Roskilde University Press

Second edition published 2006

This English edition published 2007
by Routledge
2 Park Square, Milton Park, Abingdon, Oxon, OX14 4RN

Reprinted 2008

Simultaneously published in the USA and Canada
by Routledge
270 Madison Avenue, New York, NY 10016

Routledge is an imprint of the Taylor & Francis Group, an informa business

© 1999, 2006 Roskilde University Press; 2007 Knud Illeris

Typeset in Times New Roman by
Florence Production Ltd, Stoodleigh, Devon
Printed and bound in Great Britain by
Antony Rowe Ltd, Chippenham, Wiltshire

British Library Cataloguing in Publication Data
A catalogue record for this book is available from the
British Library

Library of Congress Cataloging in Publication Data
Illeris, Knud.
  How we learn: learning and non-learning in school and beyond/
  Knud Illeris.
      p. cm.
  Includes bibliographical references and index.
  1. Learning, Psychology of.   2. Cognitive learning.   3. Social
  learning.   I. Title.
  LB1060.I438 2007
  370.15'23—dc22   2007008400

ISBN 10: 0–415–43846–2 (hbk)
ISBN 10: 0–415–43847–0 (pbk)
ISBN 10: 0–203–93989–1 (ebk)

ISBN 13: 978–0–415–43846–9 (hbk)
ISBN 13: 978–0–415–43847–6 (pbk)
ISBN 13: 978–0–203–93989–5 (ebk)

Contents

Figures

Foreword

Writing this book has been both hard work and a great pleasure. Quite special conditions prevail when one wishes to communicate the essence of almost 40 years' work as a researcher, theoretician, writer and debater in the field of learning and education while simultaneously striving towards a product with broad appeal, that can be used and is challenging. My ambition has been to write a book that covers the field as widely as possible today in relation to the subject of learning, is up to date with the most recent developments in the area, and can be read and used by a circle of readers that range from students and future teachers at all levels to professionals in the fields of psychology, pedagogy and a broad range of education programmes.

More specifically this work may be seen as a re-writing of my book *The Three Dimensions of Learning*, published in Danish in 1999 and in English in 2002. But at the same time it includes a number of new topics and has a new and more distinct structure. For me personally, the 'old' book was a kind of voyage of discovery where I tried to make sense of a field that was large and complex. When I started on my journey, I had no idea of what I would find. This book, on the other hand, after a number of further studies and numerous discussions with many people in many countries is, rather, an attempt to pass on the essence of what I have now discovered and realised in a well-structured, clear, comprehensible and engaged form.

The book is thus, on the one hand, a type of textbook that examines all the sub-elements of significant interest for understanding what learning is and why and how learning and non-learning take place. On the other hand, it is a piece of scholarly work because it not only draws on texts in the field that are already available, but adds new material, new understandings and new points of view. But, first and foremost, it presents the subject on the basis of a certain general understanding, producing a whole that has not previously been presented and which is significantly more wide-ranging, more comprehensive and more varied than the draft presented in the first version. Approximately a quarter of the book comprises thoroughly revised sections of the 'old' book, a second quarter presents fresh examinations of topics that also formed part of this book, and about half of the text deals with completely new issues and contributions that I believe it important to include in order to give an adequate treatment.

I am very grateful to all the many students, teachers, researchers and others with whom I have been in contact during meetings, discussions and lectures, by email, letter and phone concerning all possible subjects relating to learning, and naturally also to my colleagues at Roskilde University, at Learning Lab Denmark and at the Danish University of Education. There are also many to whom I owe a special thanks.

First, Hans Siggaard Jensen, Director of LLD, who ensured that I had working conditions that have made it possible to write the book during 2005 and the beginning of 2006, and in this connection also Henrik Nitschke from LLD and Thomas Bestle from Roskilde University Press, who have enthusiastically involved themselves in the production and launching of the book.

Special thanks go to three teachers: Sanne Hansen from Zahle's College of Education, Gunnar Green from Blaagaard Teacher Training College, and Palle Bendsen of the Copenhagen Day and Evening College of Teacher Training, all of whom read the manuscript and made important comments, and to my colleagues Steen Høyrup and Bente Elkjær, who have given me valuable critique during our cooperation at LLD. Mia Herskind and Christian Gerlach from LLD have assisted me with the sections on corporality and brain research, respectively, and Per Fibæk Laursen from the Danish University of Education has provided me with tips for the section on intelligence. I also received important inspiration from Mads Hermansen, Copenhagen Business School, and Jens Berthelsen, University of Copenhagen.

The many international researchers and theoreticians with whom I have discussed learning over the years have been a very important source of support and inspiration. The most important have been Peter Allheit (Göttingen), Ari Antikainen (Joensuu), Chris Argyris (Harvard), Stephen Billett (Brisbane), David Boud (Sydney), Ralph Brockett (Tennessee), Stephen Brookfield (Minneapolis), Per-Erik Ellström (Linköping), Yrjö Engeström (Helsinki), Phil Hodkinson (Leeds), Peter Jarvis (Surrey), Michael Law (Hamilton, NZ), Thomas Leithäuser (Bremen), Victoria Marsick (New York), Sheran Merriam (Georgia), Jack Mezirow (New York), Wim Nijhof (Twente), Kjell Rubenson (Vancouver), Joyce Stalker (Hamilton, NZ), Robin Usher (Melbourne), Ruud van der Veen (New York), Susan Weil (Bristol), Etienne Wenger (California), Danny Wildemeersch (Leuven) and Lyle Yorks (New York). Most of them figure in the reference section of the book.

Finally, a very special thanks to my partner Birgitte Simonsen with whom I have worked for almost 30 years and with whom I have been able to discuss all possible academic subjects and questions, and who has, of course, read this book and made very important comments.

Finally, a couple of practical comments. As a scholarly work, the book has many more, especially Danish, references than I have found it appropriate to include in the English edition. A complete literature list can, however, be found at the website of Roskilde University Press: www.ruforlag.dk/laering.

Where there are references to persons who are deceased, as far as possible I have given the dates of birth and death on the first occasion the person is mentioned.

Direct translations of quotes to English have been taken from existing works where this was possible. The book was translated by Margaret Malone with whom I have enjoyed close cooperation for many years and whom I also thank for her great and dedicated efforts.

I hope my readers will enjoy reading the book and that they will come away enriched.

Knud Illeris
January 2007

Chapter 1

Introduction

This brief introductory chapter discusses the nature of learning and provides a definition of the concept as employed in the present book on the basis of an outlined example. This is followed by an overview of the structure of the book.

1.1 What is learning?

The first reaction of most people to the term *learning* is something to do with going to school. Basically, school is the institution established by society to ensure that all members of that society acquire the learning necessary for its maintenance and continuation. All normal young people and adults have spent more than 10,000 hours of their lives at school, some have spent much more (Rutter *et al.* 1979), and this has, of course, decisively and radically influenced our growing up.

The learning situation that most people typically recall is ordinary class teaching. Let me take an example.

We enter a mathematics lesson at a school. The children are learning to divide. The teacher is standing at the blackboard explaining how to do it. She writes a typical division sum on the board and demonstrates how to solve it. Or the form of teaching may be more group oriented. In this case, the children sit in groups and help one another to work out the problem, or call on the teacher if they need help.

In both cases most of the children participate in the activities as expected. They understand what it is all about and memorise the method. They might understand it immediately, or they might have to have it shown to them several times before they have really grasped it.

But there are also some pupils who have problems with this, and some who find it hard to concentrate. They might feel that what they have to learn is abstract or boring, or they have difficulty seeing what they can use it for. They think of other things that preoccupy them to a greater extent or are more meaningful for them. There can also be those who find it difficult to understand even though they try to follow. They might not have learned to multiply properly and, therefore, cannot understand division. Or they have a bigger problem with numeracy, which requires special treatment.

It is, after all, an ordinary experience from school that not everyone learns what is expected and some pupils forget some of it very quickly. Even though most children learn a lot at school and everyone learns something, there is no automatic link between teaching and learning. Later, when the class goes on to percentages, for example, there are more pupils who find it difficult, and even more difficult when they reach differential and integral mathematics.

What happens is that the pupils who are good at school build up their self-confidence and often also their desire to learn more, while those who find it difficult learn that they are not so good at school learning. For a significant number of children, an important part of what they learn at school is that they are bad at arithmetic and mathematics.

On the other hand, one also learns a great deal outside of school. Children have already learned a whole lot of fundamental things before they ever go to school, e.g. to speak one or more languages, and they know a great deal about the social contexts they are part of. And when they are of school age, they also learn a great amount outside of school hours through play and other activities. We all learn something throughout our whole lives. But part of what we learn can be wrong or take the nature of defence or blockings, or how to avoid defeats and uncomfortable situations.

These few brief examples and reflections should be sufficient to demonstrate that learning can be many and very different processes. Learning can appear positive or negative in nature, but for the individual it always has some purpose or other that has to do with managing life and its challenges. It is, thus, an extensive and very complex field that I will attempt to capture, analyse, describe and systematise in this book, at the same time as maintaining the field's complexity rather than trying to reduce it, as has, for example, previously been the aim when learning theoreticians have attempted to find a fundamental learning form or learning process (for example, Madsen 1966, pp. 64, 75, 95).

1.2 A definition of learning

The term learning is used very broadly and partly also with different meanings. Very generally, four different main meanings can be distinguished that most frequently occur when the term learning is used in a non-specific manner in everyday language.

1   First, the term learning can refer to the *outcomes of the learning processes* that take place in the individual. Learning, here, is used to mean what has been learned or the change that has taken place.

2   Second, the term learning can refer to the *mental processes* that take place in the individual and can lead to such changes or outcomes as covered by meaning 1. These may be termed learning processes, and it is typically these processes that learning psychology is concerned with.

3   Third, the term learning can refer to both the *interaction processes* between individuals and their material and social environment, which, directly or indirectly, are preconditions for the inner learning processes covered by meaning 2 (and which can lead to the learning covered by meaning 1).

4   Finally, the term learning is very often employed not only in everyday language, but also in official and professional contexts, more or less *synonymously with the term teaching*. This shows that there is a general tendency to confuse the terms for teaching and learning.

While meaning 4 is obviously inappropriate, the first three meanings all have significance and justification. But it can often be difficult to see which meaning is being referred to, and sometimes these matters can only be separated analytically and not in practice. To overcome these uncertainties, I will therefore define learning broadly as *any process that in living organisms leads to permanent capacity change and which is not solely due to biological maturation or ageing.*

My definition is deliberately very broad and open. Expressions such as 'any process', 'living organisms' and 'permanent capacity change' have been chosen to avoid introducing unnecessary limitations. What is crucial is that learning implies a change that is permanent to some extent or other, for example, until it is overlaid by new learning, or is gradually forgotten because the organism no longer uses it. It is also crucial that the change is not just a matter of maturation of potentials that are present in the organism in advance, even though such maturation might very well be a prerequisite for learning taking place.

The term 'organism' has been selected because it is not just human beings that can learn something, and many studies of animals have been of significance for understanding learning. However, in this book it is human learning that is at the centre, and the learning of other organisms is included only where it is relevant for the understanding of human learning.

It is also important to be aware that the chosen definition implies that a number of processes termed in words such as socialisation, qualification, competence development and therapy, come under the chosen learning concept and are regarded as special types of learning processes or as special angles for perceiving learning. The term 'development' is understood as an umbrella term for learning and maturation, and I thus regard the 'classical' conflict in psychology concerning whether learning comes before development or vice versa (see Vygotsky 1986 [1934], pp. 260ff.) to be mistaken. Learning is part of development.

In my opinion it is extremely important to work with such a broad, open learning understanding, in principle because it is impossible to maintain the borders between what learning is and what, for example, socialisation or therapy is, and in practice because it is only when all the elements have entered the picture that it is possible to discern important connections and patterns of interaction.

Finally, it should be pointed out that the definition also implies limitations and distortions that can, in turn, imply quantitative and/or qualitative restrictions in what is learned also being regarded as something one learns, for example, if the volume or nature of learning options becomes unmanageable or threatening.

1.3 The structure of the book

The theory or framework understanding of learning developed in this book falls into four parts.

The first part consists of this introductory chapter and the next chapter, which deals with the basis of the understanding of learning by connecting a number of different contributions drawn from psychology, biology, brain physiology and social science.

This is followed by the book's second and central section, which has to do with the structure and nature of learning. Chapter 3 sets up a model covering the two processes and three dimensions of learning: the content dimension, the incentive dimension and the interaction dimension, and in Chapter 4 a typology covering the four fundamental types of learning is elaborated. A further number of matters concerning learning are examined in Chapters 5, 6 and 7 on the basis of each of the three dimensions, and an overview of the most important matters of significance for learning as a whole are presented in Chapter 8.

The third part, consisting of Chapter 9 alone, is about the most important types of barriers to learning that exist today, i.e. what happens when intended learning does not occur or the learning takes a different course from what has been intended. These matters are only rarely dealt with in contributions on learning theory, but here they are regarded as just as important as the discussion concerning more, or less, successful learning.

The focus in the fourth part of the book is on a number of areas comprising some of the most important of the many different conditions influencing the nature, course and outcome of learning. In Chapter 10 this concerns the learner's different types of preconditions including dispositions, abilities and intelligence, learning style, gender and social background. Chapter 11 deals with learning through the life course and at the different life ages. In Chapter 12 learning is viewed in relation to the most important practice fields or learning spaces: everyday learning, school learning, learning in working life, net-based learning and learning in activities that interest the learner. In Chapter 13 the subject is learning in connection with different types of pedagogical organisation and political conditions. Finally, Chapter 14 sums up the main points of the framework developed and places the many different contributions and authors who have been discussed in relation to the learning model.

1.4 Summary

The most important matters in this introductory chapter can be summarised in the idea that learning is a very complex and many-sided matter including 'any process that in living organisms leads to permanent capacity change and which is not solely due to biological maturation or ageing'. This definition implies that processes such as socialisation, qualification, competence development and therapy are regarded as special types of learning processes or special angles from which learning is viewed. The definition also implies that limitations and other matters that can mean a narrowing or distortion of what is learned are also regarded as something one learns. The concept of 'development' is understood as an umbrella term for learning and biological maturation.

Moreover, the chapter includes a structuring of the topic of learning and of this book in four main areas: first, an understanding of the basis of learning; second, an understanding of the structure of learning, including three dimensions and four fundamental learning types; third, an understanding of the barriers that can lead to intended learning not taking place; and fourth, that learning is influenced by a number of different conditions of an individual, social and societal nature.

Chapter 2

The basis of the understanding of learning

Chapter 2 deals with the different matters forming the basis of the understanding of learning in this book. These are the basic psychological, biological, brain and sociological conditions of learning. It is emphasised that all these areas and their interaction must be involved in a comprehensive understanding of learning.

2.1 The various sources of the understanding of learning

The broad understanding and definition of learning outlined in Chapter 1 means that many different sources must be taken into consideration if the whole complexity of human learning is to be understood.

Learning has traditionally been understood first and foremost as a psychological matter, and learning psychology is one of the most classical disciplines of psychology. But other psychological disciplines must also be involved, such as developmental psychology, cognitive psychology, personality psychology and social psychology.

In recent years, however, understanding of learning has also been taken up to a considerable extent quite outside of what we traditionally understand as psychology. This has taken place, on the one hand, on a biological basis in connection with understanding the body and brain research, and, on the other hand, on a social science basis, first and foremost in the grey area between sociology and social psychology, but also socially more broadly and right into national economy. This applies, for example, to measures to strengthen adult learning and lifelong learning with a view to economic growth and competitiveness.

In addition, within both psychology and the areas mentioned there exist different fundamental views or 'schools' that perceive the basis of learning differently. For many years, from around the beginning of the twentieth century and up to the 1980s, behaviourist psychology was dominant in research on learning, in the USA especially. But in Europe in particular there have also been many other competing basic views such as Gestalt psychology, the constructivist and the cultural historical. In the USA in the 1950s and 1960s humanistic psychology, especially, appeared as an alternative, and the Freudian or psychoanalytical view also implies a special understanding of learning. In so-called critical theory or the 'Frankfurt School' this latter psychoanalytical approach is combined with a Marxist-oriented perception of society.

I will return to this many times later in the book. What is important here is to point out that it is a fundamental view in the book that each of these academic fields and schools can have something important to contribute to a satisfactory holistic understanding. From the point of view of theory of science, a crosscutting approach such as this has often been regarded as extremely negative and suspicious, not least within psychology with its many competing schools. It has derogatorily been labelled 'eclectic', i.e. incoherent or with no clear, well-defined foundation.

However, it has always been a fundamental point of departure for me that it is impossible to arrive at an adequate understanding of the extensive and complex field of learning without relating to the results achieved in so many scholarly approaches. A great deal of energy has been wasted in the field of psychology on the different schools waging war with one another instead of working together and trying to find points of contact.

But the prerequisite for working consistently on such a basis is that a general frame can be set up as a starting point in relation to which the various contributions can be viewed, so that a coherent and well-defined foundation is, nonetheless, present to be built on. I attempt to construct such a frame in Chapter 3, and on this basis a great number of different contributions will be included, assessed and processed. In fact, the work on which this book builds is, to a high degree, in the nature of an examination of a great number of different understandings of learning which, taken together, have proved able to fill out a common frame of understanding which has been clarified and refined on the basis of the impact of the different contributions (see also Illeris 2002).

Before I turn to sketching this frame, however, in the rest of this chapter I will outline the main lines about the grounding of the understanding of learning in the psychological, the biological, the brain physiological and the sociological angles of approach, respectively.

2.2 Learning and psychology

Traditionally, psychology is first and foremost the science of human behaviour in the broadest sense. The behaviourist school has, in principle, limited itself to behaviour that can be registered directly but, nonetheless, learning psychology has, as mentioned, been a key discipline in behaviourist psychology even though learning processes are not immediately observable.

What can be observed is a part of the results of the learning processes – for example, that a child can manage a certain division sum.

But can one then conclude that the child has, in general, also understood what division is and the contexts in which it is relevant to concern oneself with division? And what about the child's emotions in this connection? The child might express joy or satisfaction if the sum is correct. But how are joy and satisfaction to be measured, how do such emotions influence learning, and how can we know whether these emotions are due only to the correct sum, or are other matters also involved? And what is the subjective value and application value of what is learned? Is the child going to remember what he or she has learned and will it be used outside of school?

Happily, other psychological schools go much further than immediately observable behaviour, and in general psychology can, perhaps, best be characterised as a science of experience. It has to do with description, systematisation and explanation of our experience of what people do and say and think etc. in all possible situations and contexts, both in everyday life and in special situations, and it also includes observations of animals in various situations. The volume of data available is thus limitless, because there seems to be no limit to what people can try to learn.

Nevertheless, there are some fundamental matters to which one always must relate when working with learning or other psychological issues. First, the human being is a biological creature born with certain specific possibilities and limitations. While there are considerable individual variations, there is also a great deal that we have in common, and there are matters that lie completely outside of our scope. For example, we cannot learn to run as fast as a panther, there are sound waves we cannot hear, etc. In other words we are limited by what our bodies and brains can achieve.

The second fundamental matter is that we live in a physical and social environment. We have to enter into interaction with this environment, we can play a part in influencing and changing it, but we cannot place ourselves outside of it. Even if one tries to completely isolate oneself, one will be influenced by the fact that that is what one is doing.

For these reasons psychology is also, by necessity, a science of how human beings in all dimensions relate, and can relate, within and in relation to the possibilities and limitations set by the organism and the environment. Understanding learning must, naturally, also relate to these existential conditions.

2.3 Learning, biology and the body

When learning is studied as a psychological phenomenon, the body can easily seem to be a sort of case that is only included if what is to be learned is wholly or partly bodily in nature, for example, when one is learning to walk, swim or cycle. Learning is primarily understood as a mental affair, and the bodily aspect is only included in special cases.

But, in fact, almost the opposite is the case. Like other mental processes, learning is something that is based in the body, and what we call mental is something that has emerged together with the development of human beings and their predecessors over millions of years. Primitive creatures can also learn, but we do not attribute any psychic or mental life to them.

In human beings, learning primarily takes place through the brain and the central nervous system, which are specialised parts of the body, and if one wishes to approach an understanding of the way in which our learning potential has developed and functions, one must go beyond the division between body and psyche, between the bodily and the mental, which has been so central in the understanding of the Western world for centuries.

The French philosopher, René Descartes (1596–1660), who formulated the famous precept 'I think therefore I am' ('Cogito, ergo sum') already in the seventeenth century (Descartes 1967 [1637]), is often mentioned as the classical example of this Western understanding. The precise meaning of this sentence has subsequently been the subject of much discussion: for example, the well-known Norwegian historian of philosophy Arne Næss is of the opinion that the translation from Latin should, rather, be 'I experience' or 'I am somewhat aware' rather than 'I think' (Næss 1963 [1962], p. 143). But what is crucial in this connection is that Descartes refers to the mental aspect as what is central to human existence, raised above the physical and the emotional, and it has precisely been such a fundamental understanding that has been dominant in the Western world.

Charles Darwin's (1809–1892) theory about man's descent in 'Origin of Species' (Darwin 1958 [1859]) created the basis for another approach, and, at the end of the nineteenth century, William James (1842–1910) and Sigmund Freud (1856–1939), two of the greatest pioneers of scientific psychology, took their point of departure in the bodily embedding of the psychological in the final analysis (James 1890; Freud 1895).

Later, it was not least Russian so-called cultural historical psychology (see section 5.3) that took up this thread. In the 1930s Aleksei Leontjev (1903–1979), especially, worked with the way in which man's mental capacity gradually emerged on the basis of the challenges it met with. This work was only published in a collected form in 1959 (Leontjev 1981 [1959]). According to the cultural historical school, the use of tools is a particularly important function. These tools are of a quite different character in people than in the few animal species that make use of something similar. People can, themselves, develop and refine their tools, and today this has led to technological development which, to a quite fantastic extent, enables us to master nature, but which at the same time, by virtue of this very fact, is well on the way to undermining the natural basis on which the whole rests. But the cultural historical understanding also regards language, cultural forms and the like, as tools we make use of in connection with learning.

Since then many other researchers have continued this approach, and today a whole branch of psychology exists that calls itself evolutionary psychology and works with this area (e.g. Buss 1999; Gaulin and McBurney 2001).

Others have worked more directly with the link between the body and the mental functions. For example, many relaxation therapists and bodywork therapists work on understanding and relieving physical tensions and inappropriate patterns of movement, and developing appropriate physical balances and bodily functions on the basis of understandings in which body and psyche are parts of an integrated context. This typically takes place either on a phenomenological (experience-oriented) basis that goes back to the French philosopher and psychologist Maurice Merleau-Ponty (1908–1961) with a starting point in body experience and body competence (Merleau-Ponty 1962 [1945]), or on a psychoanalytical basis with roots that refer directly to Sigmund Freud's own work or that of some of his followers, not least Austrian Wilhelm Reich (1897–1957) and, later, American Alexander Lowen, with a focus on overcoming the 'character armour' that can function as a barrier, or protection, against, for example, very many learning opportunities (e.g. Lowen 1967; Reich 1969a [1933]; Lowen and Lowen 1977). Mention should also be made of French-Chilean biologist Francisco Varela (1946–2001) who, with references to both Merleau-Ponty and Freud, has written about the mental as a function of the bodily ('The embodied mind', Varela et al. 1991).

Based on such approaches, it has been pointed out time and again that learning research in the Western world tends to overlook the physical elements in learning, and that learning is not only a rational matter but also builds on the bodily functions and can 'fix itself in the body' and be expressed through, for instance, bodily postures, patterns of movement, gestures and breathing.

There are many facets here, from the targeted learning of certain physical skills to more uncertain 'feelings' and more or less automatised bodily functions. It is important to maintain that these bodily aspects are the foundation that, in spite of all later developments and overlays, still emerges in our experiences, behaviour and learning and plays a greater role than we in the Western world tend to think.

In our society there is a constant, unmistakable tendency to turn the situation upside down and place the bodily side of learning as a kind of supplement to 'real' learning that is mental and rational in nature, instead of as a prerequisite and basis of this learning, both in the history of human development and the personal development of the individual. British brain researchers Mark Solms and Oliver Turnbull thus state – in line with other modern brain researchers – that, 'from the viewpoint of neurophysiology all "life events" are ultimately mediated (registered and translated) by bodily events' (Solms and Turnbull 2002, p. 233).

The presence of the body in learning is naturally most clear during the first years of life, and this has caused the well-known Swiss biologist, psychologist and epistemologist Jean Piaget (1896–1980), among others, to term the first stage in the intellectual development of the child the psychomotoric, i.e. the psychic-movement stage (e.g. Piaget 1967 [1964]).

If we return to the school situation described in the introduction, learning to divide, for example, would, on the face of it, seem to be a 'purely' mental function. It is a case of manipulating numbers that are only present as words and other symbols. Nevertheless, the bodily foundation is part of this situation in many ways.

In the first place, it is necessary that the child's brain has developed normally in the different areas that play a part in such learning. If this is not the case, acalculia, or 'number blindness', could be present, making the learning difficult or even impossible. Or there could be physical problems to do with the ability to concentrate or communicate.

In the second place, the body must be sufficiently in balance that it has enough energy to become engaged in learning rather than having to deal with countering an imbalance. For example, if one is hungry or tired, or ill or in pain, this can make school learning more difficult or even prevent it to a high degree. Or it could be a case of bad humour, sorrow, worry, nervousness or another form of mental imbalance that manifests itself in the body as unease or tension. Finally, in the school situation it can typically be because the children have had to sit quietly and concentrate on the subject matter for so long that they simply need to use their bodies.

In the third place, small children especially will feel the urge to 'physicalise' learning more directly in an arithmetic situation, typically by counting on their fingers or by making the learning content visible in another way, for example, when dividing by having a certain number of balls, apples or other objects that can be placed in different piles where number and quantity can be directly sensed.

In the fourth place, problems in managing the situation, or satisfaction in having calculated correctly will also manifest themselves physically as a kind of discomfort or well-being that can, in turn, influence the attitude to learning.

All these matters are, naturally, quite elementary. Nevertheless, they are important, not least in a society where more and more learning is an unavoidable condition of life, and one must therefore learn to learn, i.e. learn to manage and economise one's own learning. At the same time these physical matters are part of a constant interaction with motivation, which is also a part of learning and is grounded in the body, and which has the effect that the different bodily interruptions can be pushed into the background when one is highly motivated for the learning in hand, but would become more urgent if the motivation were low.

In the following, when I try to develop a great number of different matters in connection with learning in more detail, I will naturally not be able to include these basic bodily matters the whole time. But it is important to be clear about the fact that they always matter, and in contexts where the bodily factor has some special significance or other I will include it directly. There will also be a great number of references to brain functions, which are also a part of physicality.

2.4 Learning and brain functions

The brain and central nervous system is, of course, part of the body. The reason that I nonetheless place it in a separate section is because this part of the body has some quite special and very extensive functions in connection with learning. It is here, so to speak, that the individual's learning processes take place, whether they are conscious or unconscious.

Brain research has developed explosively in recent years and, on the background of advanced new technology, has been able to make an important contribution to understanding the way in which functions such as learning, thinking and memory work. I myself am merely a spectator to this development, and in the following I draw in particular on some of the best-known works by American brain researchers, especially Antonio Damasio (1994, 1999), Elkhonon Goldberg (2001, 2005), Joseph LeDoux (2002), British Simon Baron-Cohen (2003) and Mark Solms and Oliver Turnbull (2002), and German Henning Scheich *et al.* (Scheich 2002; Elger *et al.* 2004).

It should, however, be mentioned here and now that even though brain research has made colossal progress, it is as yet far from being able to give exhaustive answers to the more advanced brain functions, including learning. Its particular contribution is in a quite general and a very specific area, respectively. In the general area, the research can present a lot of results about the parts and centres in the brain that are active in different contexts, what the different centres play a part in and how impulses move between the different centres. In the specific area research can tell quite precisely what happens when impulses are transferred between the individual brain cells in the electrochemical circuit within which the brain processes move – *inter alia* about the different so-called 'neurotransmitters', i.e. the chemical substances that further and inhibit transfer between the brain cells in different contexts.

But the human brain contains something between ten and 100 billion brain cells (the figures given in the literature vary considerably), many of which are highly specialised, and each cell is directly connected with up to 10,000 other cells through several billion so-called synapses or nerve cell connections (Scheich 2002). This gives almost endless possibilities for different networks and circuits, and even if the individual never even approaches the realisation of all these possibilities, the complexity of our brains towers above what even the most advanced computers can perform. Therefore, there also exists a large 'middle ground' between the two areas mentioned above. This, first and foremost, has to do with the colossal number of different circuits that make up the neurological basis of our thoughts, emotions, experiences, understandings, consciousness etc., and which seem completely impossible to map even if some day we were to acquire the kind of technology that was able to do so (Elger *et al.* 2004).

Nevertheless, in recent years brain research has delivered some results which, in important ways, can supplement and correct existing psychological understandings, in the area of learning, among others. The most crucially significant discovery in this connection is probably that in a normal, healthy brain, what we usually term 'reason' cannot function independently of what we call 'emotions' – and thus that the classical Western and scientific ideal of 'pure reason' is an illusion (as German philosopher Immanuel Kant (1724–1804), although on a somewhat different basis, was hinting at more than 200 years ago in his 'Critique of pure reason', Kant 2002 [1781]).

In the few cases where brain damage has cut the connection between the most important brain centres for 'reason' and 'emotions', respectively, we see individuals who may have retained their reason or intelligence, but can only use it in very inappropriate ways because it is not linked to the regulations carried out by the emotions. This leads to, among other things, very great problems concerning decision-making and social interaction, which are two areas where the emotional corrective to 'reason' plays a decisive role. It is, *inter alia*, this discovery that has led the well-known Portuguese-American brain researcher Antonio Damasio to name one of his pioneering books *Descartes' Error* (Damasio 1994) – because, as already mentioned, Descartes is the classical exponent of the understanding of reason as the core of what makes us human beings.

Brain research fundamentally understands the mental functions, including learning, as a link between the body and the environment that enables the organism to react appropriately to the changing environment. In human beings this link has been decisively refined with the development of functions such as language, thought, consciousness and the self, everything that Leontjev (1981 [1959]) called 'the higher mental functions', which only exist as initial stages in the most developed primates and do not exist at all in other animals.

With respect to learning, every single learning process has its own special course that takes place in the form of certain electrochemical circuits among thousands of brain cells involved in different areas and centres of the brain. (The circuits are called electrochemical because they are electrically mediated within the individual cell, while special chemical substances called transmitters mediate the transmissions between the cells.)

Here, I shall very briefly try to present what can be involved in a quite ordinary learning process in the human brain in order to give an impression of what I regard as some important matters in the complex pattern. However, I do this with the clear reservation that it is a radically simplified account, that it by no means applies to all learning processes, and that it expresses my own selection from the many sources presenting different scientific discoveries and assumptions.

A learning process can typically start by the individual experiencing some impulses from the environment through the senses. There will often be simultaneous impulses in different sense modalities – e.g. seeing some event or other and simultaneously hearing what is said. Each of the senses forms a number of 'images' on the basis of these impulses (the concept of images is not used for visual pictures only but also for other sensory impressions, e.g. 'sound images'). These pictures or impressions are mediated on to the 'working memory' or 'short-term memory' (located in the frontal lobes of the brain above the eyes and much further developed in human beings than in even the highest primates). The double term for this centre is because it functions as both a very short-term memory and as the absolutely key coordination centre, which Goldberg calls 'The executive brain' (Goldberg 2001) and which controls our thinking, decision-making processes and everything else that forms what we think of as our 'common sense'.

The mediation from the senses to the working memory takes place simultaneously via two channels, partly through the central part of the brain, which contains the most important emotional centres, and partly bypassing these centres (Damasio 1994). In this way the working memory receives impulses that reproduce the 'pure' sensory impressions and impulses that reproduce the sensory impressions together with the emotions activated by the event. The emotional impulses come a little before the other impulses, and immediate emotional reactions can occur in this ultra-short moment: one may react with aggression before one 'has had a chance to think', or one becomes terrified and 'stiffens'.

It is important that the different impulses received by the working memory have also been 'filtered' along the way through connections with the 'long-term memory' and thus have been influenced by 'memories' which the brain immediately and subjectively 'finds relevant'. It should, in addition, be mentioned that what is called the 'long-term memory' is not in the nature of an enormous archive or the like, but consists of 'traces' or 'engrams' from previous circuits. We do not know very much about how the brain 'finds out' which traces to activate among the millions of memories that each of us has acquired, and how it finds them. Sometimes the traces can also be more or less wiped out, i.e. we cannot, or only vaguely can 'recall' what we need, or we 'remember' it only partially or mistakenly. But in most cases we are able to immediately activate what we know and feel of subjective significance for interpreting and applying the impulses we receive.

This takes place in the working memory in a fraction of a second as a combination or 'deliberation' of the different new impulses in interaction with relevant re-activated imprints of earlier experience, memories, emotions, understandings and the like, and makes the individual able to react on this basis. The reaction can be extrovert in the form of action; it can also be introvert both in the shape of changes in the body and in that a print of the event with the associated emotions and reactions fix themselves in the long-term memory and thus constitute the impulse to the learning that can later be recalled and activated in connection with relevant new events or situations.

From this simplified description it is particularly important to note that the impulses we receive are coupled together with our emotions (which reflect both our current mental and bodily situation and mood and relevant emotional 'memories', e.g. about the persons who take part in the event and the content area involved) and with the results of relevant earlier learning or experience as the foundation of both our reaction (including the judgement process that can be called a 'decision') and the lessons we learn from the situation.

It is important to point out that the long-term memory referred to is in the nature of 'traces' of an electrochemical circuit. One must imagine that these traces are thematically organised in some way or other (reference can be made here to the psychological concept of schemes, to which I return in section 4.2), so that there is a form of order or systematisation, following which they can be activated. At any rate, it is the case that the more frequently a certain trace has been activated, the greater is the probability of the trace being re-activated, i.e. that one 'recalls' the experience or knowledge or understanding that the trace represents. On the other hand, the longer the time that passes since the trace was last activated, the greater is the risk that it is weak, imprecise or has completely disappeared, i.e. has been 'forgotten'.

One must also imagine that the traces are part of connections that enable certain impulses to trigger certain associations, i.e. that we automatically put impulses in connection with memories that we subjectively 'find relevant' in precisely the given context.

It should, furthermore, be mentioned that the process outlined here is the specifically human learning process. Different animals' learning will correspond to part of this process according to how highly developed their brains are. The special developmental history of human beings is reflected in the special structure of the brain in that, generally speaking, the human brain is divided into three parts which developed consecutively.

Furthest back, and the oldest part from the point of view of development, is the brainstem (a continuation of the spine) and the hindbrain. This is where sensory impressions are received from the environment along with impulses that reproduce the state of the body, and a coupling takes place so that the functions of the body are regulated in relation to the environment, including basic functions such as breathing, heartbeat, and the maintenance of the chemical balance of body fluids. This part of the brain has also been called the 'reptilian brain', because it largely corresponds to the brains that reptiles have.

The middle part of the brain contains, first and foremost, a number of centres that have to do with processing of an emotional nature. In this connection emotions must be understood as important regulation mechanisms for security in the face of threatening situations (e.g. fear and aggression) and the carrying out of life-preserving functions (e.g. hunger and sex). The emotions regulate behaviour at a higher level than the reflexes of the reptilian brain, and the midbrain gives mammals, for example, a number of functional possibilities of a more varied kind than in reptiles. In addition, the operative centres of the long-term memory are situated in this part of the brain – while the above-mentioned 'traces' of earlier circuits that represent the content of the memory spread over larger areas.

Finally, there is the front part of the brain, which is only fully developed in humans, and which includes *inter alia* the area I have called the working memory in the above. This part of the brain makes possible what we normally term reason and consciousness – which are to be understood here as even more subtle regulation mechanisms enabling human beings to react to their environment in far more advanced ways than all other creatures, and, to a certain extent, to know and manage what they do.

The three parts of the brain are closely interrelated. New functions have emerged throughout the development process of the species in continuation of the already existing functions, which have been maintained as necessary and 'supportive' of the new functions. It is for this reason that the older functions can continue to function if the newer functions are damaged, while the more recent functions cannot manage without the older ones. Damage to the frontal lobes can strongly reduce a person's abilities, but damage to the brainstem is fatal.

From the point of view of learning this means that we can learn at different levels, from quite unconscious reflexes over more or less automatic patterns of thinking and acting to quite conscious and targeted controlled learning processes.

Finally, it should be mentioned that the brain has considerable plasticity; for example, if parts of the brain are damaged, other parts can wholly or partially take over their functions. Nor do different peoples' brains have exactly the same pattern. If, for instance, one uses a lot of time and energy on certain activities, these can take up large areas of the brain. The brain is constantly undergoing changes and developments that depend on what it is used for. The plasticity is generally larger, however, the younger we are.

2.5 Unconscious learning and tacit knowledge

The issue of the relationship between learning and consciousness in connection with learning is a continuation of the questions concerning the significance of the functions of the body and the brain. The immediate notion – and that on which learning research has very largely focused – is, naturally, that we are conscious of our own learning, that when one has learned something, then it is not only something one knows or can understand, but one also knows that one knows what one knows.

Together with language, consciousness is one of the most crucial differences between human beings and animals (although the higher primates may have some preliminary stages of what we call consciousness). My cat knows perfectly well that it is going to be fed when I fetch a certain bowl from the fridge – but it does not know that it knows it. I will not go into any more detail here on the subject of consciousness. Information about this is available from the most recent brain research, *inter alia* in the work of Antonio Damasio in his book *The Feeling of What Happens* (Damasio 1999).

In the context of this book, however, it is important to be aware of the fact that we can learn something without being conscious of it – all of us probably do this every single day. The most well-known example is probably advertisement spots in the cinema or on television that are so short as not to really be noticed but nevertheless exert influence that can have an impact on people. But this is merely a special case in relation to the volume of events and experiences we are constantly exposed to and register without being conscious of it.

It is well known that Freud was the first to deliberately and scientifically deal with the unconscious, but he was only indirectly interested in learning. Traditional learning psychology, on the other hand, concerned itself directly with learning, but was not oriented towards the unconsciousness even though practitioners worked with animals, and the production of saliva that Pavlov's famous dogs 'learned' to associate with the ringing of a bell is just as unconscious as the production of saliva in human beings when food is placed on the table.

The non-conscious side of learning would thus seem only seriously and somewhat indirectly to have loomed on the learning research horizon with the work of Hungarian-British philosopher Michael Polanyi (1891–1976) on 'the tacit dimension' (Polanyi 1966) and his 'tacit knowledge' concept which is that one can be in possession of knowledge even though this knowledge neither has, nor can be given, a linguistic form. It is also possible to distinguish between 'actual tacit knowledge' which in principle can be articulated, and 'tacit knowledge in principle', which is beyond the limits of exact language (more or less parallel to Freud's concepts of 'the preconscious' and 'the unconscious').

Another way of thematising these matters appeared later with the concepts concerning 'emotional intelligence' (Goleman 1995; see section 6.4), while Danish psychotherapist Ole Vedfelt more directly employs the expression 'unconscious intelligence' and writes, for example as follows, that:

> we can unconsciously store experiences to do with both understanding and emotion in our memories over a lengthy period, and that the unconscious intake of information is far faster and more extensive than the conscious intake. This is shocking for our common sense because it suggests that our ego and consciousness are like a small boat on a gigantic ocean of unconscious information.
>
> (Vedfelt 2002, pp. 28f.)

Nevertheless, it is only modern brain research that is now fully succeeding in establishing a general understanding of the fact that it is actually very inappropriate and unscientific that for so many years 'sensible people' have not really been willing to accept the colossal extent and significance of the unconscious processes – and also in the area of learning. For example, Antonio Damasio writes:

> The unconscious, in the narrow meaning in which the word has been etched in our culture, is only a part of the vast amount of processes and contents that remain nonconscious . . . . In fact, the list of the 'not-known' is astounding. Consider what it includes:
>
> 1   all the fully formed images to which we do not attend;
> 2   all the neural patterns that never become images;
> 3   all the dispositions that were acquired through experience, lie dormant, and may never become an explicit neural pattern;
> 4   all the quiet remodelling of such dispositions and all their quiet renetworking – that they may never become explicitly known; and
> 5   all the hidden wisdom and know-how that nature embodied in innate, homeostatic dispositions.
>
> Amazing, indeed, how little we ever know.
>
> (Damasio 1999, p. 228)

And so Damasio is back at what makes all this quite obvious. Everything is unconscious to the animals, and one of humankind's most transcending jumps in the history of evolution was the formation of what we call the consciousness. As yet brain science can only hypothesise about the mode of functioning of the consciousness. How could one imagine that we as a species have just taken the whole universe of unconscious biological modes of functioning built up over billions of years along into this eminent new construction? It is already quite fantastic that we should have been able to develop such a consciousness. To imagine that it could cover and master our whole field of functioning seems quite unrealistic, to put it mildly.

I will only rarely touch on unconscious learning in the following as research on this is rather limited. In many cases it forms part of an inseparable network with conscious learning, and perhaps without any significant differences existing other than the precise level of consciousness. However, psychoanalytical research, *inter alia*, confirms that unconscious learning of far-reaching significance for our understanding, our identity and our behaviour also takes place. This side of learning, like that to do with the body and the brain, will only be included in the following where special grounds exist.

2.6 Learning and society

Learning is not, however, something that only takes place in the single individual. On the contrary, learning is always embedded in a social and societal context that provides impulses and sets the frames for what can be learned and how. For example, there is a difference in the nature of the learning that takes place in school, the learning that takes place in working life, and the learning that takes place in everyday life outside of school and work – because the different contexts give learning essentially different fundamental conditions (see Chapter 12).

While learning theory formerly almost exclusively concerned itself with the individual side of learning, over the last 15 to 20 years there has been increasing emphasis on the social and societal contexts of learning. This has, *inter alia*, taken place with concepts such as 'social learning' and 'situated learning' (which I treat in more detail in Chapter 7), and most notably in the psychological school of understanding that calls itself 'social constructionism' (e.g. Gergen 1994; Burr 1995). In contrast to the one-sided focus of traditional learning psychology on individual learning, social constructionism claims that learning is something taking place *between* people and, therefore, is social in nature.

It is, however, a fundamental understanding of this book that learning has both an individual and a social side (this will be further elaborated in Chapter 3). This implies that both the individual orientation of traditional learning psychology and modern social orientation must be incorporated, but neither of them can, alone, offer a complete and 'correct' understanding, and formulating the problem as either–or is a fundamentally flawed view.

But it is no coincidence that in particular the social and societal side of learning and thus the context in which learning takes place has received more attention in recent years. This has taken place in parallel and integrated with swiftly increasing societal significance being attributed to learning, and the fact that this especially is about learning that takes place in certain, mainly institutional and thereby 'unnatural' contexts.

If we go back a couple of hundred years or look at existing so-called 'primitive' societies, almost all learning takes place as an integrated part of everyday life, where no distinction is made between work and spare time. Learning typically takes place, for example, in the daily life of the family, through children's play and through instruction or training in different household and daily work skills.

But with the industrial revolution, the breakthrough of capitalism and the Enlightenment in the eighteenth century and up through the nineteenth, more and more societal work was changed into wage labour, which was set apart from the rest of life in time and place and required special qualifications with respect both to knowledge and skills and to being able to sell oneself as labour to an employer who has the right to decide what should be done, why and when, within working hours.

This made demands on new forms of learning, and compulsory schooling that was determined by society gradually began to spread in the Western countries. More and more, and more wide-ranging, youth education programmes and programmes of higher education subsequently appeared, and a variegated and complex education system developed.

With the breakthrough of what has been called the 'knowledge society' or 'information society' in recent decades, learning has, however, once again entered a completely new societal situation. Learning has become a crucial parameter for economic growth and global competition, and being able to hold their own from the point of view of learning has become a decisive element in the basis of existence of societies.

This has emerged most clearly with the concept of 'lifelong learning', which has become firmly established as an international requirement of countries and their governments and populations (for example, OECD 1996; EU Commission 2000; Illeris 2004). Now it is not only the schools that have to be more efficient and, among other things, live up to different international comparisons. There is also more emphasis on learning in working life, parents are urged to stimulate children's learning in everyday life, kinder-gartens get curricula, and analyses are conducted of leisure time and life in associations on the basis of learning perspectives. Learning has been included as a quite key factor in national and international circulation.

The nature of the relation between learning and economy – for example, what it costs society if changes are implemented requiring that a large group of people must be able to perform certain tasks – might still be very uncertain, but there can be no doubt that learning has become a key societal matter subject to the economic rationality on the basis of which countries are governed (see Illeris 2004). Quite naturally, this affects the learning taking place to a high degree. Thus, apart from the individual level, learning has also become grounded to a wide extent on a social and societal level reaching right from the nature of the individual learning situation to comprehensive reforms and structuring of society's learning-related demands and services. I shall return to that in Chapter 13.

2.7 Summary

It is fundamental to the learning understanding of this book that on the basis of a general framework, contributions and understandings are included that have been developed from many angles of approach, theoretical understandings and academic disciplines, and that an attempt is made to unite these different contributions in a broad, comprehensive whole.

Learning is thus understood as a matter that is wide-ranging and complex. In order for it to be adequately understood and described, learning must be related to psychological, experience-based research within many psychological disciplines, biologically based understandings of the body and especially of brain functions, and social science analyses of the way in which learning forms part of the current structures and ways of functioning of societies, both in daily practice and in the general structuring of organised learning opportunities.

Chapter 3

The processes and dimensions of learning

This chapter describes the most fundamental matters in connection with the structure of learning and presents them graphically in a model that gives a basic overview. The matters included will, therefore, be dealt with on a general level only, while more detailed descriptions will appear in the following chapters.

3.1 The interaction and acquisition processes

The most basic understanding of how learning takes place, as I see it, is that all learning contains two very different processes, both of which must be active before we can learn anything. For the most part they will also be simultaneous and thus will not be experienced as two separate processes, but they can also take place completely or partially at different times (see section 5.5). The one process is the *interaction* between the individual and his or her environment which takes place during all our waking hours and which we can be more or less aware of – by which awareness or 'directedness' becomes an important element of significance for learning. The second is the psychological processing and *acquisition* taking place in the individual of the impulses and influences that interaction implies. Acquisition typically has the character of a linkage between the new impulses and influences and the results of relevant earlier learning – by which the result obtains its individual mark.

Up to a point in the 1980s learning research normally only concerned itself with the acquisition process. But from around 1990 important contributions began to appear pointing out that learning is also a social and interactive matter, and, as already mentioned in Chapter 1, some even went as far as to claim that learning can only be understood as a social process. For me, however, it is quite crucial for the understanding that both processes and their mutual interaction are included.

Today several learning researchers – such as British Peter Jarvis (1987; 1992) and American Etienne Wenger (1998) – operate more or less explicitly with the idea of both an individual and a social level in learning, but their starting point is not in this. However, I shall discuss this here both because it is a very fundamental matter for an adequate understanding of learning and because it provides the possibility for maintaining – as something quite basic – that learning is regulated by two very different sets of conditions.

What determines the process of interaction is fundamentally inter-personal and societal in nature and depends on the social and material character of the environment and thus on time and place. Much of the learning taking place in the industrialised countries today would not have been possible a hundred or a thousand years ago. And current learning possibilities are also very different in different countries and within different regions and sub-cultures.

The matters determining the acquisition process are, on the other hand, basically biological in nature. They have come into being through the development process that over millions of years has shaped the human being as a biological species and, especially, the central nervous system and the characteristically large brain with the high forehead which, in crucial ways, have given us some quite special learning possibilities that no other species has.

It is this duality of two sets of possibilities and conditions, each of which is enormously multiple, that fundamentally forms the frame of the almost limitless and never-ending human learning that I will try to uncover in more detail in the book. The first step is a graphic representation of the two processes and their interaction.

In Figure 3.1 the interactive process of learning is depicted as a vertical double arrow between the individual and the environment. As the environment – the outside world – is the general basis on which the whole rests,

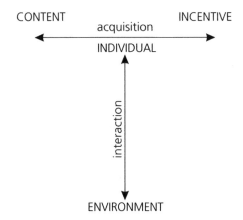

Figure 3.1 The fundamental processes of learning

I place it at the bottom in the model, while the learning individual is the specific 'case' which I place at the top. In this manner I also constitute the two levels, the environmental level and the individual level, which are part of any learning process.

I then present the acquisition process as yet another double arrow. As this is a process that exclusively takes place on the individual level, I place it horizontally at the 'top' of the double arrow that symbolises the interaction process. The duality in the acquisition process consists in this process always including an element of both *content* and *incentive*.

The content element concerns what is learned. It is not possible to speak meaningfully about learning without there being a learning content, something or other that is learned. It can be in the nature of knowledge, skills, opinions, understanding, insight, meaning, attitudes, qualifications and/or competence, and other terms can also be used. I return to all of this in Chapter 5. What is decisive here is that learning always has both a subject and an object: there is always *someone* learning *something*, and it is the acquisition of this something that is the content element of learning.

But acquisition also has an incentive element, which quite fundamentally means that mental energy is needed to carry out a learning process – in fact, a considerable amount of people's energy consumption, on average 20 per cent, goes on mental processes (Andreasen 2005, p. 60). At any rate something is necessary to set the acquisition process in motion and carry it through: there must be an incentive. This is what in everyday language is called, for example, motivation, emotions and will, and one of the most important results of the learning and brain research of the last decades is that the incentive basis of learning – i.e. the extent to which it is, for instance, fuelled by desire and interest or by necessity or force – is always part of both the learning process and the learning result (for example, Damasio 1994; LeDoux 1996). It is these moving and energy forces that constitute the incentive element of learning.

I have here divided the mental field to which acquisition is related into two broad main categories: content and incentive. I thus cross over the more traditional division of this field into three main categories: the cognitive, which concerns cognition; the affective, which concerns the emotions; and the conative, which concerns volition (for example, Hilgard 1980). This has to do with the fact that I find this tripartite division problematic in many ways. On the one hand, the division continues the separating out of bodily and motoric elements, which I have already criticised in Chapter 1. On the other hand, it separates the emotional and volitional and completely overlooks the motivational. In my opinion this distinction between different incentive forces can very well be appropriate in everyday language, but it is difficult to maintain professionally with clear categories and delimitations. I also find the bipartition between the content, the cognitive, the motoric and the rational on one side, and the incentive, emotional, motivational and volitional on the other, far more consistent and also in line with modern brain research (e.g. Damasio 1994, 1999).

Just as the vertical double arrow of the figure shows that the individual and the environment are two instances that always form part of the interactive process in an integrated way, the horizontal double arrow shows that in the acquisition process there is always an interaction between content and incentive. But the arrow, in itself, does not show anything about the nature or weighting of the two elements, only that they always contribute in an integrated way. I shall return to this later in the book.

3.2 The three dimensions of learning

As appears from Figure 3.1, the two double arrows together outline a triangular field. If this triangle is sketched in, three angles or poles appear marking what I term the three dimensions of learning, namely the content and the incentive, which have to do with the individual acquisition process, and the social and societal dimension, to do with the interaction process between the individual and the environment. (I describe in more detail in Chapter 7 the fact that the environment in connection with learning is quite overwhelmingly social and societal in nature.)

The fundamental thesis of this book is that all learning involves these three dimensions, which must always be considered if an understanding or analysis of a learning situation is to be adequate.

This can be graphically represented as the learning triangle shown in Figure 3.2.

Furthermore, as can be seen, a circle frames the learning triangle. This indicates that learning always takes place within the frames of an outer societal context which, on the general level, is decisive for the learning possibilities.

I will examine, in more detail, some general matters to do with each of the three dimensions, namely what we generally – consciously or unconsciously – aim at achieving within each of the three dimensions when we learn something, and what the overall result of this is.

As already mentioned, the content dimension is about what we learn. As signal words I will use *knowledge*, *understanding* and *skills* in full awareness of the fact that these are only some of the most important elements in learning content but not an exhaustive characterisation. This is my response to the 'cognitivism' or even more narrowly the 'knowledge orientation' that is a feature of a great deal of learning research and which is far too limited to capture the diversity of learning.

The learner's abilities, insight and understanding are developed through the content dimension – what the learner can do, knows and understands – and through this we attempt to develop *meaning*, i.e. a coherent understanding of the different matters in existence (for example, Bruner 1990;

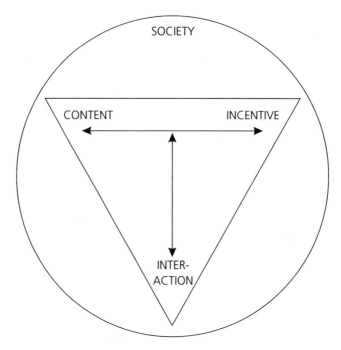

Figure 3.2 The three dimensions of learning

Mezirow 1990, 1991; Wenger 1998), and also to develop *abilities* that enable us to tackle the practical challenges of life. To the extent that we succeed in this endeavour, we develop our *functionality* as a whole, i.e. our capacity to function appropriately in the various contexts in which we are involved. This appropriateness is directly linked to our placing and interests in the current situation in relation to our qualifications and future perspectives, but quite generally, just as learning as a whole is related to the survival possibilities of the individual and the species.

As mentioned before, it is very largely the content dimension that learning research traditionally has concerned itself with, and it is also this dimension that is in direct focus when one speaks about learning in everyday language. But the learning triangle also points to other matters being at stake in connection with learning.

Acquisition has also an incentive dimension covering *motivation, emotion* and *volition* – and these are the three signal words to which I will refer in this dimension. As mentioned, it concerns mobilisation of the mental energy required by learning, and we fundamentally engage ourselves in this mobilisation in order to constantly maintain our *mental and bodily balance*. It might be uncertainty, curiosity or unfulfilled needs that cause us to seek new knowledge or new skills in order to restore the balance, and in so doing, through this dimension we simultaneously develop our *sensitivity* in relation to ourselves and our environment.

The content and incentive dimensions are usually activated simultaneously and in an integrated fashion by impulses from the interactive process between the individual and the environment (see section 5.5 about reflection). The content that is learned is, therefore, as previously mentioned, always marked or 'obsessed' by the nature of the mental engagement that has mobilised the mental energy necessary for the learning process to take place, whether, for example, it is a matter of pleasurable engagement or bitter necessity. On the other hand, the incentive basis is also always influenced by the content with which the learning is concerned. For instance, a new understanding or an improved skill alters our emotional and motivational and also, perhaps, our volitional patterns.

Learning psychology has traditionally studied the acquisition of content relatively independently of the incentive – but there have also been learning researchers who have strongly emphasised the connection, for example Lev Vygotsky (1896–1934) and Hans Furth (1922–1999), and this has later been conclusively supported by brain research (Vygotsky 1986 [1934]; Furth 1987), for example by Antonio Damasio (1994). I shall return to all of this later, in Chapter 6 in particular.

Finally, there is the interaction dimension of learning, which is concerned with the individual's interaction with his/her social and material environment on two levels: on the one hand, the close, social level in which the interactive situation is played, for example in a classroom or a working group, and on the other hand, the general societal level that establishes the premises for the interaction (a more detailed account of this will be given in section 7.1).

The signal words I have chosen for this dimension are *action, communication* and *cooperation*, which are important elements in our exchange and relation to our environment and, in connection with this, promote the individual's *integration* in relevant social contexts and communities. In this way the interaction dimension contributes to the development of the learner's *sociality*, i.e. ability to become engaged and function appropriately in various forms of social interaction between people. The development of sociality, however, itself takes place through the two dimensions of the acquisition process and is thereby marked by what concerns the interactive process and the nature of our relationship to it.

In each angle of the triangle in Figure 3.3 the signal words used for the dimension in question have been entered. Correspondingly, outside of the angles are written the key words that are used in relation to each of the dimensions to sum up the aim of learning in the dimension in question (in regular type) and what we develop on a general level in this way (in italics).

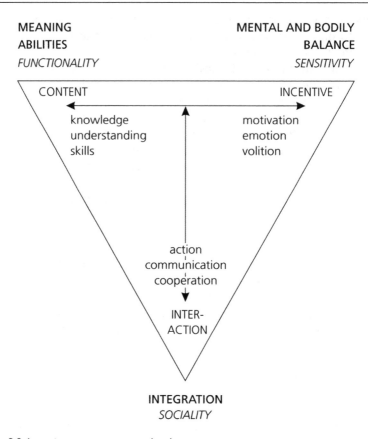

Figure 3.3 Learning as competence development

The learning triangle thereby obtains the character of a figure showing the breadth and diversity of our learning and thus meets the demand of modern society for learning as competence development. I return to this in section 8.4.

3.3 Summary

This chapter has first and foremost pointed out that all learning includes two different processes: an interactive process between the individual and the environment, and internal mental acquisition and processing through which impulses from the interaction are integrated with the results of prior learning. While the premises for the interaction are historical and societal in nature, the acquisition process takes place on a basis that has been developed biologically in step with human development over millions of years.

It was then pointed out that acquisition always includes content and incentive, thus producing the three dimensions of learning: content, incentive and interaction.

The content dimension typically concerns knowledge, understanding and skills. Through this we generally seek to create meaning and mastery, thus strengthening our functionality, i.e. our ability to function appropriately in relation to the environment in which we find ourselves.

The incentive dimension comprises motivation, emotion and volition. Through this we generally seek to maintain mental and bodily balance while at the same time developing our sensitivity.

The interaction dimension includes action, communication and cooperation. Through this we generally seek to achieve social and societal integration that we find acceptable, while, at the same time, developing our sociability.

Chapter 4

Different types of learning

This chapter sets the focus on the fact that learning can take place in different ways. A learning typology is developed covering four types of learning that are fundamentally different in nature, and which are activated under different circumstances and lead to learning results with crucially different application possibilities. In conclusion, the relation between the types of learning is discussed, together with their significance for understanding of the so-called transfer problem of the potential for using the learning in new contexts.

4.1 Learning typologies

The previous chapter was about the different processes and dimensions of learning – a fundamental area for understanding learning that has not been worked with to any great extent up to now. On the other hand, a great deal of work has been done on the question of whether there are different types of learning and how and in which areas it is possible to distinguish between such types and arrive at an adequate typology (i.e. a set of different learning types that taken together cover all learning). These are the issues I take up in this chapter.

The first clear distinction of learning research between two different learning types is probably the distinction between *signal learning* and *classical conditioning* on the one hand, and on the other hand *trial-and-error learning* and *operant conditioning*. From the early 1900s and right up to the 1970s this distinction has dominated American behaviourist learning psychology in particular.

Signal learning or classical conditioning was first discovered by the Russian physiologist Ivan Pavlov (1849–1936) by means of a series of experiments with dogs in the first years of the twentieth century. In its simplest form it concerned the production of saliva that takes place when a dog gets food. If a bell is rung at the same time, quite quickly the dog will produce saliva when the bell rings even though it does not get any food. In other words, the dog has learned to salivate when the bell rings (Pavlov 1927).

Later on, the actual founder of behaviourism, American John B. Watson (1878–1958), carried out a number of experiments with the 11-month-old Albert, who showed fright as a reaction to a high startling noise and was conditioned to react in the same way when given a white rat, which otherwise was one of his pets (Watson and Raynor 1920). This was termed emotional conditioning, and is probably the most interesting in the context of this book, because it shows that already at that point in time it was possible to think that the emotions can also be something of significance for learning.

In contrast, another of the most important American psychologists of the time, Edward Lee Thorndike (1874–1949), who is regarded as the founder of educational psychology, claimed that the fundamental form of learning takes place through trial-and-error, i.e. one tries something out and if it functions well, one learns it. In other words, a selection takes place from what is learned, and on the basis of many experiments Thorndike put forward the so-called law of effect, which states that one learns what feels satisfying and the more this is repeated, the stronger the learning becomes. If something seems unsatisfying, learning does not take place or is weakened (Thorndike 1931).

This approach was subsequently followed up and developed first and foremost by the most well-known of the American behaviourists, Burrhus F. Skinner (1904–1990), with his concept about instrumental or operant conditioning. Very briefly, this is that the learner is 'conditioned' to do something in order to get a reward. Instead of 'natural' trial-and-error learning, influences and reward provide the control so that the learner is brought to practise certain desired knowledge or behaviour, which is rewarded. In Skinner's opinion, by well-organised series of operant conditioning the most direct routes can be found to all learning targets, and in this way the method can be of quite fundamental educational significance. Skinner thought that the method could also be used to train qualities such as independence and creativity, and that its efficiency and its targeted nature could be the key to a better society – while his critics pointed out that it could equally be uniformity and depowerment (Skinner 1948, 1968, 1971).

I will not take this discussion any further here. The extensive efforts that have since been expended on instructional technology and programmed learning have clearly shown that these methods are only sustainable in practice if the participants are highly motivated and the learning content is clearly of a technical-practical nature. The efforts have also shown that elements of operant conditioning can be useful in many contexts, not least in connection with remedial teaching.

In the present context what is important is whether classical and operant conditioning are two different types of learning, and if so whether this typology is adequate and appropriate. The Danish psychologist and learning researcher Mads Hermansen has, for example, recently pointed out that in the final analysis all learning can be categorised in terms of whether it is conditioned by direct reward or indirect reward, where one has to do something one is not directly interested in to achieve something one really wants, for instance take a great number of driving lessons to get a driving licence, and that this can be understood as a generalised version of this classical typology. This would then be a typology that fundamentally relates to the motivational side of learning and thus to the incentive dimension. It has to do with what makes learning take place.

But at the same time as American learning psychology was especially concerned with the approach outlined here for half a century, other approaches existed in Europe in particular. In the first instance the most important approach came from German so-called Gestalt psychology, which, in contrast to behaviourism, was fundamentally based on the mind as an indivisible 'gestalt' to which one must relate in its totality. Viewed from this perspective the key to human learning was to develop 'insight' (cf. the learning triangle's concept of 'meaning', section 3.2), and this takes place first and foremost through problem solving. This was, *inter alia*, supported by a number of experiments with chimpanzees carried out by one of the founders of Gestalt psychology, Wolfgang Köhler (1887–1967), and subsequently through experiments on humans, especially by Karl Duncker (1903–1939). This approach gradually also won recognition in the USA (Köhler 1925 [1917]; Duncker 1945 [1935]).

In 1965 American psychologist Robert Gagné (1916–2002) set up a comprehensive typology as a summary of all of this. The typology was an attempt to summarise the approaches outlined here in eight hierarchically organised learning types: signal learning, stimulus-response learning (including trial-and-error learning and operant conditioning), learning chains (stimulus-response sequences), verbal associations, discrimination, concept learning, rule learning and problem solving. The basic idea in this typology is that the more highly placed learning types presuppose and build on those placed lower in the hierarchy, although types 3 and 4, chaining and verbal associations, are juxtaposed as two different possibilities. Problem solving presupposes and builds on rule learning, which again presupposes and builds on concept learning etc., down to stimulus-response learning, which includes trial-and-error learning and operant conditioning (Gagné 1970 [1965], p. 66).

Gagné's typology would thus appear to be concerned with the acquisition process of learning as a whole, but if one examines it more closely it becomes clear that the focus is on the content side of acquisition, and in his book the motivational side is also treated separately while the emotional side is practically absent. And even though problem solving is included in the model as the most advanced type of learning, it is obvious that it is a far cry from Gagné's set up to the holistic understanding of the Gestalt psychologists.

However, it was to be two other European approaches that emerged in the 1920s which, in the longer term, would constitute the most important alternatives to behaviourism in learning psychology. These were the cognitive and constructivist approaches in the first instance developed by the already-mentioned Swiss biologist and epistemologist Jean Piaget, and the Russian so-called cultural historical or activity theoretical approach, with Lev Vygotsky, Aleksei Leontjev and Aleksander Luria (1902–1977) as the most important names.

I will return to these approaches in more detail in the next chapter. Here I will merely note that first and foremost Piaget, as a fundamental part of his theory construction concerning learning with two well-founded biological concepts distinguished between *assimilation* and *accommodation* as two essentially different learning types and thus worked with a typology concerned with the function of the acquisition process itself (for example, Piaget 1952 [1936], 1959 [1926], 1980a [1974]; Flavell 1963).

The Russian cultural historical approach does not work with learning types as such, but with the concept of *the zone of proximal development* (to which I return in the following chapter). Vygotsky nevertheless approaches a typology as learning in this zone has a different character than learning within the already established field (Vygotsky 1978) – a distinction which, to a certain degree, is parallel to Piaget's concepts.

This approach was later further developed by the Finnish learning theoretician Yrjö Engeström (1987), who builds on the cultural historical tradition and compares it with a learning typology that is system theoretical in nature and drawn up by the English-born zoologist, ethnographer, cyberneticist, philosopher etc., Gregory Bateson (1904–1980). It has five learning types:

- *Learning 0* is quite mechanical – the impulse is accepted without any correction.
- In *learning I* the impulse can be corrected within a set of alternatives.
- In *learning II* a corrective change can be made in the set of alternatives from which the choice is made.
- In *learning III* a corrective change can be made in the system of sets of alternatives, which can be a great strain and even cause illness.
- *Learning IV* is an imagined future form of learning that transcends the possibilities in learning III.

(after Bateson 1972, p. 293)

As can be seen, Bateson's typology is rather speculative in nature. Levels 0 and I are so simple that they are only relevant for human learning very early and in special situations – Mads Hermansen characterises them as at an 'amoeba stage' – and level IV is non-existent. On the other hand, almost all human learning takes place at level II, and to make this more useful Engeström also divides this into a IIa and a IIb level, which correspond to Piaget's assimilation and accommodation. Level III remains as a superior level which human learning can reach under special conditions. Engeström's term for this is *learning by expanding*, and I return to this also later in the present chapter.

Here I should first and foremost like to stress that with his concepts on assimilative and accommodative learning Piaget laid the ground for a learning typology which, in my opinion, has the clear advantage of being based on fundamental differences in the nature of the acquisition process and which, therefore, I shall take further in the following. It should also be noted that Vygotsky's, Bateson's and Engeström's understandings contain elements that may be regarded as parallel to Piaget's fundamental distinction. A further two important theoreticians in the field of learning in working life have, in their different ways, worked with a corresponding bipartite typology, namely the American Chris Argyris, who makes a distinction between single-loop and double-loop learning (Argyris 1992; Argyris and Schön 1996) and the Swede Per-Erik Ellström, who uses the terms adaptation oriented and development oriented (Ellström 2001). Finally, it can be mentioned that already in 1979 the international report 'No limits to learning', very much in line with Ellström, distinguished between 'maintenance learning' and 'innovative learning' (Botkin et al. 1979; Jarvis 2005b, p. 117). I will deal with all of this in the following, but first I would like to make a further two introductory remarks.

First, the learning typology I develop in this chapter solely concerns the acquisition process of learning. As mentioned in Chapter 3, the acquisition and the interaction processes of learning are essentially different in nature and cannot, therefore, be covered by a common typology. In Chapter 7, I will provide more details concerning a typology for the interaction process and the way in which the two typologies can interact.

Second, the division between formal, non-formal and informal learning utilised in the supra-national literature about lifelong learning (e.g. the EU Commission 2000), is first of all problematic (see Colley et al. 2003) and, in the second place, does not concern learning in itself but only the context in which it takes place. For these reasons I do not regard this division as a learning typology.

4.2 Piaget's understanding of learning

In the further work of developing a learning typology I choose to take a point of departure in Piaget's categories not because I regard his theory as more 'correct' than other learning theories (I myself have written a critique of parts of Piaget's theory – Illeris 1996). As already stated, there are many approaches to learning, all of which have something to contribute that can have different significance for different contexts. My grounds for preferring Piaget in this case are, as appears from the previous section, that his approach is an appropriate choice because his two fundamental learning types, assimilation and accommodation, have to do with the nature of the acquisition process itself, and thus also the nature of what is learned.

Piaget is, indeed, almost exclusively concerned with the cognitive aspect of learning (even though a collection of lectures was posthumously published in the USA on the role of the emotions in learning, lectures he held at the Sorbonne in Paris in 1953–54 – Piaget 1981). What he fundamentally wanted to do was to uncover how the human intellect develops, and he did this very thoroughly (closer examinations of Piaget's theory can be found in the works of Flavell 1963 and Furth 1981, among others), so that today he is generally acknowledged to be one of the pioneers of psychology – as the English sociologist Anthony Giddens writes: 'the influence of Jean Piaget's work has been not far short of that of Freud' (Giddens 1993, p. 72).

In the present context there are both a number of fundamental factors concerning Piaget's approach and some central features to his theory which, in my view, make it highly appropriate to choose this particular theory as a starting point – even though there are also, in my opinion, a number of problematic factors and limitations, which I will return to later.

Quite basically I consider it a vital strength that Piaget, who originally trained as a biologist, constructs his theory on a genetic-biological basis, which is to say that he views the human ability to learn as a characteristic that has developed phylogenetically through the struggle for survival of the various species, in line with other species-specific characteristics. This view Piaget shares with many others, including Vygotsky, the Russian learning theorist mentioned previously, and other representatives of the cultural historical school, as well as modern brain research.

Another fundamental strength, which has come to the fore particularly in the years following Piaget's death in 1980, is the constructivist approach, which holds that a person constructs his or her own comprehension of the surrounding world through learning and knowledge – which excludes any form of learning approach as a filling process, in which someone, a teacher, for example, transfers knowledge and skills, to others, for example, pupils (an approach which many other learning theorists have also dissociated themselves from, the most well known perhaps being the Brazilian Paulo Freire (1922–1997) with his rejection of all that he calls 'banking education' – Freire 1970, pp. 58ff.).

Besides these two very important basic factors there are a number of important matters in the very construction of the theory to which I also ascribe vital significance.

First, Piaget differentiates between the dynamic and the structural aspects of learning – somewhat analogous to the differentiation between the incentive and the content dimensions in this presentation. The dynamic aspect is concerned with what drives learning, where the motive comes from, and the 'why' of learning, and Piaget specifically emphasises that he does not deal with this aspect of learning. The structural aspect is concerned with the content and nature of learning, the 'how' of learning. It is this aspect of learning that Piaget's theory is mainly concerned with, and in which he has involved himself in such detail.

To this are added Piaget's view and analysis of developmental stages. Piaget's stage theory is regarded by most as central to his work and has always been highly controversial. This holds that cognitive development from birth to puberty runs through a number of developmental stages that Piaget perceives as essential and unavoidable, and that they come in a particular order according to age. The ages may vary slightly, but not significantly.

The extensive criticism of the stage theory has partly been aimed at the definition and age determination of individual stages, but there has also been a more general criticism that the process is less clear-cut than Piaget describes it, and that the stages can set in at different times for different spheres within the same individual, depending on influence and interests (see Donaldson 1986). However, it is my opinion that the four main stages in Piaget's construction – i.e. the sensory-motor period in roughly the first two years of life, the preoperational period up to around school age, the concrete operational period up to around puberty, and the formal operational period after that – stand largely unchallenged by such criticism. In any case, the stage theory is of minor importance for the structural aspect of the learning theory.

More fundamental in my view is the criticism of Piaget relating to his quite dominant focus on the intellectual or cognitive side of development, most convincingly put forward by the American development psychologist Daniel Stern on the basis of his studies of the early development of the infant (in particular, Stern 1985). Even though Piaget was aware of the problems in only dealing peripherally and sporadically with emotional, social and personality development, it is clear that he has not been able to avoid these problems. This one-sidedness has led to inadequate understandings on decisive points, also in the cognitive area, because these different areas cannot be fully understood independently of each other. It is, therefore, always important to keep this limitation in mind when dealing with Piaget's work.

However, this problem has no direct bearing on the point that what I might call Piaget's actual learning theory is centred on the concept of learning as a process of equilibration. The individual strives to maintain a steady equilibrium in his or her interactions with the surrounding world by means of a continuing adaptation, i.e. an active adjustment process by which the individual adapts himself or herself to his or her environment, as well as attempting to adapt the environment to meet his or her own needs. This adaptation takes place in a continuing interaction between precisely the assimilative and the accommodative processes, which tend to balance each other all the time.

Assimilation is about taking in something in an already existing structure. We speak, for example, of assimilating immigrants in another society, and biologically organisms can assimilate various nutrients by transforming them chemically so that they can be utilised by their digestive systems. In learning, this is about incorporating new influences in established patterns of movement, potential actions, structures of knowledge or modes of understanding.

In accommodation it is the receiving organism that changes itself in order to be able to take in influences from the environment, e.g. when the eye accommodates the size of the pupil to the strength of the light. In learning this is about breaking down and restructuring established patterns of movement, potential actions, structures of knowledge or modes of understanding in accordance with new impulses.

Piaget regards these two processes as contributions to maintaining a cognitive organisation or structure, but this point of view can be expanded to apply to mental organisation or structuring as a whole. In line with modern brain researchers, Piaget emphasises that everything a person has acquired cannot possibly be stored in an unorganised manner in the brain. When to an amazing extent it is possible to 'retrieve it' or 'come to think of it' precisely when it is relevant for the individual, then there must be a structure making this possible.

In section 2.4 I have tried to sketch the way in which brain research imagines this structure in the form of neural 'traces' in an enormous and complex network of mutually connected electrochemical circuits. Piaget uses, instead, the psychological concept of 'schemes' containing coherent memories, knowledge, understanding and acting potential within a sub-jectively delimited area.

What is important here is irrespective of whether one speaks of traces or schemes, these are terms for grounded ideas about the structure that must necessarily exist for our 'memory' in the widest sense to be able to function. They are not words that are to be understood literally, because both terms are undifferentiated and inflexible in relation to the almost incomprehensibly complex network structure in the brain that is being referred to. The brain is, naturally, not full of anything as crude as schemes, nor can traces be an adequate term for the billions of circuits through the myriad of synaptic cell connections involved. But it is necessary to use such metaphors in order to be able to relate in any analytical way to the question of what goes on in the brain in terms of learning, thinking and memory.

It is, therefore, only in the context of such auxiliary constructions that one can begin to concretely relate to the way in which the acquisition process of learning comes to consist in a linkage between present impulses and already established structures, i.e. between a new impulse or experience and the ever-changeable result complex from earlier impulses and experiences represented by the traces or schemes.

Learning something means linking something new with what is already there and, according to Piaget, this can take place either assimilatively as an addition or accommodatively as restructuring. The Piaget-inspired American learning researcher David Ausubel has formulated it thus: 'The most important single factor influencing learning is what the learner already knows' (Ausubel 1968, p. vi).

A similar view also forms part of Daniel Stern's psychological perspective on 'the present moment' (Stern 2004), and also fits with the view of brain research as outlined in section 2.4.

Also inherent in this linkage is the explanation that even though a group of people is exposed to the same impulses – e.g. a school class that is being taught – each of them will learn something different because the traces or schemes each has already developed are different. It is only in very special circumstances that what they learn is more or less the same (see Chapter 7).

It is very important to recall these fundamentally structural understandings when, in the following, I examine the four basic types of learning which I call cumulation, assimilation, accommodation and transformation. They come into being by my separating out a special group called cumulative from Piaget's assimilative processes, and correspondingly separate the transformative out from the accommodative processes.

4.3 Cumulative learning

Naturally, many researchers have worked on elaborations or adaptations of Piaget's theory, both major and minor. First I will look at some elaborations described by the Danish psychologist Thomas Nissen in a small book entitled *Learning and Pedagogy* (Nissen 1970) – which, even in Denmark, is not well known and is somewhat inaccessible. In this book he separates out the special learning type he calls *cumulation* from assimilative learning, and also works with the circumstances under which the three learning types – cumulation, assimilation and accommodation appear, and what characterises the learning to which each gives rise. This is highly interesting because it aims directly at making learning psychology more useful in connection with teaching and other forms of activity directed at learning.

Cumulative learning occurs in situations where the learner does not possess any developed mental scheme to which impressions from the environment can be related, i.e. when the first element in a new scheme is established. Nissen presumably found it necessary to take this situation into consideration because he was concerned with basic forms of learning such as those that occur in a number of animal experiments, on which American traditional behaviourist learning psychology has largely focused.

Cumulative processes in humans are, by their very nature, of particular importance in the earliest years of life when a great number of mental schemes are established, but situations also occur later in which it may be necessary to learn something that is in no way connected with anything of which one has any previous knowledge. A good example of this is the practical task of learning telephone numbers off by heart. The first few numbers may refer to a geographical area, and this makes them easier to remember: there is something to connect them with. But the last numbers are always random and have no systematic connection with anything; these must either be learnt off by heart, or one must 'invent' a connection to something one knows, a kind of mnemonic. If you learn them off by heart, that is cumulative learning – which may also be termed *mechanical learning*. If you make up a mnemonic, what is happening is that you are linking them to something already known, a scheme previously established, and that is therefore assimilation.

In the context of education cumulative processes typically relate to the old-fashioned learning by rote of hymns, lists of kings and vocabulary, but cumulation also occurs in the acquisition of the first hesitant motor skills in, for example, riding a bicycle or skating. To summarise, it may be said that cumulative learning is, first and foremost, characterised by rigidity.

The results of cumulative learning are characterised in particular by it only being possible to 'remember' them or recall them in situations that are subjectively experienced as corresponding to the learning situation. This makes learning not very useful in a changeable world, and it is cumulative learning that is most important to human beings as a beginning of something more. The situation is quite different for most animals who do not have the potential to get any further than isolated cumulative courses of learning, or for the higher developed animals which can only to a limited extent develop coherent schemes through assimilation. Cumulative training has the character of dressage, a certain impulse or stimulus that triggers a certain reaction or response.

Therefore, knowledge of this form of learning can also contribute to an explanation of why, as a rule, animal experiments are of limited significance for understanding human learning. Quite simply, animals do not have, or have to a very limited degree only, the possibilities for going further with more complex forms of learning upon which the greatest part by far of human learning is based.

4.4 Assimilative learning

Sensory impressions from the environment are taken in and incorporated as additions to, and development of, already established mental schemes through assimilative learning. Therefore, one can speak of *additional learning* in connection with assimilation, and it should be noted immediately that this is the ordinary form of learning that we all practise in the many contexts of everyday life.

The situation from a mathematics lesson sketched at the beginning of the book can be taken as a typical example. This situation presupposes that the pupil has already acquired a certain knowledge of arithmetic and mathematics, i.e. that mental schemes have been developed to hold and structure the acquired mathematical knowledge. The way it is supposed to work is that when the teacher explains a new arithmetical operation that has not previously been dealt with in class, the pupil acquires the new knowledge by means of an assimilative extension of the pupil's mathematical scheme.

In assimilative learning, the learner adapts and incorporates impressions from his or her surroundings as an extension and differentiation of mental schemes built up through earlier learning. The learning products are typically knowledge, skills and experiential opportunities that can be activated in a broad spectrum of situations with certain specific common characteristics, and thus the products can, to a certain extent, be adapted to altered situations with new learning so long as they are subjectively related to the same scheme.

In its 'pure' form, assimilative learning is characterised by a steady and stable progressive development in which the learning products are constructed, integrated and stabilised. This category can include the majority of knowledge and skills learning that is traditionally aimed at in our education system, where systematic attempts are made within the various subjects to comprehensively extend the knowledge and skills structures that exist.

At the same time, it can be a disadvantage that learning is linked to the subjects and to school and can be rather inaccessible in other contexts – one cannot remember it even though it could be relevant. For example, physics teachers often complain that the pupils do not mobilise their mathematical knowledge during physics classes, or literature teachers say that the pupils do not link authors with what they have learned in history about the era in question.

What is learned assimilatively is thus characterised by being bound to certain mental schemes, and this can have its limitations in a modern world where things change so quickly and unpredictably. In principle we could imagine that all learning is built up assimilatively – and this is actually behind traditional curricula where all teaching is organised in subjects and lessons with a certain teacher and a certain syllabus. We could learn everything we needed in this way if we lived in a stable and unchangeable world. But we do not live in such a world, and, therefore, the fact that we have other, more flexible possibilities is precisely human beings' fantastic strength in relation to all the other species (perhaps with the slight exception of the highest developed primates). This is what the following sections are about.

4.5 Accommodative learning

As already mentioned, *accommodation* concerns whole or partial restructuring of already established mental schemes. It is a form of learning we can activate when we are in situations in which impulses from the environment cannot immediately be linked to the existing schemes due to some inconsistency or other, something that does not fit. To create the necessary context, we can carry out a whole or partial breakdown of the relevant schemes and, by effecting a change or restructuring, create the basis to allow the impulses to enter in a coherent way.

Accommodation thus implies a qualitative going beyond, or a transcendence of, the readiness already developed, and can be characterised as *transcendent learning*. When the necessary preconditions are present, the accommodative processes can be short and sudden: the learner understands immediately how something works. But it can also be a lengthy process, in which the learner struggles with a problem or a difficult relationship and gradually, or step by step, develops a new comprehension or a solution.

It should also be mentioned that while most accommodations are about overcoming a problem situation by creating a new context and, therefore, can be described as 'offensive accommodations', in special cases there can also be 'defensive accommodations', where the problem is solved by a transcending withdrawal that implies the establishment of a defence against a realistic experience and handling of the problem field in question. I shall return to this in section 9.3.

Under all circumstances it is, first and foremost, through accommodative learning and restructuring that the character of the learning changes in a decisive way. The accommodative restructurings are characterised to a high degree by individual understandings and particular forms of comprehension, and even in relation to the clearest structures in, for example, the field of mathematics and formal logic, there will be individual ways of perceiving the subjects. Piaget declared that individuation – the differences that make us develop into separate and distinct individuals even under uniform external conditions – lies in the diversity of accommodations:

> There is a great diversity in structures. – Accommodation gives rise to unlimited differentiations. – The fact that a number is the same for everyone, and the series of whole numbers is the same for everyone, doesn't prevent mathematicians, taken one by one, from being unique as individuals. There is such diversification of structures . . .
>
> (Piaget 1980b, quoted from Furth 1987, p. 4)

However, the individuation of accommodation also leads to individuations in the assimilative processes. For when the schemes are individuated by means of accommodation they will, of necessity, take on an individual stamp, and when assimilation to individualised schemes takes place, the assimilations will very often be different, even though the influences are the same for several individuals. Therefore, there will always be differences in even the most educated logicians' or mathematicians' knowledge schemes: even if they apparently 'know' the same thing, they do so in different ways, which may lead to differences when this knowledge is recalled and what likelihood there is for it to be transcended.

It is thus equally important for a teacher to be interested in what the pupils already know as in what he or she wants them to learn. At the same time this approach makes it clear why pupils very often learn different things even though they have all received the same teaching: each pupil has unique and individually developed mental structures, and when the meeting between specific impressions and these different structures brings about learning, the results will, in principle, be different.

With respect to the relationship between the assimilative and the accommodative processes, there is an interesting difference between Piaget's and Nissen's conceptions. Piaget's position is perhaps best expressed in the following summary by John Flavell:

> However necessary it may be to describe assimilation and accommodation separately and sequentially, they should be thought of as simultaneous and indissociable as they operate in a living cognition. Adaptation is a unitary event, and assimilation and accommodation are merely abstractions from this unitary reality. – Some cognitive acts show a relative preponderance of the assimilative component; others seem heavily weighted towards accommodation. However, 'pure' assimilation and 'pure' accommodation nowhere obtain in cognitive life; intellectual acts always presuppose each in some measure.
>
> (Flavell 1963, pp. 48–49)

It should, however, be noted that in spite of this basic view there are, nevertheless, numerous places where the two types of processes are treated individually in Piaget's work.

This is almost the opposite in Nissen's work. As I have done here, he starts by separating assimilation and accommodation as two essentially different forms of learning, but at the same time he makes *a general reservation*:

> In the following, three forms of learning are postulated: cumulative, assimilative and accommodative learning. – They are less 'pure' than they appear, but examination of them may . . . be treated as an attempt

to construct search models that can perhaps point out important points in learning.

(Nissen 1970, p. 43)

In following the same procedure as Nissen, I make the same reservation. In principle it is undoubtedly correct that assimilation and accommodation are more or less linked together and they are at any rate mutually dependent processes. But from a pedagogical viewpoint, there is much to be gained in considering and analysing each of them separately. In this way it is easier to see their different fundamental conditions and the qualities in the learning to which they give rise.

It is, first and foremost, important to be aware that accommodation in general is a considerably more demanding process than assimilation. It is far more straightforward to add to an already existing scheme than to perform the necessary complicated demolition, reorganisation and restructuring implied by accommodative learning. In particular, breaking down or giving up an insight or understanding that has already been acquired would seem to be a strain. We do not simply give up positions we have struggled to gain and which we at any rate have become accustomed to building on. This requires considerable mobilisation of mental energy and again requires the presence of subjectively convincing reasons to do so, or as Nissen himself has formulated it: 'The actual accommodative learning process is a strain for the individual, characterised by anxiety, bewilderment and confusion, and requires a certain amount of strength'(Nissen 1970, p. 68).

Accommodative learning, in general, requires more energy than assimilative learning, and therefore there is also a tendency to avoid this type of learning if we do not have any particular interest in learning the item in question, or for accommodations to be blocked by mental defence or resistance (I go further into this in Chapter 9). In return for these efforts, however, we build up some learning results through the accommodative processes that are generally more long-lasting and applicable in nature. Through the breaking down and reorganisation, a liberation from the established schemes can simultaneously occur that can lead to more coherent understandings that one remembers more easily and which can more easily be used to build on.

For example, when one is faced with a problem or one has been puzzled about something one cannot make any sense of for a long time and then one finds a solution through an accommodative process, then, at the same time, one establishes a more sustainable understanding that can be used across the lines of several mental schemes. To express it more simply, the learner has 'realised' the (subjectively) right context and this is an experience that makes an impression and sticks. The Danish psychologist Jens Bjerg, who has worked closely together with Thomas Nissen, has expressed it as follows: 'Accommodative processes provide the individual with opportunities for action, for use in various situations, whatever the context. Here we are dealing with the basis for openness, sensitivity, creativity, flexibility and the like' (Bjerg 1972, p. 19).

In more general terms it can be pointed out that accommodative learning presupposes, first, that relevant schemes that can be reconstructed are already in place (e.g. presuppositions regarding a subject, attitudes or social relations); second, that the individual needs or is keen to mobilise energy for a reconstruction of that type; and third, that the individual in that situation perceives sufficient permissiveness and safety to 'dare' to let go of the knowledge already established. These three kinds of preconditions for accommodative learning are not separately absolute in nature, but occur in a reciprocal interactive relationship, such that strong motivation for advancement, for example, can reduce the need for preconditions and security – or vice versa.

In more popular terms, accommodative learning can be related to concepts such as reflection and critical thinking (to which I return in Chapter 5), and it is clearly a form of learning of key importance for the current concept of competence (which will be discussed in section 8.4). It is, to a high degree, through accommodation that our learning obtains the general applicability in different, unpredictable situations that is precisely at the centre of the concept of competence.

4.6 Transformative learning

Over the last 10–20 years, however, and especially in connection with requirements concerning lifelong learning and the development of adult education programmes, an urgent need has arisen to realise that there is a form of learning that is even more far-reaching in nature than that which Piaget characterised as accommodation. Viewed in relation to the already outlined learning types character of foundation, development and reorganisation, respectively, of mental schemes, this concerns the learning that takes place when a large number of schemes are reorganised at the same time and with relation to all three dimensions of learning.

Historically, this is a type of learning that has been known for a long time in the field of psychotherapy, but which has not been understood in relation to the concept of learning and has not at all been regarded as something that could have to do with schooling and teaching. The oldest term referring to this type of learning is probably the concept of *catharsis*, developed by Freud already at the end of the nineteenth century as a term for the mental breakthrough that successful psychoanalytical treatment could trigger (Freud and Breuer 1956 [1895]).

The first to relate such a breakthrough to a learning understanding would, however, seem to have been the American psychotherapist Carl Rogers (1902–1987), who is regarded as one of the key figures in the previously mentioned humanistic psychology. In the course of his extensive work he dealt, *inter alia*, with the link between psychotherapy and learning and developed the procedures which he called client-centred therapy and student-centred teaching (Rogers 1951, 1959, 1961, 1969). In these contexts Rogers developed the concept about significant learning, which involves 'a change in the organization of the self'(Rogers 1951, p. 390), as it involves 'the whole person, both his emotions and the cognitive aspects are involved in the learning' (Rogers 1969, p. 5), and which he subsequently defined more precisely in the following statement:

> By significant learning I mean learning which is more than an accumulation of facts. It is learning which makes a difference – in the individual's behaviour, in the course of action he chooses in the future, in his attitudes and in his personality. It is a pervasive learning which is not just an accretion of knowledge, but which interpenetrates with every portion of his existence.
>
> (Rogers 1961, p. 280)

It is immediately obvious that Rogers's formulation about 'the organisation of the self', 'the whole person' and 'every portion of his existence' exceed what above is described as accommodation. Nevertheless, there is a parallel to Nissen's formulation about the strain involved in accommodative learning when time and time again Rogers points out that:

> any significant learning involves a certain amount of pain, either pain connected with the learning itself or distress connected with giving up certain previous learnings . . . learning which involves a change in self organization – in the perception of oneself – is threatening and tends to be resisted . . . all significant learning is to some degree painful and involves turbulence, within the individual and within the system.
>
> (Rogers 1969, pp. 157–158, 159, 339)

Significant learning is something one only becomes engaged in when faced by a situation or challenge exceeding what one can manage on one's existing personal basis, but which one unavoidably must win over in order to get further – i.e. a crisis that is often existential in nature.

However, since the time Rogers formulated his concept of significant learning society has developed in a way that leads more people into such existential crises while at the same time having a higher degree of expectations of the education system, and adult education in particular, to handle such crises. The extremely rapid rate of change in social development, globalisation's breaking down of borders and cultures, and breakdown in a long series of traditional patterns of interpretation of, for example, religious, ideological, class and traditional natures, all bring more and more people into exile, sudden involuntary unemployment, divorce and other losses of close relations that create deep personal crises. At the same time there is a rising economically conditioned societal interest in such crises being quickly resolved, at least to such an extent that the person in question can return to the labour market.

When attention is paid to what is actually going on in the adult education programmes offered to ordinary people with no special educational qualifications, it becomes obvious that this is to a high degree a form of crisis help requiring 'significant learning', but that naturally cannot be resolved to the necessary extent through lengthy and costly individual psychotherapy. This is why the people in question end up in different types of adult education as participants who need 'rehabilitation', 'retraining' or 'personal development' (see Illeris 2003b, 2004). It is striking that throughout the same period and independently of each other (at least) three different learning concepts have been developed that have thematised these matters in a learning theory context on the basis of very different approaches.

First, there is Finnish Yrjö Engeström's concept of *learning by expanding*, which I have previously discussed (section 4.1. – Engeström 1987). As mentioned, it has been formulated by combining the cultural historical learning approach and the concept of the zone of proximal development with Gregory Bateson's system of theoretically oriented learning typology – and the main point is that this special type of learning appears when the learner transcends the premises and fundamental conditions that apply to the person's 'general' assimilative and accommodative learning.

Second, there is the German sociologist and biography researcher Peter Alheit's concept of *transitory learning* (Alheit 1994, 1995). In the terms of this concept learning is regarded in relation to the learner's life cycle or biography, which precisely through societally determined occurrences is faced with requirements concerning transcending the previous life foundation as a transition from one life phase to another.

Third and finally, there is the American adult educator Jack Mezirow's by now thoroughly documented and discussed concept of *transformative learning*, which he has most recently defined as follows:

> Transformative learning refers to the process by which we transform our taken-for-granted frames of reference (meaning perspectives, habits of mind, mind-sets), to make them more inclusive, discriminating, open, emotionally capable of change, and reflective so that they may generate beliefs and opinions that will prove more true or justified to guide action.
>
> (Mezirow 2000, pp. 7–8)

It should be noted here that although Mezirow's definition is immediately more cognitively oriented than the other mentioned here, both here and in other contexts he also always refers to emotion and action.

Thus, as a whole, I view the concepts of significant, expansive, transitory and transformative learning as expressions that fundamentally cover the same type of learning on the basis of different perspectives. In the following I have chosen to utilise Mezirow's concept of transformative learning solely because it is the most widespread and best known of the terms mentioned and because linguistically it is in line with the concepts already introduced about cumulative, assimilative and accommodative learning.

At the same time, however, I would stress that this concerns learning that – as formulated by Rogers – implies a restructuring of the organisation of the self and thereby also a coherent restructuring and coupling of a great number of mental schemes that lead to change in the individual personality. It is very important to maintain this when, as here, the concept is included in a learning typology, because neither Rogers, Engeström, Alheit nor Mezirow lay down clear criteria for where the borderline goes between this type of learning and other learning. Mezirow, in particular, includes many examples of learning that are termed transformative, even though it would probably be understood as accommodative in the typology outlined here.

It is obvious that transformative learning is extremely demanding and a strain, and only takes places when the learner is in a situation with no other way out that can be experienced as sustainable. As Engeström, in particular, has pointed out, in some cases such learning can take place as a sudden breakthrough, but perhaps more commonly through a lengthy process in which social relations play a significant role. Under all circumstances this is what one more familiarly would call crisis resolution and what is typically experienced as a release mentally and frequently also physically. One can feel born again as a new and better person, and suchlike expressions, which I have often come across in my own research on the Danish adult education programmes.

But it is also clear that the adult education programmes and their staff rarely have an educational background that can meet the demands that learning of this nature can involve, and that, therefore, it is often in spite of this, and to a high degree driven by the learner's own efforts and tenacity, when adult education programmes trigger such a learning process, and that in all likelihood there are many cases where it cannot take place under the given conditions.

4.7 Connections and transfer potentials

I have now examined four different learning types, each of which is basically characterised by its relation to our mental schemes. The order in which I have examined them is clearly not random, but characterised by a rising degree of complexity and, at any rate in the case of the last two, of experienced strain and use of mental energy.

It should not, however, be concluded on this basis that the more advanced learning types are 'better' than those that are less advanced. What is 'good' or appropriate is that one is in a position to flexibly alternate between the learning types and to activate the type of learning that is relevant in a given situation. There is particular reason to point out that there can be a double tendency to make use of ordinary assimilative learning especially, partly because traditional teaching, and thus also our immediate understanding of what learning is, typically set the stage for assimilative processes, and partly because the accommodative processes are, as mentioned, more demanding, and modern people are often mentally over-strained and have a tendency to avoid accommodations – not to speak of transformative learning, which for good reasons we are only inclined to embark on if this is the only way out of an urgent problem or crisis. As mentioned, these matters will be taken up separately in Chapter 9 under the headings of mental defence and resistance.

Finally in this chapter on types of learning, however, I will briefly look at one of the most classical areas of learning psychology, namely the problem of transfer of learning from one context to another, because this issue takes on another character and transparency in the light of the learning typology outlined here.

In practice, the transfer problem originates in particular in the well-known situation that it can be difficult to apply or recall what one has learned in school or in an educational context when one encounters other contexts, and, more generally, that in order to be able to make use of it, much learning requires a situation which, to a greater or lesser extent, is reminiscent of the learning situation. For this reason, almost as long as learning psychology has existed, it has been imperative to discover what it would take for learning to obtain utility value outside the learning situation.

The classical answer to the question was formulated by the previously mentioned American psychologist Edward Lee Thorndike together with his colleague Robert Woodworth (1869–1962) with the theory that 'identical elements' must be present in the learning and application situation for transfer to occur (Thorndike and Woodworth 1901). In answer to this, however, a couple of years later yet another American psychologist, Charles Judd (1873–1946), put forward another theory that was more open and optimistic to the effect that general principles, rules and theories could form the basis for transfer (Judd 1908).

Ever since, these two fundamental positions seem to have been opposites at the same time as other explanations have been sought relating to the nature of the learning content, features of the learner, or the nature of how what is learned is to be used (Illeris *et al.* 2004).

But it is inherent in the definitions of the four types of learning in the above that, in themselves, they imply different transfer possibilities, and in this connection it is interesting that the English education researcher Michael Eraut, who has also done a great deal of work on the transfer issue, without referring to any form of learning types has reached a similar understanding of four different kinds of knowledge which he terms repetition, application, interpretation and association (Eraut 1994).

In this way there arises a general understanding of four different main categories for learning, knowledge, transfer and application possibilities:

• Through cumulative learning, delimited, repetition-oriented knowledge is developed that can be used in situations that are the same as the learning situation in a decisive way.
• Through assimilative learning, knowledge oriented towards application to a subject (or scheme) is developed and can be used in situations that bring the subject in question to the fore (cf. the theory of identical elements).
• Through accommodative learning, understanding- or interpretation-oriented knowledge is developed which can be flexibly applied within a broad range of relevant contexts (cf. the theory of general principles).
• Through transformative learning, personality-integrated knowledge is developed on the basis of which associations can be freely made in all subjectively relevant contexts.

It should be noted that the word knowledge has been retained throughout this presentation even though other terms such as meaning and understanding would, perhaps, be more appropriate in step with the complexity in the categories of the presentation. The important point has been to illustrate the fact that there are crucial connections between the nature of the learning that takes place, the learning product that is developed, and the application possibilities available.

4.8 Summary

In this chapter a learning typology has been developed covering the four learning types of cumulation, assimilation, accommodation and transformation, which relate to the acquisition process of learning and are characterised by their relation to the mental schemes that organise our knowledge, understanding, thinking and memory. The four learning types are realised in different contexts and lead to learning of different kinds and with different application and transfer potentials.

It is important to maintain that the more complicated and advanced (and, therefore, more demanding and straining) learning types cannot be understood as 'better' than the more ordinary learning types, but that learning that is appropriate and developing for the individual presupposes the ability to make use of the learning types that are relevant in the situation. In daily life alternation between assimilation and accommodation will usually promote progressive learning, while cumulation and transformation can be mobilised in more unusual contexts.

Chapter 5

The content dimension of learning

This chapter starts by stating that the content of learning must be understood far more broadly than the usual pedagogical idea of knowledge, skills and attitudes. On the basis of such a broader concept of content, the chapter examines a number of more recent, different learning researchers and learning theories, which in their different ways relate to such a broader learning perspective. The chapter concludes with two sections, of which the first deals with reflection and meta-learning, respectively, as two key concepts in an up-to-date understanding of the content dimension of learning, and reflexivity and biographicity as two key concepts when it comes to the increasingly urgent aspect of learning that has the learner's own self and self-understanding as its content.

5.1 Different types of learning content

In section 3.1 it was maintained as something quite fundamental that all learning has a content – there is otherwise no point in speaking of learning – and it was stated that the content could, for example, have the character of knowledge, skills, opinions, understanding, insight, meaning, attitudes, qualifications and/or competence. But it can also be seen in a broader perspective and have the character of more general cultural acquisition, or it could be related to the method of working or have the character of 'learning to learn', as it is called in more popular terminology. Moreover, important personal qualities such as independence, self-confidence, responsibility, ability to cooperate, and flexibility are also elements that to a high degree can be developed and strengthened through learning. But this is something that also involves the two other learning dimensions and which I, therefore, will return to in Chapter 8.

It is at any rate clear that the content dimension of learning goes considerably further than the traditional view has prevailed in educational contexts, where the objective of learning from the point of view of content has typically been related to the categories of knowledge, skills and, perhaps, attitudes. For example, as late as 1987 a modern learning researcher such as Peter Jarvis defined learning as 'the transformation of experience into knowledge, skills and attitudes' (Jarvis 1987, p. 8), a definition that he has since expanded considerably (Jarvis 2006, p. 13).

It can, naturally, be practical to limit the number of the many different and overlapping terms to a few categories that are important and adequate. But it is a notable reflection of the limited understanding of education that was developed in industrial societies – and it also is connected with the one-sided orientation towards assimilative learning pointed out in the last chapter – that, for example, none of the words understanding, insight, opinion, overview or anything similar is among the three classical peda-gogical aspects – not to mention the more cultural, social or personal qualifications. This does not, of course, imply that an attempt has not been made to give the pupils and students an understanding of the material and personal development, and some might also claim that knowledge in some way or other includes both understanding and personality development. But this is not something regarded as being so central that it has been maintained as independently valuable.

With respect to the concept of 'qualifications', which has mostly been used in connection with vocational education, there is linguistic usage which specifically speaks of the 'hard' qualifications, i.e. knowledge and skills, and a more modern form that also covers the 'soft' or 'personal' qualifi-cations (for example, Andersen *et al.* 1994), thus bringing the term into line with the new concept of 'competences'. I also return to this in Chapter 8.

Within learning research and learning theory, traditionally there has also been a tendency to regard the content dimension in learning very narrowly as knowledge and skills. With the general interest in discovering a fundamental form of learning or learning process, which was already mentioned in the introduction to this book, the main emphasis has been on acquisition of the simplest forms of knowledge and skills. At the end of the nineteenth century, German learning researcher Hermann Ebbinghaus (1850–1909) even went so far as to focus on the learning of meaningless syllables such as nug, mok, ket, rop etc. to avoid any distorting influence that the meaning might have on the learning (Ebbinghaus 1964 [1885]).

Others have, of course, transcended this limitation, and it has been a feature of many of the most important learning researchers that not least the acquisition of understanding and meaning has been at the centre of their work. But the more personal, dynamic, social and societal aspects have often only been included as matters that can influence 'learning itself', which has been understood as the acquisition of knowledge and skills. In the following I will concentrate in particular on learning researchers and concepts that have played a part in taking the content dimension beyond the narrow confines of knowledge and skills – which should, naturally, not be taken as meaning that I do not consider the acquisition of knowledge and skills as a very important and considerable part of learning.

It should also be noted that the previous chapter has already laid an important basis for treating the content dimension with a review of some of Jean Piaget's most basic assumptions, which are first and foremost relevant for this dimension. In this chapter I will go further with a number of other and largely new researchers who have gone beyond Piaget's understanding in relation to the content of learning in important areas.

5.2 Kolb's learning cycle

American psychologist David Kolb is a well-known learning researcher who has taken his point of departure in Piaget, among others. In an article written together with Roger Fry in 1975 (Kolb and Fry 1975), he outlined the learning model that he later developed further in his book *Experiential Learning* (Kolb 1984). It may be said that the learning theory Kolb developed in this book can seem somewhat problematic in places, with some rather uncertain conclusions on a basis that is not always clearly developed, but it also contains some important elaborations of Piaget's concept, including a transcending of the limitations that result from Piaget's restricted interest in learning in formal logic spheres, where it is clear what is right and what is wrong.

There is, however, a vast distance from the certainty of formal logic to the numerous structuring possibilities that exist in other spheres, e.g. in the acknowledgement of the chaotic mass of conditions and impressions that characterise everyday life in a modern society. In concentrating on logical structures, Piaget attempted to get to what he viewed as the core of knowledge, and was thereby able to uncover some fundamental features in the nature of knowledge. At the same time, though, other features that have far more importance in ordinary life were pushed out onto the periphery or even right out of sight. Kolb's work can provide a partial remedy to that, and therefore I will here concern myself with Kolb's theory and concentrate on what I find of significance in order to reach his treatment of the question of the ambiguity and unambiguity of learning.

Kolb starts by referring to Piaget together with the American philosopher and educational theorist John Dewey (1859–1952) (see section 8.2) and the German-American Gestalt psychologist Kurt Lewin (1890–1947). By transforming the essence of these three learning approaches into three somewhat crude models, Kolb finds that they all understand learning as a process with four stages or adaptive learning modes, which can be inscribed in a learning cycle (Figure 5.1) from concrete experience through reflective observation and abstract conceptualisation to active experimentation, and then back to a new concrete experience (Kolb 1984, pp. 30 and 32–33).

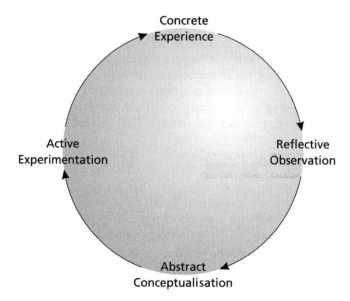

Figure 5.1 Kolb's learning cycle (see Kolb 1984, p. 33)

This juxtaposition and inscription in a common model – which Peter Jarvis *et al.* have called 'probably . . . the most well known of all illustrations about learning' (Jarvis *et al.* 1998, p. 48) – is undertaken by Kolb on the basis of very different elements in the three theory formations. He refers to the practical process in Lewin's model for action research and laboratory training (Kolb 1984, p. 21). From Dewey he refers to a very general description of 'how learning transforms the impulses, feelings, and desires of concrete experience into higher-order purposeful action' (p. 22). And from Piaget he takes the order of the characteristic learning patterns in the four main stages from newborn to adult from the stage theory mentioned earlier (pp. 24–25) – and thus not at all the single learning process.

From one viewpoint it is not obvious that these three very different elements in the three theories can be taken to express the central themes in the three learning concepts, and Kolb does not discuss this problem at all. However, it can also be seen as an important innovation in Kolb's work that he was able to spot a parallel not immediately apparent because of the very great differences between the three theorists' approaches.

At any rate, Kolb's learning cycle constitutes a systematisation of the learning process which may in some contexts be a valid analytical blueprint, but which also involves a vigorous rationalisation of the diversity of reality. In that way it makes one think of differing scientific methodological models that produce systematised interpretations of research processes. But neither learning nor research take place in the real world, according to that kind of logical systematism. In both cases it is more a case that one starts off with what one knows and regards as important or striking, whether it is a question of experiences, observations, knowledge, understanding, conjectures or problems, and from there one attempts to make progress in a combined acquisition and clarification process. This is documented by, among others, another American psychologist and learning theorist to whom I will frequently return, namely Donald Schön (1931– 1997), who has studied how 'reflective practitioners' cope with different situations by drawing on, and combining in parallel, the relevant elements that they have at their disposal (Schön 1983 – there is a brief corresponding criticism of this element in Kolb's theory in Mezirow 1991, p. 103).

The next step in the development of Kolb's theory that I wish to cover here is that after a lengthy discussion on the nature of learning, he reaches the conclusion that there are two dimensions present in all learning, a grasping, or to use Kolb's own term, 'prehension', and a transformation, in which that which has been grasped is embedded as an element of the learner's psychological structures. There is a clear parallel between this distinction and my understanding of the two integrated sub-processes of learning (see section 3.1). But there is also a clear difference. While Kolb's transformation dimension is rather similar to what I term the internal acquisition process, Kolb's prehension dimension is also a consistently individual matter in contrast to the interaction process with the environment on which I focus. Thereby, according to Kolb learning as a whole also becomes a completely internal phenomenon, while in my understanding it is, at the same time, both an internal and an interactive process. Thus the social dimension is quite absent from Kolb's learning understanding, just as it is in Piaget.

Thus, the most innovative aspect of Kolb's work, in my view, lies not in his learning dimensions as such, but in his further analysis of them, for he finds that they each stretch between two dialectically opposed adaptive orientations which, together, are identical to the four stages in the learning cycle. The prehension dimension stretches as a vertical axis in the learning cycle between an immediate apprehension that points towards concrete experience, and an adapted or reflective comprehension that points towards abstract conceptualisation. And correspondingly the transformation dimension stretches as a horizontal axis in the learning cycle between intention, pointing out towards reflective observation, and extension, pointing out towards active experimentation. According to Kolb, the structural basis of the learning process lies in the interaction between these four orientations (Kolb 1984, p. 41). Thus, Kolb develops a learning model that can provide an inspiring picture of the structure of the acquisition process of learning (Figure 5.2).

The two interacting dimensions mark out four spaces or fields within the learning cycle that are filled by four adaptive orientations or basic

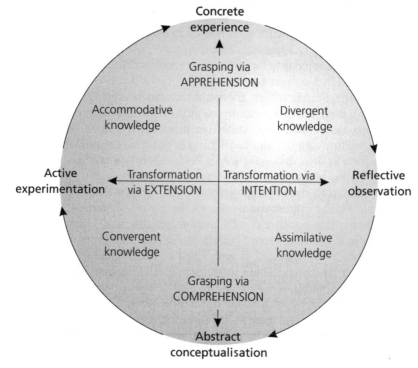

Figure 5.2 Kolb's learning model (Kolb 1984, p. 42)

forms of knowledge. In his further work, Kolb drops the problematic succession in the learning cycle and instead concentrates on these forms of knowledge, and it is in this that I regard him as having transcended Piaget.

This emerges clearly from the naming of the forms of knowledge as assimilative, convergent, accommodative and divergent knowledge, respectively – the assimilative and accommodative concepts are clearly taken from Piaget, while the convergent and divergent concepts come from Joy P. Guilford (1897–1987), the American researcher into intelligence and creativity. Convergent (unambiguous) knowledge concerns concentration on a specific output from a given input, i.e. what we typically call inference or deduction, while divergent (ambiguous) knowledge means the development of various potential outputs from the same input, i.e. what we typically understand by creativity and diversity (see Guilford 1967, pp. 213f.).

In addition the model indicates the typical conditions for each of the forms of knowledge thus:

- assimilative knowledge typically develops from comprehension and intention;

- convergent knowledge typically develops from comprehension and extension;
- accommodative knowledge typically develops from apprehension and extension;
- divergent knowledge typically develops from apprehension and intention.

In comparison with Piaget, it could be considered problematic that the four forms of knowledge in the model are of equal standing. This is not immediately in accordance with Piaget's theory of equilibrium. But it is still possible to conceive of assimilation and accommodation as the two basic types of processes, and then, on the basis of Kolb's work, make the important addition that both these types of process can have a nature that to some extent favours the direction of the convergent or the divergent. Thus a very important differentiation from Piaget's concept emerges, as many relationships in life cannot be interpreted with certainty and with clear criteria for what is right and what is wrong. In addition Kolb's model to a certain extent – although only on a more theoretical level than in Nissen's description – indicates which situations tend to advance the various forms of knowledge.

5.3 From activity theory to cultural psychology

As mentioned in section 4.1, the cultural historical tradition in psychology and the activity theoretical approach derived from this have their roots in the inter-war period in Russia, where the big names were Lev Vygotsky, Aleksei Leontjev and Aleksander Luria. The tradition became very widespread in the post-war period, among other places, in Scandinavia, Germany and the USA (for example, Holzkamp 1983, 1995; Engeström 1987, 1996; Cole 1996; Engeström *et al.* 1999; Chaiklin *et al.* 1999; Chaiklin 2001).

The definition 'cultural historical' refers to the basic view that mankind's phylogenetic development, and that which separates humans from animals, centres on the human development of culture, and that mankind's fundamental psychological structures have developed in interaction with the development of culture. Leontjev (1981 [1959]) was among the most important contributors to have thoroughly elaborated this view, and, in addition, Luria tested and confirmed this approach through an investigation of changes in the knowledge processes of farmers in Uzbekistan, who experienced an abrupt change in the early 1930s from a primitive feudal farming society to a modern communist farming collective (Luria 1976 [1974]).

The central point in the approach of this tradition is that psychological factors can only be understood in a historical perspective and based on interaction with the cultural environment. This interaction takes the nature of what Leontjev terms as object reflection:

> The organisms' adaptation, which is always . . . a kind of reflection of properties of the environment by them . . . acquires the form . . . of reflection of affective properties of the environment in their objective connections and relations. This is also a specific form of reflection for the psyche, object reflection.
>
> (Leontjev 1981 [1959], p. 45)

This concept of object reflection is, to a certain extent, in accordance with Piaget's constructivist approach, for both concepts involve an active development of psychological structures based on an interaction between the individual and his or her environment. But in the cultural historical approach, the psychological structures are developed from a reciprocal mirroring process, while Piaget deals with a construction which, to a great extent, can involve interpretations and deviations from the conditions of the environment.

In the cultural historical approach, mankind's interaction with the environment is characterised by the key concept of activity. Through activity, the individual acquires the cultural conditions that he or she is a part of, and at the same time he or she influences cultural development within the society:

> What is the concrete link between the psychological features of man's individual consciousness and his social being? – The answer to that stems from the basic psychological fact that the structure of man's consciousness is linked in a regular way with the structure of his activity. – Man's activity then can only have a structure that is created by given social conditions and the relations between people engendered by them.
>
> (Leontjev 1981 [1959], p. 231)

It must be emphasised that activity is defined as *goal-directed* endeavours. It can only be considered activity when the individual pursues definite aims through his or her efforts. Activity is seen as different actions that can, again, be divided up into different operations, and it is characteristic that in his or her activity, a person can make use of different tools, which are not simply material instruments and devices, but can also include language, social conventions, theories and so on.

There are many kinds of activity, but the most important – which activity theorists return to time after time – are *play*, *learning* and *labour*, which are the predominant forms of activity in the pre-school age, school-age and adulthood, respectively. The Danish learning theorist Mads Hermansen finds, however, that in this connection learning is better characterised as a result of activity, and that the prevailing form of activity in the school-age years should probably be called school activity (Hermansen 1996, pp. 63f.).

Thus we enter the sphere of the more specific learning approach of the cultural historical tradition, as developed by Vygotsky, in particular in connection with his central work on thought and language (Vygotsky 1986 [1934]) – and at this point it seems to me characteristic that while object reflection and activity are the general comprehension categories, Vygotsky deals with learning as something more specific that occurs in school and other 'educational' situations. I think it is no coincidence that Vygotsky perceives learning as a particular form of activity on a level with play and work, for the concept is related to contexts in which the very fact that someone is to learn something is vitally important to the situation, and the underlying thought pattern seems to involve an interaction between one person who is more capable, and others (one or more) who are less so – one who represents the evolved culture, and others who are to acquire it.

This is particularly the case regarding two concepts that play a central role every time there is an attempt to set Vygotsky's learning concept into pedagogical theories, instructions or practice, namely, the concept of the zone of proximal development (Vygotsky 1978, pp. 84ff., 1986 [1934], pp. 187ff.) and the concept of scientific concepts (Vygotsky 1986 [1934], pp. 146ff.). Vygotsky defined the zone of proximal development as 'the distance between the actual developmental level as determined by independent problem solving and the level of potential development as determined through problem solving under adult guidance or in collaboration with more capable peers' (Vygotsky 1978, p. 86). Scientific concepts are concepts that are real and genuine, i.e. they must be precise and defined in a systematic context.

I have always been somewhat sceptical of these two key concepts in the cultural historical tradition because it is so clearly adults and those in power who are able to decide both what the specific zones of proximal development are for children or participants in education, and what concepts can be characterised as scientific. Therefore, applying Vygotsky's learning concepts, teaching easily becomes a predominantly teacher-directed form of encounter which, in turn, can easily result in the nearest zone of proximal development being conceived of in the perspective of academic systematism, e.g. the next chapter in the textbook (whereby logical and psychological arrangement become confused, which Dewey so strongly warned against – Dewey 1902). Hence, scientific concepts will become synonymous with the concepts of those in power.

Though it was hardly Vygotsky's intention it appears that his learning conception and account may easily lead to a form of goal-directed activity in which it is the teacher or the adults that control the process to a very great extent. In Denmark in the late 1970s and early 1980s we saw what this can lead to in practice, when Vygotsky-inspired so-called 'structured learning', which was very much pedagogically controlled, was a widespread ideal in Danish pre-school institutions (Brostrøm 1977). But there have been other experiments in Denmark, also based on Vygotsky's learning concept, without that same dogmatic kind of teacher control, and in which more emphasis has been placed on the pupils' own contributions to the concept development (Hedegaard and Hansen 1992).

As I see it, the cultural historical tradition has, first and foremost, used the historic-genetic approach to build up an important basis for the understanding of the biological, historical and societal anchoring of psychological processes. It has moved in the tension field between the content and the interaction dimensions of learning, but even though Vygotsky has expressed understanding of the significance of the emotions clearly enough (Vygotsky 1986 [1934], p. 8), it has in general not been particularly prominent in the activity theoretical picture. And perhaps because the tradition was developed within the ideal of a contradiction-free communist society, in its fundament it lacks an understanding of societal conflicts and their fundamental structural importance – and in extension of this an idea may very well emerge that transfer of cultural and societal matters to a particular individual can take place as a more or less frictionless process. This might mean a simplification of the understanding of the learning conception and could, in practice, cause a number of problems with respect to authority.

However, some of the passing on of the cultural historical approach to the learning understanding of recent years would seem to have transcended these problems. I refer here, in particular, to the already mentioned Finnish learning researcher Yrjö Engeström, who in connection with the development of the theory of learning by expanding (section 4.6), in my opinion has taken a decisive step ahead. For example, while Engeström has adopted Vygotsky's concept of the zone of proximal development from the cultural historical tradition – he has not done so without criticism. On the contrary, he makes a critique similar to what I have put forward here – and after a lengthy discussion of this, he ends by endorsing the following reformulation of Vygotsky's definition of the zone of proximal development, proposed by the Americans Peg Griffin and Michael Cole:

> Adult wisdom does not provide teleology for child development. Social organization and leading activities provide a gap within which the child can develop novel creative analyses . . . – a Zo-ped [author's note: zone of proximal development] is a dialogue between the child and his future; it is not a dialogue between the child and an adult's past.
>
> (Griffin and Cole 1984, p. 62)

But Engeström does not stop at this reformulation. Such a radical alteration of the definition of the concept must have further consequences. A dialogue between the child and his future in the form of new analyses clearly indicates creative processes, and, therefore, the reformulation involves an understanding of the zone of proximal development as a space for creativity. This is a clear expansion of Vygotsky's comprehension, and in Engeström's opinion it is a necessary one: we must stop talking about the acquisition of what has already been developed, and understand that what are important are creative processes (see Engeström 1987, pp. 169ff.).

However, the precondition for such processes taking place is that the individual must have a pressing problem or conflict of interests that cannot be solved within the existing set of alternatives. A transgression of this nature can typically occur when the learner in a problem situation asks him- or herself questions such as: 'What is the meaning and sense of this problem in the first place? Why should I try to solve it? How did it emerge? Who designed it, for what purpose and for whose benefit?' (Engeström 1987, p. 151).

Problem solving and the social and societal context move into the centre, and in this way Engeström also indirectly allies himself with a constructivist understanding of learning.

In this connection it is also natural to mention American psychologist Jerome Bruner. Back in the 1940s he started with various studies in personality psychology and cognitive psychology, which increasingly challenged and exceeded traditional behaviourism and played a part in the development of cognitive science (Bruner *et al.* 1956, 1966). It was on this basis that in 1957 he was elected chairman of the group of experts who were to reform the American education system after the 'Sputnik shock' (when the Russians sent the world's first satellite into space) had shaken belief in American technological and scientific supremacy. This resulted, among other things, in the books entitled *The Process of Education*, *Toward a Theory of Instruction* and *The Relevance of Education* (Bruner 1960, 1966, 1971), which were central for the spread of the so-called science-centred curriculum, i.e. the pedagogical idea that educational processes should be organised as a gradual development of understanding where, to a high degree, the learners themselves uncover the way in which things are structured and create meaning (for example, Taba 1962).

But Bruner gradually became more humanistically and culturally oriented in his approaches, and in his books *Actual Minds, Possible Worlds*, *Acts of Meaning* and not least *The Culture of Education* (Bruner 1986, 1990, 1996), which he published at the age of 82 and which will probably be regarded as his main work, he moved into a cultural psychological position in which learning is about acquiring and developing cultural expressions actively and together with others.

In this way, throughout his long life Bruner went all the way from a narrowly cognitive and individual-oriented starting point to a broadly humanistic and socially oriented view. He has often stated that he has gone through this course by standing on the shoulders of both Piaget and Vygotsky, both of whom he knew personally. And, finally, he has in particular come close to the cultural historical tradition and at his great age participated in some of the seminars and conferences related to this tradition.

But he has at the same time adopted the narrative understanding, in terms of which people's life history, the story one has about oneself and which constantly develops and is interpreted anew, is the red thread running through life, self-understanding and learning. As late as in 2002 Bruner published *Making Stories: Law, Literature, Life* (Bruner 2002) – and in June 2005, at the age of 90, he was the main speaker at a conference on 'Culture, Narrative and Mind' in Copenhagen.

5.4 Adult education, transformation and critical thinking

Another important approach to the content dimension of learning was developed in relation to adult education in the USA and Canada. This approach does not have a clear, common theoretical basis, but nevertheless it has a certain common inspiration pointing back to John Dewey (e.g. 1916, 1965 [1938]), and especially his colleague at Teachers College, Columbia University in New York, Eduard Lindeman (1885–1953), in the first half of the twentieth century, and to Malcolm Knowles (1913–1997) and Canadian Allen Tough (Lindeman 1926; Tough 1967, 1971; Knowles 1970, 1973) in the 1960s and 1970s. Here I will discuss Jack Mezirow and Stephen Brookfield as two of the most important more recent learning theoreticians in this approach.

Jack Mezirow has many years of practice behind him as a consultant in the field of adult education in different developing countries before returning to the USA at the end of the 1970s and beginning to formulate himself more theoretically. As well as the above-mentioned more general North American tradition of adult education, three other sources of inspiration were very important to Mezirow. First, Brazilian Paulo Freire (see section 7.7), who has worked with liberation pedagogy for poor illiterates in developing countries (Freire 1970). Second, German philosopher and sociologist Jürgen Habermas with a background in German critical theory (in particular, Habermas 1984–87 [1981] – see section 7.4). And third, experience from the American women's movement, which in the 1970s was behind a number of activities for adult women wishing to return to the education system (Mezirow 1978).

The concept of transformative learning is central in Mezirow; I have already referred to this in section 4.6, where Mezirow's definition of the concept is also quoted. According to Mezirow, we organise the under-standings we build up through our learning, partly in a series of *meaning schemes* for different areas of content roughly corresponding to Piaget's understanding, and partly more generally in some *meaning perspectives*, which constitute the key frame of reference for our creation of meaning.

We develop most of our meaning perspectives up through childhood and youth, and they then function both consciously and, to a high degree, unconsciously as governing our attitudes and modes of understanding (Mezirow 1990, 1991, 2000).

Transformative learning is about being conscious of, considering and reviewing one's meaning perspectives and the habits of mind that follow from them. This typically occurs when one discovers in one or other connection that the meaning perspectives do not fit with what one experiences or does. Then dissonance or a dilemma arises which one feels one must solve, and this takes place first and foremost through reflection, leading to revision or transformation of the meaning perspectives, i.e. through transformative learning.

Mezirow repeatedly stresses that transformative learning involves emotional aspects to a high degree:

> Cognition has strong affective and conative dimensions; all the sensitivity and responsiveness of the person participates in the invention, discovery, interpretation, and transformation of meaning. Transformative learning, especially when it involves subjective reframing, is often an intensely threatening emotional experience in which we have to become aware of both the assumptions undergirding our ideas and those supporting our emotional responses to the need to change.
> (Mezirow 2000, pp. 6–7)

Nevertheless, it is remarkable, and has been pointed out by many, that Mezirow's description of the transformative process is, to a high degree, grounded in cognition and content. This has to do with the transformation of meanings and modes of understanding, and, when the emotions are mentioned, they typically appear as a kind of accompanying phenomenon more than as a part of what is transformed. Nor does the social and societal dimension seem to be a direct part, even though Mezirow's thinking is clearly associated with pedagogical considerations and strong social and democratic engagement (see Illeris 2004).

In relation to the way in which I have defined and used the concept of transformative learning in the last chapter, there is thus a tendency for Mezirow's own understanding of the concept not to emphasise the significance of the three dimensions of learning to the same degree. He also sometimes makes use of the concept in connection with learning which, in the terms of this book, would be regarded as accommodative, and he has even mentioned that in some cases transformations can take place through assimilation (Mezirow 1998, p. 191). Nevertheless, I do not think that there are any decisive differences with respect to the intentions that Mezirow and I link to the use of the concept, but rather in the academic traditions on which we build.

Stephen Brookfield was born, brought up and educated in England, but since the 1980s he has lived and worked in the USA, where he also was one of Mezirow's colleagues at Teachers College in New York.

Although Brookfield's approach greatly resembles Mezirow's, each of them has been careful to hold on to their set of concepts and their special angles. Where transformative learning has been central for Mezirow, for Brookfield it is *critical thinking* and *critical reflection*, which he has clearly explained, inter alia, in this formulation:

> In terms of Mezirow's transformational theory it is clear that transformative learning cannot happen without critical reflection being involved at every stage. Given this, it might seem logical to extrapolate from Mezirow's comments that the two processes are equivalent – synonyms for each other. Yet this would be a mistake and Mezirow carefully avoids it. Critical reflection is certainly a necessary condition of transformative learning, in that the existence of the latter depends on the presence of the former. However, it is not a sufficient condition; in other words, just because critical reflection is occurring does not mean that transformative learning inevitably ensues. An episode of critical reflection on practice does not automatically lead to transformation. As Mezirow acknowledges, the assumptions one holds can be exactly the same after critical reflection as they were before.
>
> (Brookfield 2000a, p. 142)

It is thus Brookfield's opinion that critical thinking or reflection can be very valuable and something that is important to promote in itself, even if it does not lead into demanding and onerous transformative learning. For Brookfield, being able to think critically and getting used to critical thinking is what is central, while transformative learning is something that can accompany this under certain circumstances.

According to Brookfield, critical reflection is something different from, and more than, merely reflection in general. It is about:

- identifying challenging assumptions;
- challenging the meaning and the context;
- trying to use one's imagination and exploring other possibilities;
- and that these notions and explorations lead to reflective scepticism.

(Brookfield 1987, pp. 7ff.)

(Brookfield uses the expressions 'assumptions' and 'sets of assumptions' more or less as Mezirow uses 'meaning schemes' and 'meaning perspectives').

Brookfield regards critical reflection and thinking as fundamental in a democratic society, from daily life and work to the political level, and thereby also in adult education programmes. Likewise, in his most recent book (Brookfield 2005) he examines the concept of *critical theory* in a broader and more general understanding than that which only refers to the so-called Frankfurt School (to which I return in section 7.4).

Brookfield also regards the key tasks of adult education teachers as encouraging the participants to practise critical reflection, and he points out that they themselves must master and practise such an approach (e.g. Brookfield 1990a, 1995). He has, moreover, been greatly interested in how this can be done in practice in many different ways, e.g. through the participants' analysis of situations which they themselves have experienced as critical (Brookfield 1990b).

What is always crucial for Brookfield is that one constantly questions one's own problems and reasons, that one questions the assumptions and reasons of others, and that one questions the contexts that set the stage for the situations and matters to which one relates.

Like Mezirow, he explicitly stresses that 'critical thinking is both emotional and rational' (Brookfield 1987, p. 7) – but, as for Mezirow, for Brookfield it is nevertheless content and the cognitive that come to the fore in his descriptions. He primarily concerns himself with thinking and reflection and less with experiences, feelings or interaction. But where Mezirow, as mentioned, first and foremost deals with the learning processes that were termed transformative in the previous chapter, although he has no clear delimitation to the accommodative processes, in Brookfield the opposite is almost the case. His focus is predominantly on the accommodative processes implied by critical thinking and reflection, while transformative learning is seen as something that can be an extension of this in special cases.

5.5 Reflection and meta-learning

In connection with the content dimension of learning, I will here finally discuss some very topical concepts extending beyond ordinary immediate learning through acquisition, namely *reflection*, which I take up together with meta-learning in this section, and *reflexivity*, which I discuss along with *biographicity* in the next section.

The word 'reflection' can encompass two different main meanings, both in everyday language and that of academic study. One concerns *afterthought*: one reflects on or gives further thought to something, perhaps an event or a problem. The other can best be characterised as *mirroring* – in line with the word's original optical meaning: an experience or comprehension of something is mirrored in the self of the learner, i.e. the significance for the self is in focus and the experience is evaluated with the personal identity as a yardstick – which is why the word *self-reflection* is also used in this sense. It is, particularly, the ability for, or inclination to, this form of reflection that is today often defined as *reflexivity*, although it must be said an accurate vocabulary does not always occur in this sphere.

For the time being, however, I will concentrate on reflection in the cognitive sense of afterthought. In recent years this has increasingly been part of both the political and the academic learning debate, to such an extent that functions of this nature have been seen as an important general objective for education and socialisation and thus also as a central element in a modern ideal of formation.

What seems to characterise this kind of reflection is that new impulses arising from interaction with the environment do not occur directly – the words afterthought and reflection contain this element of time lag. Of course, the process is sparked off by interaction with the environment, and it is also quite possible that some immediate learning from this interaction has taken place. However, something remains unfinished, the impulses have not been completed, there is an element of cognitive dissonance (Festinger 1957), and when a suitable situation appears, perhaps a quiet moment, the afterthought makes itself felt. As Jack Mezirow has pointed out, reflection also occurs when what has been learnt is to be used in a later context or an examination or justification of acquired comprehension (Mezirow 1990, 1991).

In psychology this situation was first considered by the German psychologist I have already mentioned, Karl Duncker (1945 [1935]), who was one of the first to systematically research the psychology of problem solving – and it is characteristic that afterthought in one form or another always takes the nature of problem solving. The original interaction has left behind something uncertain or unsolved, some problems, which must be put into place by means of elaboration later. As a learning process, reflection can, therefore, be characterised as accommodative learning that does not occur immediately in connection with the trigger impulses, but after a time lag implying a further elaboration of the impulses.

Reflection is thus basically of the same nature as other accommodative learning processes, but it includes a further consideration. Therefore, reflection will also require more psychological energy, and at the same time involves a potential for further elaboration in relation to the immediate accommodation.

Reflection has become a keyword in the present debate on pedagogics and learning theory. This is because in recent years there has been strongly increased awareness that what is learned in school and education programmes must be able to be used in practice, especially in working life, and it has become clear that reflection plays a decisive role in this context. Very often it is only through reflection and processing that the accommodations take place that can contribute to this transfer (see section 4.7). For this reason the pedagogical structure must ensure that such reflection takes place in a community and in the individual, and that what is learned in this way is linked to relevant practice situations.

This is also an important part of the background for reflection being a key element in a number of modern learning theories, e.g. as already mentioned in Mezirow and Brookfield with their concept about critical reflection. Above-mentioned American organisation psychologist Donald Schön speaks directly of 'the reflective turn' in education programmes (Schön 1991), but it should be noted here that his own concept of 'reflection-in-action' (Schön 1983), does not fall within the concept of reflection after a time as described above.

For Schön, reflection-in-action is a process in which one immediately reacts to a problem or a situation by finding new potential solutions, drawing on one's familiarity with the field in question – and if there is no element of examination or new thinking, then it is a typical example of what I have dealt with in the previous chapter as an 'ordinary' accommodation, i.e. a direct learning reaction to impulses in an interaction with the surrounding world (see Mezirow 1990, pp. 112ff.).

However, Schön's language use shows at the same time that it can be difficult to maintain this distinction, because according to Schön reflection-in-action can also include the situation where one stops in the middle of an action, thinks, and finds out how to continue, and then goes on. This is actually a brief shift in time but nevertheless within a certain process – and it may be more precise to speak, like Australians David Boud *et al.*, of 'reflective practice' as a process where action, experience and reflection more or less flow together (Boud *et al.* 1985; Boud and Walker 1990).

With respect to the concept of meta-learning, there are also two different understandings or approaches. The one is about what more popularly has been termed 'learning to learn', i.e. an idea that today learning is so important that one must also learn how best to tackle it. The other is about accustoming oneself to thinking critically and analytically about one's own learning, i.e. placing one's own learning in a personally and societally general perspective.

The popular phrase 'learning to learn' is a modern catchphrase which, when viewed from an academic perspective, can be traced back to the observation within learning psychology that if an individual constantly applies him- or herself to learning within a given field, there will typically occur a gradual increase of learning speed (presumably because one gradually has more and more relevant presuppositions at one's disposal, a closer net of structures is woven, or however one may like to put it – see Bateson 1972, pp. 166ff.). However, this original meaning seems to have been lost, and the modern catchphrase seems more like a mystification, as if one has to be trained to be able to learn something.

Therefore, it must be maintained, as pointed out earlier, that the ability to learn is one of mankind's innate skills – and, moreover, in the next chapter it will emerge that this also fundamentally includes the desire to learn: learning is basically libidinal. When the catchphrase appears time and time again in debate, however, there must naturally be a response to it – and part of that response surely lies in the fact that institutionalised learning in schools and institutions can tend to undermine the desire to learn, at least in certain contexts and under certain forms.

Naturally this does not mean that it sometimes cannot be sensible to acquire appropriate habits and procedures in connection with different forms of learning, including for example reflection, testing and application, or quite external matters such as arranging suitable and well-organised learning situations and developing a helpful and empathetic climate of cooperation. But calling this 'learning to learn' is quite an exaggeration. It is surely rather the case that it takes quite an effort to prevent people from learning – even though they might not always learn what others think they should.

Dealing with the concept of meta-learning is more complicated – or *meta-cognition*, which is the somewhat broader term employed (e.g. Engeström 1987, p. 128), understood as a general learning category that places other learning processes in a collected overall perspective. One, perhaps, comes closest to it with the previously mentioned category 'learning III' in Bateson's learning theory, which involves acquiring something qualitatively new by understanding the fundamental conditions for ordinary assimilative learning and partly also accommodative learning and practical training in an area.

This is, however, precisely the way Engeström has gone in developing his concept about expansive learning, which I placed on a level with transformative learning (in section 4.6). Similarly, if one looks at Mezirow's definition of transformative learning, here it is also the case that it is the underlying meaning schemes and meaning perspectives that must be reconstructed to arrive at a more overall understanding.

The conclusion is that meta-learning understood in this way is the same as accommodative learning if it is a matter of a relatively limited field, and as transformative (or expansive) learning if it is a case of a larger area that also includes a more personal element. The difference would seem only to be that when one speaks of meta-learning one sees it typically from a content or academic perspective and therefore, perhaps, seeks an academic solution or approach, whereas the other concepts are defined on the basis of the learner's perspective and therefore also indicate to a higher degree a solution or approach based on the learner's situation.

It is, however, worth maintaining that meta-learning can occur whenever there is a significant conflict of interests and there is the potential for a transcendent adaptation. The learning process may take the form of coming through a crisis, in which the learner struggles for a certain length of time with a problem which is of urgent subjective importance – this is both reflection and meta-learning. But meta-learning can also occur as a shorter and more intense process, even like a kind of explosion in the most concentrated cases.

In modern creativity theory, precisely this kind of conflict-filled and chaotic situation can be seen as a typical background for creative transcendence (e.g. Joas 1996 [1992]), and the Swede Feiwel Kupferberg has noted that project work can form a pedagogical framework that contains possibilities of this kind (Kupferberg 1996). A more general pedagogical observation is that there must be challenges that the learner feels obliged to deal with, and that there must be the potential for, and input to, a relevant processing of such challenges if learning of this kind is to take place.

5.6 Reflexivity and biographicity: the self as learning content

In recent years reflexivity in the sense of mirroring has become a central concept in a number of current sociological, cultural theory and socialisation theory approaches – e.g. from English theorists such as Anthony Giddens and German theorists such as Ulrich Beck, Niklas Luhmann (1927–1998) and Thomas Ziehe. This has to do with the transition from industrial society to the service and knowledge society – or, viewed in a cultural and consciousness perspective, to 'late modernity' or 'postmodernity'.

In relation to learning and personal development, what the German youth and culture theorist Thomas Ziehe has called cultural liberation (Ziehe and Stubenrauch 1982, pp. 17ff.) is central to this development. We – and particularly the young – have been liberated from all the old norms and traditions that previously controlled our lives, for good or bad, to choosing and forming our own lives to a far greater degree. This means that individuality has come into focus in a new way, and this involves one constantly putting what one learns in relation to oneself, i.e. to one's understanding of oneself, and what meaning the influences one faces have for oneself. Ziehe very briefly defines reflexivity as 'the opportunity to relate to oneself' (Ziehe 1985, p. 200), and describes it in another context as:

> if we were constantly filming ourselves with a video camera, observing ourselves and commenting on it. All members of modern society are basically part of that structure, but it is most obvious among the young. . . . To be 'modern' today means to be able to name and formalise definite goals for oneself, which one relates to strategically and uses in one's self-reflection.
>
> (Ziehe 1997, p. 29)

Ziehe later suggested the term 'the second modernisation' for these developments and their societal background, and he points out that pedagogical changes that have taken place from the 1970s onwards are no longer on a level with the situation and forms of consciousness of the young (Ziehe 1998).

The English sociologist Anthony Giddens is also very interested in these matters and sees them from a slightly different perspective:

> It is often said that modernity is marked by an appetite for the new, but this is not perhaps completely accurate. What is characteristic of modernity is not an embracing of the new for its own sake, but the presumption of wholesale reflexivity – which of course includes reflection upon the nature of reflection itself. . . . Modernity is constituted in and through reflexively applied knowledge, but the equation of knowledge with certitude has turned out to be misconceived. We are abroad in a world which is thoroughly constituted through reflexively applied knowledge, but where at the same time we can never be sure that any given element of that knowledge will be revised.
>
> (Giddens 1990, p. 39)

Both Ziehe and Giddens stress that reflexivity is not only an intellectual phenomenon but, to a great extent, also concerns experiential and emotional matters and self-comprehension and formation of the identity, generally. And Giddens goes further: he also uses the expression *reflexivity of the body* for the modern upgrading of body awareness, identifies a hidden *institutional reflexivity*, i.e. that society's organs and institutions today must also function reflexively, constantly referring to and legitimising their existence and function – and talks generally about *reflexivity of modernity* as a characteristic of the time (Giddens 1990, 1991).

On the same level the German sociologist Ulrich Beck characterises the new epoch as *reflexive modernisation* because reflexivity has become an individual and societal necessity, and in the light of the breakdown of the grand narratives, the dominance of market mechanisms, globalisation etc., he talks of the *risk society*, because the individual must choose his own life course without any certainties to guide him or her (Beck 1992 [1986]).

Finally, I would like to mention in this connection the German sociologist Niklas Luhmann, whose approach can be termed system theoretical – the concept of system being used about individuals, groups, organisations, and function systems such as markets – and these systems are characterised by being self-referential, self-reproductive and closed to the surrounding world that does not form part of the system, but is a condition for its existence. Luhmann sees the world today as being characterised by an emergent order, i.e. that it cannot be understood from any overall principle, but each sphere and each system has its own basis. As self-referential systems, late-modern people must thus control their own existence and function in an ever-changing world, and this demands reflexivity – which in this context seems to appear as a central condition for existence for people today (for example, Luhmann 1995 [1984]).

At first glance there appears to be a relationship between the focus of these modern observers on the individual's relationship to him- or herself, and a number of classical orientations within humanistic psychology, e.g. Gordon Allport's (1897–1967) ideal of 'the mature personality' (Allport 1967), Carl Rogers's 'fully functioning person' (Rogers 1961), or Abraham Maslow's (1908–1970) notion of 'self-actualization' as the ultimate goal for existence (Maslow 1954; see section 6.5). But while such orientations have been open to criticism for being individualistic and without roots in society, the concepts referred to here take societal conditions as a starting point for the comprehension of typical developments in the individual. Central to these developments are reflexivity or self-reflection, which are both psychological categories that describe characteristic human modes of function in late modernity, and sociological categories concerning society's modes of function and the relationship between the individual and society.

The late-modern concept of reflexivity is, therefore, not primarily concerned with learning and thinking but, nevertheless, involves considerable consequences for the nature of learning. It can be broadly linked to the development of personality and various more specific personal qualities, but in relation to learning reflexivity concentrates first and foremost on the development of the self and the functions of the self.

The self is a philosophical and psychological concept with a somewhat turbulent history, which can be interpreted as a mirroring of the development in the relationship between the individual and society at different times. The central point is that the self takes the nature of a relation, i.e. the relation or the perception the individual has to, or of, him- or herself – in contrast to the concept of personality, which centres on qualities the individual has or is attributed with. But within the psychoanalytical tradition, there is also a lengthy and more detailed discussion of the definition of the self, the psychology of the self, and the relationship between the self and the ego (for example, Kohut 1977; Goldberg 1978).

In the present context, however, I would like to refer to the concept of the self that was developed by the American psychotherapist mentioned earlier, Carl Rogers, because he directly links changes in the organisation of the self with the concept of 'significant learning', which I have discussed earlier. Rogers basically perceives the self as an innate tendency for activity which, through interaction with the environment, develops into 'the organized, consistent conceptual gestalt composed of perceptions of the characteristics of the "I" or "me" to others and to various aspects of life, together with the values attached to these perceptions' (Rogers 1959, p. 200).

If we maintain the parallel between 'significant learning' and transformative learning (see section 4.6), this leads to the assertion that changes in the self occur through transformations concerning the organised, consistent conceptual whole, which structures the individual's perception of him- or herself and others, and of various aspects of life. This is, therefore, a specific type of transformative learning characterised by the involvement of self-experience and self-relationing, i.e. the individual relates to him- or herself – and it is precisely this that is implied in the concepts of reflection and mirroring.

Several of the previously mentioned analysts in this sphere also emphasise that such reflexivity is not necessarily limited to internal processes, but can also occur through interpersonal communicative processes, in which one uses other people as a kind of sparring partner, and performs the mirroring actively and externally as an aid to gaining insights into one's own self-comprehension by observing the reactions of others, and listening to their evaluations.

Today, reflexivity must, first and foremost, be understood in relation to the general societal conditions that mean that the individual constantly has to choose his or her way, not only externally, between all sorts of offers, but also internally, in terms of life course, lifestyle and identity. But with this, reflexivity also comes to have significance for some of the personal characteristics such as independence, self-confidence, sociability, sensibility and flexibility, which are highly valued on today's labour market. But it should also be mentioned that these processes cannot always be immediately comprehended as being forward-looking or positive. Personal development and reflexivity may also involve the development of resistance, defensiveness, distortions and blocks which, in various ways, can be rigid and restrictive for the person in question. I return to this in Chapter 9.

Biographicity is another important and closely related concept that can be said to cover both reflexivity and personal development. The concept was launched by the German biography researcher Peter Alheit, whom I have mentioned previously in section 4.6 in connection with 'transitory learning'. He describes biographicity as the experience modern people have of being able to form their own lives to a great extent:

> Biographicity means that we can redesign again and again, from scratch, the contours of our life within the specific contexts in which we (have to) spend it, and that we experience these contexts as 'shapeable' and designable. In our biographies, we do not possess all conceivable opportunities, but within the framework of the limits we are structurally set we still have considerable scope open to us. The main issue is to decipher the 'surplus meanings' of our biographical knowledge, and that in turn means to perceive the potentiality of our unlived lives.
>
> (Alheit 1995, p. 65)

Such biographicity has been quite widespread in recent years, in step with 'normal biography' construction principles breaking down, i.e. there might not be a natural continuity between family background, education, work and identity, but a perception that those are issues one can, and must, take a stand on.

It is important to be aware that biographicity is something that concerns how we perceive and interpret our lives in relation to the opportunities we have and the choices we make. For in this lies also the fact that biographicity can be understood as an overall framework for learning through reflexivity, which, after the breakdown of the external traditional norm-oriented framework, holds the individual's self-comprehension and identity together.

Finally, it should be mentioned that the concepts of reflexivity and biographicity, which concern learning in relation to the self and self-understanding, do in this way enter into a special aspect of the content dimension of learning. But as the self and self-understanding include the whole individual and thereby all three dimensions of learning, this learning simultaneously points to the two other dimensions and is thus on the edge of the holistic learning in all three dimensions, which I take up in Chapter 8.

In addition, in various current approaches of a 'social constructionist' and 'postmodern' nature (see section 7.8) there have been strong objections to the validity of more traditional views of the self today. For example, American Kenneth Gergen has described the self as 'saturated' (Gergen 1991; see section 7.8), and English-Australian Robin Usher has characterised the typical present self as weak and incoherent (Usher *et al.* 1997; Usher 2000; see section 7.8), while Australian psychologist Mark Tennant has criticised these views as being too extreme in their deconstruction of the self and is of the opinion that it is precisely through learning, e.g. in adult education programmes, that work can be done on a reconstruction of the participants' selves with a view to creating 'a certain degree of contours and continuity . . . rather than fragmentation and discontinuity' (Tennant 1998, p. 165).

In the present context, however, precisely to maintain the possibility of working with the self in the context of learning, I will refer back to the definition developed by the previously mentioned American Carl Rogers.

5.7 Summary

The content dimension of learning is about *what* is learned. Traditionally this content has been viewed in the categories of knowledge, skills, and also attitudes in some contexts, and these are, naturally, very important aspects or parts of the content. But in modern society the content of learning must also be understood in some much more far-reaching categories.

First, and quite centrally, it must be maintained that learning – and accommodative and transformative learning to a special degree – also concerns everything we describe with words such as understanding, insight, meaning, coherence and overview. It is inherent in human brain capacity, and thus in our nature, to try to create meaning in what we learn, and precisely this aspect of learning increases in step with society becoming more and more complex. Despite all the television competitions in fingertip knowledge, the acquisition of knowledge without understanding is becoming increasingly inadequate in relation to the reality in which we live.

Next, it is important that learning content also includes a more general acquisition of the culture and the social contexts of which we are a part. This is what was termed 'formation' in traditional educational language and formulations of objectives, but where earlier there was an attempt to define 'top-down' what such formation covers, today there is such cultural diversity and constant innovation that it is hardly meaningful any longer to retain it in fixed content-describing formulations. To a far higher degree it is about acquiring a general readiness to understand, follow and critically relate to the world around us. In this connection reflection is understood as afterthought and fresh evaluation of increasingly greater significance for learning.

Finally, an increasingly urgent content field for learning would seem to be learning about ourselves, getting to know oneself, understanding one's own reactions, inclinations, preferences, strong and weak sides etc. as a prerequisite for making meaningful decisions, and thus, to a certain degree, participating in managing one's own life course. Reflexivity and bio-graphicity become learning challenges of key significance in this connection.

Chapter 6

The incentive dimension of learning

Learning's incentive dimension concerns the matters we usually speak about in terms of emotions, motivation and volition. It is on the basis of these we mobilise the energy that is the necessary motive power of learning. They thus also become part of our learning processes, influencing the quality of the learning that takes place, for example with respect to permanency and utility. The relation between the content and incentive dimensions is taken up on the basis of a fundamental comparison of Piaget's and Freud's understandings. Then two more modern approaches are presented concerning emotional intelligence and a learning oriented phenomenological personality theory. In the last sections of the chapter, the focus is on motivation psychology, on disturbances and conflicts as motivation, and on problems of motivation in present society.

6.1 The divided totality

As already stated in Chapter 3, the acquisition process of learning has both a content and an incentive dimension. Learning research has previously almost exclusively concerned itself with the content dimension, while incentive concerns have typically been dealt with in personality psychology, developmental psychology, motivational psychology and clinical psychology.

As I have also already stated, the classical distinction between the cognitive and the affective or the emotional exists not only in psychology as an academic discipline, but is a general feature in our culture and language, which can be traced back as far as the ancient Greek distinction between logos and psyche. With respect to learning, in plainer terms this has resulted in a distinction between, on the one hand, how we learn something, and on the other hand how we become who we are. As a typical example I can refer to the previously mentioned American learning researcher, Robert M. Gagné, from the introduction to his main work 'The Conditions of Learning':

In the most comprehensive sense of the word 'learning', motivations and attitudes must surely be considered to be learned. But the present treatment [author's note: Gagné: *The Conditions of Learning*] does not attempt to deal with such learnings, except in a tangential sense. Its scope is restricted to what may be termed the intellectual or subject matter content that leads to improvement in human performances having ultimate usefulness in the pursuit of the individual's vocation or profession.

(Gagné 1970 [1965], p. 25)

Against this is a personality and developmental psychology that is typically broadly concerned with human psychological development, but seldom takes any interest in the acquisition of concrete knowledge, skills or qualifications and thus places a considerable part of most educational processes beyond their horizon.

A similar tendency can implicitly lie in much of current progressive educational thinking. There is an interest in human development as a whole, societal and subjective conditions are brought in, learning is conceived of as an interaction between an acting individual with presuppositions both personal and created by society, and a surrounding world permeated with economic structures, power structures, media and ideological structures – but there is very little interest in the fact that most education also includes a subject matter content which it is extremely important to acquire, both for the individual and for society. Just consider how much we care that our bus drivers, mechanics, social workers, doctors and so on should all be properly qualified.

An adequate learning theory must thus transcend the classical division and concern itself with the human being as a whole, both the rational and subject matter content and the incentive and emotional sides, and, not least, the interaction between them.

6.2 Freud's understanding of drives

Just as I took my point of departure in Piaget's learning understanding in the above because I regard him as one of the most classic and pioneering researchers with respect to the content dimension of learning, in this chapter I will start with Sigmund Freud as the most classic and pioneering figure when it comes to the incentive perspective. And just as, in the case of Piaget, I addressed his fundamental learning understanding and circumvented his more well-known stage theory, I will go directly to Freud's understanding of drives, which is the basis of the incentive dimension, and set aside the better known theories about the psychosexual development stages (the oral, the anal and the genital phase) and the personality theory of the mental levels (the ego, the id and the superego).

Fundamentally, it is worth noting here that it is a spontaneous element in both Piaget and Freud – even though neither of them directly expresses it in this way – that it is from the incentive, emotional area that the learning processes emerge. This is where motivation comes from and where energy is collected. In this they are in line with modern brain research, which regards emotions (general states of feeling) and feelings as a kind of regulation mechanism that receives impulses from both the body and the environment and initiates unconscious and conscious reactions to these impulses in the form of actions, thoughts and thus also learning (for example, Damasio 1999, pp. 35ff.).

Freud regarded this whole field as being regulated by our drives, but changed his understanding of the fundamental conditions concerning the structures of drives several times. What is, without doubt, best known is his distinction between a basic life or Eros drive, which is concerned with desire, sexuality, nutrition and other life-supporting functions, and a death or Thanatos drive, which has to do with aversion, aggression and the like, and in the final analysis seeks towards death. But this was an understanding he only developed around 1920, and which was subsequently subjected to fierce criticism from several sides. How can such a death drive, for example, be compatible with an otherwise fundamentally Darwinist conception of the struggle for the survival of the species? Was this thinking not merely a result of the many negative forms of behaviour that Freud was constantly confronted with through his clinical work?

It can, therefore, make sense to return to the earlier version of the theory of drives where Freud distinguished between ego drives (e.g. nutrition etc.), serving to maintain life, and sexual drives, which serve the maintenance of the species (e.g. Freud 1940 [1915]) – the two drives that later were combined in the category of the life drives. This fits far better with Freud's fundamental views, with motivational psychology developed later, and with modern brain research. But what, then, about the death drive, about aversion and aggression and inexplicable self-destructive forms of behaviour? In my opinion Freud himself has given us the key to answering a part of this difficult question through his concept about defence mechanisms. Another part of the answer has to do with our potential for resistance. I return to both in Chapter 9.

Freud's theory of drives can also be problematic in other areas, among others his notion that the total psychological energy is constant, just as energy is constant in physics, and particularly concerns the idea that when a need is repressed, the energy that is connected to bringing it about gets transferred to other spheres: 'The energy of the nervous system appeared to Freud like steam in a steam engine. It pushes and presses to get out, and in so doing, makes the wheels go round' (Olsen and Køppe 1981, p. 329).

This is, naturally, naive as a general notion. Human beings have the possibility to mobilise and restore energy in many ways. But this does not exclude energy being linked to, for example, maintaining a mental defence and being released if such defence is overcome.

But why, then, should one concern oneself at all with Freud's theory of drives? First and foremost because Freud was the very first to think systematically along lines that concern the mobilisation of mental energy and thus the most fundamental precondition for learning. Next, because with his concepts of ego drives, sexual drives and life drives, Freud points to what it is basically about: namely, that the human being's fantastic potential for learning is embedded in the biologically and genetically developed urge for life-realisation, that it is essentially a survival potential, and that, therefore, in its realisation, it is fundamentally libidinal in line with other life-maintaining activities. This is worth holding on to as a point of departure in a world in which society exerts constant pressure to learn a lot of things throughout our whole lives that we might not always find particularly interesting or relevant.

The Austrian-American psychologist and Piaget specialist Hans Furth has written a book that he has called *Knowledge As Desire* (Furth 1987), in which he tries to combine the learning understandings of Piaget and Freud. I return to this in the next section (and I have also dealt with it fully in Illeris 2002, pp. 64ff.). Here it suffices to maintain that Piaget and Freud with their constructivist approaches to the two dimensions of the acquisition process have created a basis that makes it possible to analyse learning as the fundamentally life-maintaining, developing, qualifying and libidinal process it basically is, and thereby also to consider what is at stake when this is not always the case in today's world of reality.

6.3 Structures of content and patterns of incentives

Before I continue further with the incentive dimension, I should like to return to the divided whole I referred to at the beginning of this chapter and examine a little more closely the connection between content and incentive. In doing this I will continue with the above-mentioned book by Hans Furth (1987), because he concentrates on the relation between the two theoreticians, Piaget and Freud, from whom I have also taken my starting point.

In his introduction, Furth stresses that not only did Piaget and Freud develop the best known and most comprehensive theories in the cognitive and personality spheres, respectively, but that they also – despite the apparently huge difference in their theories – share some important fundamental features: they were both trained in biology, and they both anchored their theories in the biological development of the child, which they had studied empirically in detail.

However, Freud did not directly deal with the concept of learning, and even though many of his deliberations concern matters that belong under this book's learning concept, his contribution regarding the relationship between cognition and incentive is on a completely different level to the deliberations concerning learning with which I am dealing here.

The case is somewhat different when it comes to Piaget, however, because even though he did not work a great deal with emotional matters, some distinctive statements can be found in his work of many years. For example, the following:

> All schemes, whatever they are, are at the same time affective and cognitive.
>
> (Piaget 1946, p. 222, quoted from Furth 1987, p. 127)

> Affective life, like intellectual life, is a continual adaptation, and the two are not only parallel, but inter-dependent, since feelings express the interest and the value given to actions of which intelligence provides the structure. Since affective life is adaptation it also implies continual assimilation of present situations to earlier ones – assimilation gives rise to affective schemes or relatively stable modes of feeling or reacting – and continual accommodation of these schemes to the present situation.
>
> (Piaget 1951 [1945], pp. 205–206)

> Obviously for intelligence to function, it must be motivated by an affective power. A person won't ever solve a problem if the problem doesn't interest him. The impetus for everything lies in interest, affective motivation. . . . If the problem at hand is the construction of structures, affectivity is essential as a motivation, of course, but it doesn't explain the structures.
>
> (Piaget 1980b, quoted from Furth 1987, pp. 3 and 4)

These three quotations were formulated over a period of 35 years, and it is, therefore, no surprise that they are not immediately consistent. The first quotation concerns schemes that have to do with both incentive and content at one and the same time. The second refers to incentive schemes that can, however, be characterised as 'relatively stable modes of feeling or reacting', i.e. they are not of the same nature as the content schemes that Piaget usually characterises as structures. In the third quotation, incentive lies outside of the structures, but is necessary as motivation. How can these differences be explained and elucidated?

In examining this question I will go first to an approach developed in German 'Critical Psychology' (see section 7.5), in which Ute Holzkamp-Osterkamp, in particular, has concerned herself with the same problem:

> As we have been able to show with a thorough functional-historical analysis of the conditions for the differentiation of emotionality from

the life process . . . the emotions consist of evaluations of environmental conditions perceived cognitively with their subjective meanings and the individual action potential as a standard. The emotions are thus a significant defining element for actions concerning cognitively perceived circumstances and events.

(Holzkamp-Osterkamp 1978, p. 15)

For Holzkamp-Osterkamp, content and incentive are clearly perceived as two distinct spheres, functioning in close interaction in a particular way. This perception appears to parallel closely the last of the Piaget quotations, which concerned cognitive structures motivated by an affective power. But Holzkamp-Osterkamp continues:

The response concerning the evaluation of the adjustment of the individual behaviour reflects the individual organism not separately for each level in the environmental conditions, but as a 'compound quality', i.e. as a compound emotional mood that automatically sums up all single evaluations into a compound action direction, and only that can make goal-directed action possible.

(Holzkamp-Osterkamp 1978, p. 15)

The influence of incentive on content is thus perceived as an overall function, characterised by converting a differentiated influence from the surroundings into one overall impression. Although this summarising is described rather categorically by Holzkamp-Osterkamp – after all, one can easily experience both differentiated and contradictory emotions in a given situation – there is a certain parallel to Piaget's approach in that it concerns 'relatively stable modes of feeling or reacting'. In both cases there is a form of mediation of the diversity of the emotional possibilities, but no fixed structure, as in the cognitive sphere. Or to put it another way: where as a rule it is clear what one knows and does not know, what one understands and how one understands it, on the emotional level it is more a case of gradual transitions which, for the individual at any rate, follow a certain pattern that can change over time – and these changes occur, according to Piaget's approach in the second of the three quotations, by assimilations and accommodations in the same way as for the content structures. Where the individual builds up structures and schemes in the content sphere, in the emotional sphere it could be a case of developing incentive patterns.

However, Holzkamp-Osterkamp continues with another observation that is of interest in the present context:

Normally such emotional evaluations come forward only when there are 'disturbances' of the customary and 'automated' consequences of action and when there are actual threats to the ability to act, or in 'new' situations, requiring increased 'attention'. Thus they are characteristic for phases in which the organism 're-orients' relations with the surrounding world.

(Holzkamp-Osterkamp 1978, pp. 15–16)

If this is translated into the Piagetian and Freudian terminology used here, it can be seen that Holzkamp-Osterkamp perceives the emotions as more or less unconscious in assimilative processes, while in accommodation they come more to the forefront, and become conscious. If, for example, you work at actually acquiring the principles and history of social legislation, you are typically not very conscious of the emotions you attach to the matters being discussed, but if in that work you begin to grasp what some of these matters mean for people you actually know, the emotional aspect of the case can become conscious and very insistent. Using Piaget's sporadic declarations as a basis, and with Holzkamp-Osterkamp's approach as a filter, I am able to summarise the structural relationship between content and incentive after the relative separation that occurs around the age of six years as follows.

In learning, one can distinguish between the cognitive or epistemological aspect, which is concerned with the content of learning, and the incentive aspect, which is concerned with the dynamics of learning. Through the cognitive processes, content structures and schemes are developed, while emotional experience develops incentive patterns of a relatively stable nature. Both the content structures and the incentive patterns change and develop through an interaction of assimilative (additive, consolidating) and accommodative (transcendent, restructuring) processes. In assimilation the incentive aspect typically functions unconsciously for the most part, while in accommodation it typically becomes more conscious.

However, content and incentive develop from a common totality and always function in close interaction. So the next question has to be: what is this interaction like, and what is its function? Here, I would like to come back to another of Furth's many Piaget quotations:

Take, for instance, two boys and their arithmetic lessons. One boy likes them and forges ahead; the other . . . feels inferior and has all the typical complexes of people who are weak in math. The first boy will learn more quickly, the second more slowly. But for both, two and two are four. Affectivity doesn't modify the acquired structure at all.

(Piaget 1980b, quoted from Furth 1987, pp. 3–4)

The example is clear, plausible and unquestionably correct – and yet it does not tell the whole story, and it suffers from a weakness in Piaget's approach that was noted earlier: it only concerns a learning situation in which what is right and what is wrong can be clearly distinguished, i.e. convergent knowledge.

But what if it concerns divergent knowledge, in which the learning situation is ambiguous and there can be many equally 'correct' learning results? Do the emotions in that case still not have any significance for what is being learnt? And although in terms of content, both boys learn the same thing, have the emotions or the motivation no significance for the nature of the learning result, e.g. how well it is remembered, how inclined one is to use it in new contexts (transfer potential), or how it is at one's disposal as an element in connection with new learning?

If one moves just a little beyond Piaget's very straightforward example, it is easy to see that incentives will have a significance for the learning results, even if what is being learned is apparently the same. The well motivated boy will, as a rule, be better at remembering his maths, even if the less motivated boy slaves over it and eventually learns the same. The well motivated boy will be inclined to use his maths skills in all relevant contexts, while the less motivated one will tend to avoid such contexts, or avoid seeing them from a mathematical point of view – and this, in turn, will also make him more likely to forget it.

More generally, the incentive aspect of learning will always affect the learning result, even if it does not influence the epistemological content itself. To use an expression from Freudian terminology, we can say that cognitive learning is always affectively 'obsessed': there are always emotional tones or imprints attached to the knowledge being developed. And generally it will be the case that the stronger the incentives that are present in the learning situation, the stronger the emotional obsession will be – just think of the powerful tensions that characterise the Oedipal drama as described by Freud, and how this influences the individual for the rest of his or her life.

However, the interaction works in both directions. The emotions are also influenced by knowledge: 'In the study of feelings, when you find structures, they are structures of knowledge. For example, in feelings of mutual affection there's an element of comprehension and an element of perception. That's all cognitive' (Piaget 1980b, quoted from Furth 1987, p. 4).

Comprehension and perception, knowledge and insight all also influence the incentive patterns. But since these patterns differ in nature from the content structures and have a less manifest nature, the interaction is also different. It cannot be stated that particular emotional features are 'obsessed' by a particular comprehension. The incentive patterns have the nature, as Piaget expresses it, of 'relatively stable ways to feel and react', and precisely this 'relatively stable' means that the patterns typically shift gradually through processes of assimilative nature under the influence of impulses from the individual's constant interaction with the environment, including the building up of new knowledge.

However, strong content accommodations can also be accompanied by strong accommodative restructurings in the incentive patterns. If a sudden event, or the kind of cognitive processes that have earlier been referred to as reflection or meta-learning, causes a radical reconstruction of the individual's comprehension of certain sets of conditions and contexts, there may also be a correspondingly radical shift in the emotional patterns, not as obsessions, but more what could be described as a toning: the nature of particular parts of the emotional patterns shift generally in strength and direction. For example, if, on the basis of various experiences and influences, one reaches a point of eliminating one's prejudice concerning the opposite sex or other ethnic groups, it will probably also bring about general shifts in the emotions concerning these groups.

6.4 Emotional intelligence

Prior to 1990 the incentive dimension in relation to learning was almost exclusively dealt with in motivational psychology only, but during the 1990s, against the background of modern brain research, a number of important contributions appeared with a wider orientation. In this and the following section I will discuss what I regard as two important approaches in the area, which, in an innovative and inspiring manner, connect emotional life as a whole with learning and teaching. This section concerns the work of American Daniel Goleman on emotional intelligence (in particular Goleman 1995), and the next section considers British psychologist John Heron's phenomenological theory of personality (Heron 1992).

With respect to Goleman, it should be noted that he is not a researcher in the traditional academic sense, but a scientific journalist. However, having done a Ph.D. in psychology, his academic background is in order, and taking his point of departure in modern brain research he has performed highly qualified work in investigating and communicating what the emotions mean for our daily life and our ability to handle it.

What has especially made Goleman's work known all over the world is his use of the concept of 'emotional intelligence'. Ordinarily the concept of intelligence is connected with common sense, thinking and being gifted, i.e. with the cognitive area (which is connected with the content dimension in this book). But, not least, American psychologist Howard Gardner, with his concept of the multiple intelligences, paved the way for a broader view (Gardner 1983, 1993; see section 10.2). Goleman himself says that he has taken over the concept of 'emotional intelligence' from a book by Peter Salovey and John Mayer (Salovey and Mayer 1990).

Although Goleman does not provide any actual definition of the concept, he characterises it on many occasions in his book in different contexts and with a slightly different choice of words. For example, he writes that it includes:

> competencies such as self-awareness, self-control, and empathy, and the arts of listening, resolving conflicts, and cooperation . . . being able

to motivate oneself and persist in the face of frustrations; to control impulse and delay gratification; to regulate one's moods and keep distress from swamping the ability to think; to empathize and to hope ... a *meta-ability*, determining how well we can use whatever other skills we have, including raw intellect.

(Goleman 1995, pp. xiv, 34 and 36)

In his introduction he refers to the following quotation from Aristotle (384–322 BC): 'Anyone can become angry – that is easy. But to be angry with the right person, to the right degree, at the right time, for the right purpose, and in the right way – this is not easy' (Aristotle, quoted after Goleman 1995, p. ix).

Basically Goleman finds that people have two minds, the rational and the emotional, and that they constantly interact. The emotional mind is the original and, as polemically formulated on the front cover of the book, it also 'can matter more than IQ':

Ordinarily there is a balance between emotional and rational minds, with emotion feeding into and informing the operations of the rational mind, and the rational mind refining and sometimes vetoing the inputs of the emotions. Still, the emotional and rational minds are semi-independent faculties, each ... reflecting the operation of distinct, but interconnected, circuitry in the brain. .... As the root from which the newer brain grew, the emotional areas are intertwined via myriad connecting circuits to all parts of the neocortex (including the working memory, ki). This gives the emotional centers immense power to influence the functioning of the rest of the brain – including its centers for thought.

(Goleman 1995, pp. 9 and 12)

On the one hand, Goleman agrees with Gardner's view that intelligence is much more than intellectual abilities, but on the other hand he criticises him for not according sufficient importance to the emotions. He gives a great number of examples of situations where the emotions are completely decisive for the ability to function appropriately, at the same time as he stresses the crucial significance of the reason with respect to rational deliberations and decisions.

Goleman also emphasises that a high IQ is far from being a guarantee that one will manage well in life, and that the ability to use and control one's emotions in appropriate ways is at least as important. He strongly recommends that the school be transformed in such a way that our children get to know their own emotions and how to relate to them appropriately. In a later work he also deals with the significance of emotional intelligence in working life in general and in connection with career development

(Goleman 1998), and, together with two co-authors, in connection with management (Goleman *et al.* 2002).

With his strong emphasis on the importance and necessity of the emotions on an equal footing, and in interaction with, the reason, Goleman is in line with, and a strong advocate of, the understanding of the importance for learning of the incentive dimension, which is one of the central themes of this book.

6.5 Heron's theory of feeling and personhood

The contribution of British psychologist John Heron is a broadly based theory of the person, the application possibilities of which he has chosen to illustrate in relation to learning. Heron's theory is based on 'a wide-ranging phenomenology of human experience ... and the philosophy of human relations and of the person' with references to 'the self-actualization psychologies' (Maslow, Rogers), 'spiritual philosophy and psychology' (Fawcett, Hyde), 'transpersonal psychology' (Grof, Wilber) (Heron 1992, p. 1), and also East Asian philosophies and system theory are implied. For Heron is it axiomatic that one can neither separate the mental from the physical nor the reason from the emotions. In his book *Feeling and Personhood: Psychology in Another Key*, he sets up a comprehensive and quite complex model of the person (Heron 1992; Yorks and Kasl 2002). Here I will only present the main features of this model that are important for the understanding of learning (Figure 6.1).

First and foremost, Heron defines four different, fundamental 'modes of psyche' or 'primary modes of functioning', which he places partly in a quite complicated model of the person rather reminiscent of Kolb's learning circle (see section 5.2), and partly within what he terms an 'up-hierarchy', which 'is not a matter of the higher controlling and ruling the lower', but 'of the higher branching and flowering out of, and bearing the fruit of, the lower' (Heron 1992, p. 20).

The lowest mode in the up-hierarchy is the affective, stretching out between feeling and emotion. This is followed by the imaginal mode, between intuition and imagery. The third level is the conceptual, stretched out between reflection and discrimination. On the top is the practical mode, stretched between intention and action:

> The up-hierarchy metaphor points to what is going on in the psyche all the time, even if this is in a tacit, distorted and unacknowledged form because of blocks and deformations. In its unimpeded form it portrays a dynamic programme for the continuous functioning in an integrated person.
>
> (Heron 1992, p. 21)

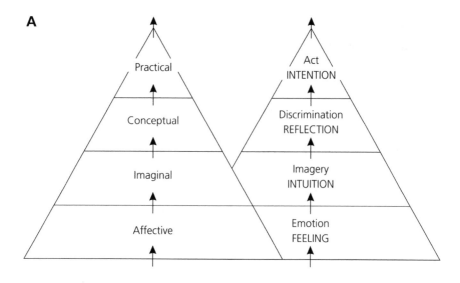

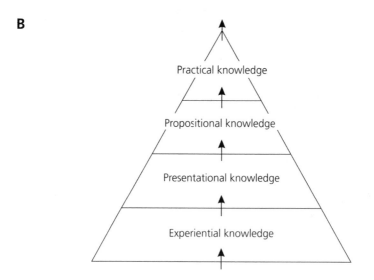

Figure 6.1 Heron's conceptualisation of mental orientations and modes (A) and forms of knowledge (B) (after Heron 1992, pp. 20 and 174)

The other up-hierarchy corresponds to the four mental orientations and includes four forms of knowledge. The lowest mode here is the experiential, stretched out between feeling and imagery. The presentational comes next, stretched out between notions and concepts. Then follows the propositional, stretched out between concepts and practice. Finally there is the practical mode, stretched out between practice and feeling. It is noted that in the forms of knowledge there is a clear circular movement from feeling, over notions, concepts and practice and back to feeling – and here the parallel to Kolb's learning circle is very clear.

However, Heron points out that when it comes to formal learning in schools, education programmes and the like, or whenever one consciously strives to learn something, the process is different in that the two middle modes change places in such a way that the conceptual comes before the notional and the propositional before the presentational. When one decides to learn something specific, or when one organises the learning processes of others, one first sets up some frames or concepts which one then tries to fill out, but in everyday learning content comes first and concepts and contexts later.

In my opinion, like Kolb, Heron can be criticised for erecting systems that are far too extreme with, among other things, clear rules of sequence with respect to the different mental processes and levels. Learning does not function like this in practice. The human brain is much too flexible for this in its mode of functioning and it is able constantly to make use of precisely the processes it finds relevant – just as illustrated by Heron on a general level through differences in formal and incidental learning. Nevertheless, such general systems can provide an overview and inspire many readers. One must simply be careful not to understand them as fixed systems applying at all times and in all situations, and Heron seems to be more prepared than Kolb to maintain a flexible attitude to his own systems. What is important for him is that both the person and the learning are regarded holistically and dynamically, and that there is constant interaction between experience, feeling, reason and social practice, which create learning and balance in personal development. For this reason, learning approaches must also provide space, inspiration and input for this interaction, and here relations between the participants play a decisive role.

That Heron's understanding can be used can be seen illustrated by, for example, American Lyle Yorks, who has described a course on racial identity in cooperation with Elisabeth Kasl, organised and implemented with inspiration from Heron (Yorks and Kasl 2002), and together with Judy O'Neil and Victoria Marsick, on a similar basis, has published the book entitled *Action Learning*, which provides important input for an up-to-date type of staff education (Yorks *et al.* 1999; Illeris *et al.* 2004).

6.6 Emotion, motivation, volition and attitudes

As appears from the title, this chapter is about what I have termed learning's incentive dimension, but in the discussions above I have often only referred to feelings and emotions and, among other things, contrasted this with cognition and learning content. It is, however, important to maintain the general broad concept of the incentive, even though reference is only made to the emotions both in everyday language and in many scholarly contexts – and there is a great deal of linguistic fuzziness in this area that can easily cause confusion.

There is, in general, a long series of mental states that we immediately understand as emotions, for example, joy, anger, sadness, fear and hate, which are usually counted as the five 'basic emotions', (e.g. Campos *et al.* 1983, p. 814). But there are numerous other emotions in both the language of every day and in professional psychology, and even if, for instance, it can be proved that there exist certain states of the brain and certain other more or less automatic reactions relating to different emotions, it is characteristic that they cannot be defined precisely and sharply separated, and one can after all experience many emotions at the same time. In addition, a distinction is often made both in brain research and in psychology between immediately experienced feelings, which come and go in step with the individual's interaction with the environment, and the underlying more general emotions, which often have a more permanent nature and set their mark on our 'mood' and thus also on the experience of, and reactions to, the single more specific feelings (for example, Damasio 1999).

But the incentive dimension also contains matters such as motivation, volition and attitudes that do not normally come under the concept of emotions – even though the borders here are also unclear – but form part of the picture to a high degree, not least where learning is concerned. For example, there is far more mention of the participants' motivation than of their feelings when it concerns learning in schools and education programmes.

Here, also, we enter an area with unclear definitions and boundaries. For example, if one has the will to learn something specific, this is clearly also a form of motivation, and certain attitudes can also be motivating or de-motivating in relation to certain learning measures. In everyday language, as a rule we have no difficulty in handling these concepts and understanding what we ourselves and others are referring to, because each of the concepts has its own special meaning and field of application with which we are very familiar. But there are problems connected with a more specific theoretical definition, and there have been a great number of attempts to define and order the terms without any definite and generally recognised terminology having been established.

In connection with learning, it is, first and foremost, important to maintain the incentive dimension as a whole and as an important, integrated element in all learning. If one wishes to go into more detail, it is probably most appropriate to be satisfied with distinguishing between emotion more directly linked to the learning situation, and motivation – also including volition and attitudes – that more generally concern the relation to the content and the context of which the learning forms a part.

In the first part of this chapter, which dealt with characterising the incentive dimension and placing it in the totality of learning, emotions played the greatest part because they are what traditionally, both professionally and in everyday language, are at the centre of the idea of matters to do with incentive. In this section I will look more closely at the motivational element in incentive. It is rather clear to anybody who deals with learning in one way or the other that motivation plays a key role in this connection. Motivation psychology has also traditionally been a discipline referring more to learning than to emotions and, at the same time, an area usually taken up in all kinds of teacher training.

The first motivation theory as such that is usually mentioned is that of American William McDougall (1871–1938) from the beginning of the twentieth century about man's 12 instincts (McDougall 1963 [1908]). It is characteristic that much of, in particular American, motivational psychology has dealt with listing and discussing various motives or types of motivation – and thereby to an even greater extent than emotional psychology ended in a blind alley where the categorisation of motives has been at the centre instead of the significance and functions of motivation, the complex patterns of interacting and contradictory motives, and, not least, the contexts of which motivation is a part and by which it is formed.

The most widespread and popular motivation theory is in all likelihood that presented by American psychologist Abraham Maslow in 1954 and subsequently formulated in his famous needs or motive hierarchy (Maslow 1954). Maslow, in line with Carl Rogers, was one of the key figures in American humanistic psychology of the time, which in this context manifested itself in particular in his placing the motive for self-actualisation at the top of his hierarchy. The idea in the hierarchy is also that all the different needs or motives are placed in approximate groupings and that these groupings are hierarchic in the sense that the lowest and most basic motives must be satisfied to a reasonable extent before the next group of motives come to the fore.

Thus at the bottom of the hierarchy Maslow has placed the basic physiological needs (hunger, thirst, sex etc.). Next come safety needs (stability, security, protection etc.). Then follow the social needs, first what could be called community needs (belongingness, love etc.), and after them esteem needs (self-esteem, achievement, reputation etc.). Finally at the top lie first the cognitive needs (knowledge, understanding, insight, etc.), next the aesthetic needs (beauty, harmony, etc.), and finally, as mentioned, the self-actualisation needs (realising oneself and one's potential), from which

Maslow later separated out a special 'transcendence need', which is about finding a meaning in, and a holistic view of, life (Maslow 1971).

Apart from the chosen groupings, the hierarchy thus contains a somewhat doubtful assumption about a certain order. It is a little reminiscent of the categorical interpretation of the hierarchy in the three main areas of the brain (see section 2.4), which was widespread earlier but has today been replaced by a far more subtle understanding of the way in which the later areas developed from the earlier ones in a manner that has ensured an enormous network of connections, cooperation and division of labour. Correspondingly it can be said that an argument could be made for a certain tendency in the direction of what Maslow has claimed. But in the world of reality things are far more complicated, and people's needs and motives constitute a complex pattern which, in the individual and in different population groups, develops and is used differently on the basis of their experience, their current situation and their future perspectives.

At any rate it is not difficult in everyday life to find examples that are in disagreement with Maslow's hierarchy, for example, people who defy hunger, security and social relations to achieve something that is more important to them. The key problem is that these need categories are assumed to exist as general human entities apart from the context in which they exist. As soon as one has realised this, one can easily come to see the well-meaning hierarchy as a picture of the ideals of the rising white American middle class in the 1950s. On the other hand, and as an extreme example, it can be difficult to explain the behaviour of contemporary suicide bombers on the basis of Maslow's need hierarchy.

Another very well-known and widespread American view of motivation from around the same time was expressed in the extensive research of David McClelland (1917–1998) *et al.* of the achievement motive (McClelland *et al.* 1953; McClelland 1961). Interest in precisely this motive had to do with its economic significance in the widest sense. Among other things, McClelland, referring to sociologist Max Weber (1864–1920) (Weber 1904), was of the opinion that if in the developing countries, for instance, people's ideology could be influenced so that they bring up their children to develop a stronger achievement motive, this could further economic growth, and he tried to prove empirically the connections between the single steps in this process (McClelland and Winter 1969).

McClelland's research is open to criticism because all his subjects were white male college students who formulated stories on the basis of some pictures depicting men only. It is, to phrase it politely, not without problems to generalise matters to do with all human beings' motivation on this basis (see Horner 1974). In addition, his ideas about the spread of white American middle-class norms for upbringing seem precarious.

I have taken these two central examples from motivational psychology as an illustration of an important point, namely that even though all seem to agree that motivation is of crucial importance for learning, this discipline has not contributed very much to the understanding and organisation of learning in practice. This has primarily to do with the tendency to focus on various categories of motivation as decisive, instead of looking at different groups of learners and what motivates or de-motivates them, what is behind this on the individual and the societal levels, and the conclusions that could be drawn from this regarding consequences for the structure and conditions of learning.

But there are, naturally, very many teachers and others, including the learners themselves, who think along such lines to a high degree, and this will inform in many ways both the rest of this chapter and the book, although direct reference is not always made to the concept of motivation.

6.7 Motivation through disturbances and conflicts

Motivation through disturbances and conflicts of different kinds is an important example of the significance of motivation in learning practice. Precisely in connection with the significance of the incentive dimension for learning, one often becomes aware that learning, which is different from, and more than, acquiring subject matter, rarely proceeds as a smooth, progressive process, and the possibilities for learning that simultaneously contribute to personal development often take their starting point in one form or other of disturbance of the current personal or social balance. This might be a question of simple 'cognitive dissonance' (Festinger 1957), i.e. that one experiences something that is in conflict with one's ideas, or there are small or larger contradictions in one's social relations and self-understanding. British learning researcher Peter Jarvis (see section 8.6) utilises in general the expression 'disjuncture', which he regards as something that in some form is the point of departure for all learning that is not merely additional in nature (e.g. Jarvis 1987, 1992, 2004, 2005a, 2005b, 2006).

The classic psychological contribution in this area is Canadian Daniel Berlyne's (1924–1976) theory concerning curiosity as learning motivation (Berlyne 1960). The core here is that conflict that implies a discrepancy between the understanding of a current situation and already existing knowledge or an expectation, if experienced as challenging without being overwhelming, leads to the form of motivation that Berlyne calls 'arousal', a mental countermove originating in an 'arousal potential' that can be understood as the side of general human readiness that I later discuss (in section 9.5) as 'resistance potential'. On the level of action, according to Berlyne, the consequence is curiosity that can either be perceptual and lead to exploratory behaviour, or conceptual, leading to response-seeking or epistemic behaviour. What is pedagogically central in Berlyne is that learning is promoted by appropriate challenges that must not be either too small (then one does not learn very much) or too great (then one gives up and circumvents the situation). This is a fundamental understanding that many teachers have internalised.

Chilean biologists and system theoreticians Huberto Maturana and Francisco Varela (1976–2001) later took up the same theme in a more general form in connection with their theory about 'autopoiesis' (i.e. self-maintaining systems – Maturana and Varela 1980), while others went further in the area of learning with discussions of the possible significance of big and small conflicts for learning. In the work of the well-known German-American developmental psychologist Erik H. Erikson (1902–1994) conflicts and crises are what create the transition between different stages of life. For example, in the years of youth a crisis arises concerning liberation from the childhood environment, which must be solved in a sustainable way for appropriate identity formation to take place (Erikson 1968), and this can be understood as a far-reaching transformative learning process (see Chapters 8 and 11).

In Denmark, psychologist Jens Berthelsen has worked with deliberately using dilemma situations with a view to personal development and self-awareness in the psychology study programme (Berthelsen 2001). A dilemma means choosing between two evils, and one should probably be careful about introducing such situations of choice as part of the education programme. However, precisely when it comes to the training of psychologists conducted by other and more experienced psychologists, Berthelsen has shown that it both can be relevant and be practised in a fruitful and accountable manner, and the example shows something about how far one can go in taking a point of departure in contradictions.

Across the board, from the slightest challenge to dramatic personal conflicts, from the point of view of learning it is a matter of providing impulses furthering accommodative and transformative learning processes and thus lift teaching above the usual reproductive level where one can manage with assimilative processes. This is something that can be done by the individual teacher or more generally be built into educational concepts as, for example, project work or other problem-oriented concepts.

It is rather clear that precisely such challenges that originate in small disturbances over contradictions and problems to dilemmas are, in general, suited for taking learning further in a decisive way. But, and keeping Berlyne's theory in mind, it is also important to understand that irrespective of the level one is on, there is in principle a risk of going too far so that the challenge is no longer 'appropriate' in relation to the participants. For the individual learner, learning will always, to a greater or lesser extent, take place in interplay between situations with smoothly progressive development marked by assimilative processes, and situations that in general can be described as 'learning leaps', where accommodative or perhaps transformative processes dominate and one can decisively come further in one's development (see Bjerg's learning model, section 8.7).

Even though the challenges in themselves can easily be kept at a content and cognitive level, it is, however, not least in these contexts that the incentive dimension in the learning can soon have key significance, because disturbances, challenges and conflicts appeal at least as much to the emotions and motivation as to insight and understanding.

6.8 Motivation problems in modernity

Today we are living in what has frequently been called a globalised knowledge society, among other things, with increasingly keener international competition in which the competence level of members of society, and thus also their learning, forms a key parameter of competition. In the different countries this situation has led to growing awareness of, and growing pressure for, more learning and personal development, both generally and especially in the areas regarded as commercially relevant. In the political arena the pressure takes the form of campaigns, legislation and administration, ranging from the introduction of more tests in the primary school to initiatives about lifelong learning in adult education programmes.

This is a situation directly concerning economic growth, educational reforms and educational management. But it also impacts the social and pedagogical climate at educational institutions to a high degree, and today the pressure has a great effect on most educational programmes and on the single teaching situation. Moreover, it influences both teachers and participants in the education as an undercurrent which means that one often feels under pressure, directly financially by tighter framework conditions with respect to, for example, class quotas, access to counselling, teaching materials etc., but also from the point of view of learning. There is more pressure, both generally and for the individual, not just to learn more, but also to learn the right thing and in the right way in order to enter society and workplaces smoothly and constructively.

Therefore, in almost all parts of the education system we also find ourselves more or less constantly in situations where the motivation of the participants is under pressure. There is, of course, also pressure in the content and interaction dimensions, but the pressure is most intense in the incentive area in the form of motivation problems and ambivalent feelings. In Chapter 13, I will return to this on a more general level, but here I will more directly address the motivation problems that are appearing with increasing strength in most parts of the education system.

In the concrete contexts it is usually a matter of double pressure on the motivation. This comes partly from within the individual in the form of uncertainty, about what and how one should preferably try to learn and if one is good enough at it. At the same time, it also comes from the outside in the form of requirements, expectations, stricter rules and more control.

There are probably some who like this situation where the pressure makes them work harder, and there is positive reinforcement when they experience being able to manage it and improving. But my experience from many different parts of the education system is that especially those who are the weakest to start with have difficulty in handling it. They become more insecure and their motivation becomes very ambivalent: at one and the same time they would like to qualify themselves, because this is after all necessary, but they also strongly wish they could escape it, because it is a strain and they are afraid of adding yet more defeats to those they have already experienced.

Today it is not necessary to go very far up in the primary school before motivation problems begin to appear and influence both the working climate and the learning. This situation merely becomes worse in youth education programmes where it is, not least, an important part of the background for the far too high drop out rate (see Illeris 2003a). In the broad, non-academic education programmes, ambivalent motivation proved to be a key problem in an extensive participant-oriented project some years ago (Illeris 2003b, 2004), and when it comes to learning in working life, this is also the case especially among the low-skilled (Illeris *et al.* 2004; Illeris 2006).

The reason why these problems exist on such a broad scale is naturally because they are an extension of some key matters appearing in society in general and the education sector in particular, namely, the pressure on learning caused by everything we sum up in the concept of the knowledge society. Therefore, it is not something that can just be got rid of by means of some suitable education reforms. The framework conditions can naturally be made better at tackling this side of the situation, for example, through better economy and better teacher training, but it is important to understand that these conditions influence motivation in particular and make it ambivalent for most people, i.e. both positive and negative at one and the same time. Only then it will be possible in everyday life at schools, educational institutions, in counselling and in working life to relate to the ambivalence by systematically seeking to build on its positive element, accommodate the participants, ground the activities in relation to their situation and interests, listen to their concerns, give them the highest possible degree of self-determination and adjust the challenges so that they are as relevant as possible from the perspective of both participants and education programmes, at the same time as efforts are made equally systematically to avoid supporting the negative side by acting over the heads of the participants, treating them impersonally, playing on their insecurity and otherwise 'happening to' do some of the small things in everyday life to which they are sensitive and easily experience as humiliating.

Very briefly and primarily, this is about relating to the participants as equals, consciously, in detail and constantly, whether they are adults, young people or children. This sounds very simple but in practice it is not.

On the other hand, practice also shows that to the extent it is successful, it is really possible to contribute to considerably reducing the motivation problems.

6.9 Summary

Learning's incentive dimension covers the matters concerning the scope and character of the mental energy that is the driving force of learning, i.e. typically the motivation, emotion, attitudes and volition invested by the individual in a learning situation or course of learning.

In the acquisition process of learning there is close interplay between the content and the incentive dimensions, so that what is learned is influenced by the nature and strength of the mental energy, at the same time as the motivation, the emotions, the attitudes and the volition are influenced by the content side of the learning. While mental schemes and structures of a relatively manifest character are developed on the content side, in the incentive dimension relatively stable motivational, emotional and volition patterns are developed. In connection with assimilative learning, the incentive dimension functions largely unconsciously, while learning is typically more conscious in nature in connection with accommodative and transformative learning.

It is important to maintain that the incentive dimension is an important and integrated element in all learning, and that its results in the form of motivational, emotional, attitude and volition patterns are at least as important as the content results of the learning for the ability of the individual to function appropriately and in a targeted way in society. It is these matters that have been termed 'emotional intelligence'.

What is central to the incentive dimension of learning seems to be that the learning-related challenges are in agreement with – or at least not fundamentally in conflict with – the learner's interests and qualifications, and at the same time that they are balanced, i.e. neither too small to give rise to any significant learning nor so big that they are experienced as unattainable and therefore lead to avoidance tactics. With the pressure that is on learning in present society at almost all levels, there is a tendency for the challenges, especially for participants with relatively weak content and motivational qualifications, often to be inappropriately great and/or be experienced as imposed to a degree that the learning is reduced or fails.

Chapter 7

The interaction dimension of learning

This chapter presents a more detailed elaboration and analysis of the interaction dimension of learning. The starting point is that all learning is 'situated', i.e. that it takes place in a certain situation, a certain learning space, which both determines the learning possibilities and marks the learning process and the nature of the learning that takes place. In addition, the situatedness of learning can be understood on different levels, and here a distinction can first and foremost be made between the immediate social situation and the underlying societal framework conditions. The interaction between the learner and the environment can, itself, also be different in nature, and six typical forms of interaction are identified. Next I deal with the way in which social and societal conditions influence the nature of the learning that takes place and how one can relate to this. Finally, there is discussion of the relation between the concepts of social learning, collaborative learning and collective learning.

7.1 Situated learning

This chapter deals with the dimension in learning that concerns the interaction between learner and environment. This signals departure from the individual level and the internal acquisition process to instead focus on the connection between the individual and the social and societal level. Simultaneously the basis shifts from the human being's biological-genetic constitution and its individual and societal development in this relation, to society's historically developed structures and customs of which the individual forms a part. For the internal psychological dimensions, the individual is the setting, while the action takes place through the individual's meetings with the environment. For the interaction dimension, it is the environment that is the setting, and the actions are the individual's deeds in relation to this environment.

From the point of view of learning, the necessity of including the environment as an element in learning, as already pointed out in Chapter 3, lies in the fact that all learning is 'situated', i.e. that the learning situation not only influences, but also is a part of, the learning. This is a quite fundamental condition which we all know about and have an intuitive experience of, but it is only in the last decades that it has seriously been included in learning research, and the very concept of situatedness was only introduced in 1991 with the book by Americans Jean Lave and Etienne Wenger entitled *Situated Learning* (Lave and Wenger 1991).

However, Lave and Wenger were not aware that this situatedness always has a dual nature, and this may be part of the reason why this fundamental feature has not been included in the extensive literature that has been inspired by their approach, e.g. in Wenger's own books on communities of practice and two Italian edited books on forms of knowledge in organisations (Wenger 1998; Wenger *et al.* 2002; Nicolini *et al.* 2003; Gherardi 2006).

This dual nature consists in the fact that the learning situation always, and at one and the same time, can be regarded as both the immediate situation that the learner or learners find themselves in, e.g. at a school, a workplace or leisure-time activity (see Chapter 12) and as a societal situation that is more generally influenced by the norms and structures of the society in question in the widest possible sense. Thus a triangular model can be set up for the interaction situation, which is a reversal of the learning triangle developed in Chapter 3. In this model the baseline is stretched out on the social level between the immediate social situation and the underlying general societal situation, and the interaction is aimed at the individual's acquisition process as a whole. The two triangles can then be joined thus producing the somewhat more complex learning model shown in Figure 7.1.

There are a number of important comments to be added to this learning model.

First, it could be asked why I did not immediately set up this model in Chapter 3. The answer is that I find it important as a basic model to illustrate how learning directly proceeds for the learner, and in this perspective it is clearest to picture the environment as such as the antipode with which the learner interacts. Thus the complex model only becomes relevant to the degree there is a need to specify the environment in more detail.

Second, it is very important that while learning on the individual level can only reasonably be specified between content and incentive because this corresponds to the way in which our brain has developed and functions, the environment can be specified in many different ways according to what one wishes to emphasise. It is thus my choice to point out the difference between the immediate and close situation and the underlying societal

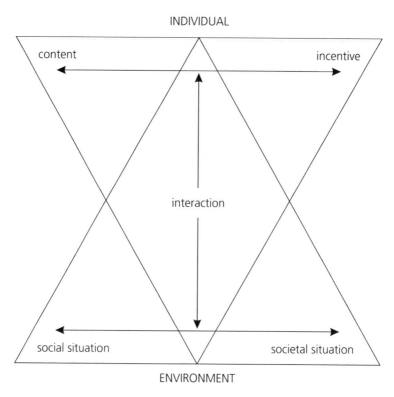

Figure 7.1 The complex learning model

conditions as the most important specification of the environment viewed from a general learning perspective. This can be viewed as contrasting with my emphasis in the book entitled *Learning in Working Life* (Illeris *et al.* 2004, pp. 44ff. and pp. 67ff.), where I chose a specification between the technical-organisational and the social-cultural sides of the workplace as learning environment, in agreement with a model of 'workplace learning' developed by my colleagues Christian Helms Jørgensen and Niels Warring (Jørgensen and Warring 2003), and more generally corresponding to the polarisation between the 'system world' and the 'life world' developed by German sociologist and philosopher Jürgen Habermas within the frames of so-called 'critical theory' (Habermas 1984–87 [1981]).

Third, it must be pointed out that the great majority of the above-mentioned current literature on situated learning in this context relates to what I have called the immediate and close side of the learning situation. In relation to the significance of the underlying societal situation for learning, a basis is rather to be found within the critical socialisation and educational literature of the 1970s (e.g. Bernstein 1971; Bourdieu and Passéron 1977 [1970]; Willis 1977), and in the more sociologically oriented literature on the area from the 1990s and on (e.g. Giddens 1990, 1991; Beck 1992 [1986]; Jarvis 1992; Castells 1996; Usher *et al.* 1997; Sennett 1998; Bauman 1998; Beck and Beck-Gernsheim 2002). To this can then be added the specifically social-constructivist contributions, to which I return later in this chapter (e.g. Gergen 1991, 1994; Burr 1995).

Finally, it may be surprising that even though the interaction situation of learning concerns an interaction between the individual and the environment in the broadest sense, I have, nevertheless, defined this environment on a directly social and a more general societal level. Whatever has happened to the interaction with the material environment, the localities that surround the learning situation, the tools and instruments one utilises, and the institutions in which a great part of learning takes place?

Naturally the individual is involved in interaction with the material surroundings all the time, but the nature of this interaction is always transmitted socially and societally. In today's society this transmission is predominant and very visible – the imprint of mankind on the material world is so widespread today that it is extremely difficult to find an element of 'untouched nature'. Viewed in relation to learning, the material aspect of the environment is under submission to the more dominant social side. This fundamentally means that mankind's mental condition is that of a social being, his psychological functions can only develop in a social space – because we are talking of humans the societal dimension is given.

And although it may be possible to find a piece of untouched nature, our perception of this nature is necessarily socially influenced – we know that it is called the 'sea' or they are called 'stars', and that people relate to these phenomena in specific ways: that the sea is something you can swim in, sail on and even drown in, and that the stars form various constellations and that they are inconceivably distant from us etc. Thus it is not possible to separate interaction with the material surroundings from interaction with the social surroundings – in psychological and also in learning conditions they make up a totality that is always transmitted socially.

In addition, the important factor in today's society is that this transmission can occur both in a direct social interaction and indirectly through a large number of different media that stretch from written and artistic expressions to the vast range of electronic equipment. Naturally this is of great practical significance for learning opportunities but, when it concerns learning, the forms of transmission must not be treated on the basis of a media perspective but, rather, psychologically, from the perspective of how the individual as learner confronts his or her surroundings, whether they are transmitted directly or through media.

7.2 Forms of interaction

There would, in general, seem to be limitless possibilities of variation for the way in which the interaction between the learner and the environment can take place. There are neither a finite number of interaction forms nor a finite number of ways of experiencing them, and therefore it is not possible to develop an adequate typology with respect to forms of interaction in the same way as in connection with the inner acquisition process. Nonetheless, one can attempt to achieve an overview and make some suggestions regarding some of the most important and widespread forms of interaction. I will attempt to do so in the following with the reservation that it cannot be a typology per se, but merely an attempt to obtain an overview that is as appropriate and adequate as possible.

From the point of view of psychology, it can be said that interaction begins with what can be called *perception* in its simplest form, where the surrounding world comes to the individual as a totally unmediated sense impression. The individual is passive, but an impression encroaches and is registered – this can be most simply illustrated with a scent impression, which people rarely seek actively, but typically perceive when it imposes itself on them.

Something different happens when we talk about *transmission*. This aspect of interaction typically involves someone from outside having an interest to some degree or other in passing on something to others, or in influencing someone, in transmitting specific sense impressions or messages either generally or to specific others. The receiver can be more or less interested in the transmission in question, and accordingly will be more or less active in relation to it.

Most generally in relation to interaction we talk of *experience*. In general language use, both perception and transmission can be included in the term 'experience', but one can also choose to limit the use of the word so that experience presupposes a particular activity, i.e. that the learner is not simply receiving, but also acts in order to benefit from the interaction. (In Chapter 8, I will return to the concept of 'experience' and try to establish a more qualified definition.)

A particular form of considerable interest in learning where the learner actively complies with the learning opportunities is *imitation*, in which the learner attempts to do something in the same way as another person acting as a model or, in a more goal-directed form, as an instructor. Imitation is a very widespread form of interaction in the pre-school years, both in direct copying and in role-play and so on, where the children more generally copy others as they perceive them. But imitation also plays a large role in teaching and similar situations – the American Dreyfus brothers point out, for example, that one reason computers will never be able to replace teaching and social learning is because they do not have the capacity for imitation (Dreyfus and Dreyfus 1986).

The next extensive form of interaction I would like to address is *activity*, which, as previously explained (see section 5.3), implies that the learner actively seeks influences that can be used in a particular context that the person concerned is interested in.

And finally I would like to mention *participation* as the most extensive, and also the most general, form of interaction. This is characterised by the fact that the learner is in a common goal-directed activity, a community of practice, as Etienne Wenger (1998) calls it, in which the person concerned has a recognised position and thus also an influence.

As has emerged, this sketch of various categories of forms of interaction is structured on the basis of the learner's involvement in the interaction. It would be easy to think of other categorisations based on other parameters, but in terms of learning, the choice of the involvement dimension as the structuring element includes the notion that the likelihood of learning occurring, and the degree of attention and 'direction' (as opposed to chance) in this learning, generally follows this parameter – i.e. that the more active one is and the more one becomes engaged, the greater is the chance of learning something significant, and that one learns it in a way that one is able to remember and make use of in relevant contexts.

It should also be noted that if the forms of interaction listed here – perception, transmission, experience, imitation, activity and participation – are compared with the typology concerning forms of acquisition developed in Chapter 4, there is a certain parallelism. The more simple forms of acquisition, cumulation and assimilation, will tend to figure more frequently in connection with the less activity- and engagement-influenced type of interaction forms, while there is a greater likelihood of accommodation in connection with the active and engaged forms of interaction. With respect to transformation, in particular, this form of acquisition rarely appears in connection with a single situation, but is most often triggered through processes that include activity and/or participation, also including courses of education and therapy.

Finally in this section it should once more be pointed out that the categorisation of interaction forms set up serves here only to provide some structural ideas of how interaction can work, and hint at the significance of active involvement in this connection; I do not intend to use these forms of interaction as starting points in the following sections, since they are not clearly defined and substantiated, and in practice they often overlap. But they can provide a sort of reference framework when I refer to various approaches and theories I believe to be significant in the understanding of the interaction processes that are found in learning.

7.3 The social embeddedness of learning

The close interpersonal interaction processes that are of direct significance for learning have traditionally not been dealt with in learning psychology, but in social and group psychological contexts, and only with diffused or limited references to learning contexts. An overview of this can be gained, for example, in edited works from the 1960s and the early 1970s (e.g. Krech *et al.* 1962).

The concept of *social learning* was first established in earnest at this time with American Albert Bandura's work on the significance of close social ties for learning. It primarily concerned model learning and learning through imitation – phenomena that had often been dealt with before, not least by Piaget (1951 [1945]) – and which Bandura and his work associates studied in a traditional behaviouristic fashion. One result they came to was that the learning is influenced not only by the behaviour of the model, but also by the positive or negative response the model receives to his or her own behaviour, as witnessed by the learner.

From this they developed the theory of *vicarious learning*, which asserts that the reinforcing influences of learning are not aimed directly at the learner – which again presupposes that certain mental adjustment processes occur that cannot be measured or registered and which therefore reach beyond the comprehension horizon of the traditional behaviouristic paradigm (Bandura and Walters 1963; Bandura 1977). Bandura's work was thus primarily linked to the type of interaction processes that are here called imitation, and was also transcending in that it revealed the limited opportunities for explanation of the behaviouristic approach to learning.

At the same time as Bandura opened the way for an elaboration of the prevailing conceptions of social learning, the learning concepts of Vygotsky and, particularly, Piaget began to make a serious impression on American psychology. This can be seen in the work of some of the most central figures in pedagogical psychology at that time, e.g. Jerome Bruner (1960) and David Ausubel (1968). And around the same time the Brazilian Paulo Freire published *Pedagogy of the Oppressed* and turned a considerable part of the comprehension of learning upside down with his convincing references to South American agricultural workers' societal conditions (Freire 1970; see section 7.7). Also, in Europe the previously mentioned new Marxist and socio-linguistically oriented socialisation theories began to place both developmental psychology and social psychology in a new perspective. Thus the traditional American disciplines of group and social psychology and the new concept of 'social learning' came under pressure, and attention was increasingly directed to the significance of societal conditions.

Currently an ambiguous picture is emerging in extension of this. The traditional group and social fields of psychology have returned to a certain extent, but in new and more complex forms, in which they mingle with many of the impulses from the 1970s that now most often appear in more moderated forms. The term 'social learning' crops up in many contexts, but even so has never quite achieved the status of an independent sphere of research – the term is not, for example, used by one of the currently most prominent figures in the sphere, the British learning researcher referred to earlier, Peter Jarvis, who prefers to talk about 'learning in a social context' and similar expressions. I will in any case briefly summarise Jarvis's conception here, as I view him as a typical representative of the concept of social learning today, within the English-speaking currents at any rate.

Jarvis emphasises that learning occurs in a tension field between the individual and the social:

> The process of learning is located in the interface of people's biography and the sociocultural environment in which they live, for it is at this intersection that experiences occur. . . . When children are born, they are born into a society whose culture preceded them and will almost certainly continue after their lives are over. Culture, therefore, appears to be objective and external. But the children have inherited no, or minimal, instincts to help them live within society and conform to its culture; thus they have to acquire that culture. In the first instance, then, learning is a matter of internalising and transforming something that is apparently objective to the individual. . . . However, there comes a time when they begin to think for themselves, ask questions, and generally experiment. . . . Children gradually become more independent; they usually develop a mind of their own and then process the external cultural stimuli and respond to them in a variety of ways. . . . Individuals begin to act back on the social world that has formed them.
>
> (Jarvis 1992, pp. 17, 22 and 23)

There is no doubt that Jarvis recognises both the internal acquisition processes and the interaction processes, as they are called in this book. His starting point was sociological and philosophical, but he has gradually also included psychological matters and emphasised the active role played by the learner. In this way he represents a trend to incorporate the internal processes into the perspective of the social processes, with the social processes here including the more general socialisation, more goal-directed teaching and influence processes and the learner's own self-directed activities (what I have termed transmission, experience and activity), while imitation has more or less slipped out of sight.

However, in recent years Jarvis has published a steady stream of books about adult learning and education (e.g. Jarvis 1997, 1999, 2001a, 2001b, 2006, Jarvis et al. 1998; Holford et al. 1998; Jarvis and Parker 2005), and his interests have, not least, referred to the slogan about lifelong learning, about which he is enthusiastic, at the same time as becoming increasingly critical about the way the slogan is put into practice (for example, Jarvis 2002). In this process Jarvis has also gradually moved from a predominantly social to a more existentialist approach. I shall return to that in section 8.6.

7.4 Critical theory and socialisation

Socialisation denotes the process through which the individual acquires current societal norms and structures, thus becoming part of the society in question. The process includes both an individual and a social-societal aspect in line with this book's conception of learning. Rather than signify a particular part of the learning process or a particular form of learning, socialisation may, therefore, be perceived as a specific viewpoint on learning and development, namely, the societal viewpoint. In this lies the notion that the significance of learning is perceived based on the relationship that develops between individual and society, and which can occur directly through teaching and other forms of goal-directed transmission, and to a great extent also indirectly, by the individual gaining experience of how things work and how different people behave.

There have thus always been considerable elements of socialisation theory in learning, developmental, personality and social psychology, but a more direct and targeted socialisation theory approach first seriously developed in extension of the work of the so-called Frankfurt School concerning the scientific school of thought called *critical theory* (for a broader understanding of this concept see Brookfield 2005).

It concerns the approach that developed in the years between the two World Wars at the 'Institut für Sozialforschung' in Frankfurt, other places in Europe and especially the USA after Hitler came to power in 1933, and from the early 1950s again in Frankfurt. Central people in the first generation of the Frankfurt School were particularly Max Horkheimer (1895–1973), Theodor Adorno (1903–1969) and, later, Herbert Marcuse (1898–1979). The main academic point lay in the intersecting field between philosophy, sociology and psychoanalysis, and, in many ways, the problems that were focused on concerned the relationship between individual and society, often seen in a contemporary historical perspective. The approach was primarily a coupling between the Marxist conception of society and the psychoanalytical conception of the individual – but both in a critical inter-pretation in which there was also room for other approaches, while certain Marxist and psychoanalytical interpretations were rejected (not least the dialectical materialistic conception of Marxism that was predominant in the Soviet Union) – and the theories were applied to current societal and political problems.

A major work from the early period was Horkheimer and Adorno's *Dialectic of Enlightenment* which took the form of outlines and dialogues, but still describes the Frankfurt School's objective of critical enlightenment (Horkheimer and Adorno 1944). For Adorno, too, aesthetic and artistic dimensions took a central position. Of more direct interest in the present context is the extensive investigation of the authoritarian personality structure that was perceived as a basis for the success of Nazism (Adorno *et al.* 1950)

– I return to this later in the present chapter. Finally, it must be mentioned that Marcuse gained some degree of status as the student rebellion's philosopher, particularly with his books *Eros and Civilization* (Marcuse 1955) and *One Dimensional Man* (Marcuse 1964), which, in different ways, deal with new forms of alienation in the post-war period.

The second generation of the Frankfurt School is most strongly signified by the philosopher Jürgen Habermas, who took over management of the institute in Frankfurt in 1965. Habermas has dealt with a broad range of subjects, including the relationship between theory and practice (Habermas 1988 [1963]), the elucidation of various interests in knowledge (Habermas 1989a [1968]), and a number of books on language, communication and public life (especially Habermas 1989b [1962] and 1984–87 [1981]). To summarise very briefly, Habermas attempts to oppose modernity's technical or instrumental rationality that increasingly characterises society, with a communicative rationality, discourse, the ideal speech situation and life-world, as approaches that can maintain a humanistic emancipatory practice and 'knowledge-constitutive interest'.

Habermas has also addressed the theory of socialisation in a short work (Habermas 1971), but it was with the 'branch' of the Frankfurt School that has sometimes been called the Hanover School that this interest first became concentrated on the socialisation theory approach.

The key work in the Hanoverian School's treatment of the socialisation concept is the draft of a materialist theory of socialisation drawn up at the beginning of the 1970s by Alfred Lorenzer (1922–2002), precisely in an attempt to combine the approaches of Marx and Freud:

> This investigation pursues the question: how can the child's development be seen as a natural process and as a social process of development at one and the same time? . . . What is alluded to here is not the harmless old cliché about a weaving together of natural aptitudes and cultural influences. Rather, the investigation is fully concerned with the confrontation between two theories that seem mutually exclusive: psychoanalysis and historic materialism. . . . If psychoanalysis under-stands human structures of experience – action, thought, feelings, perception – as determined by drives, historic materialism must maintain that these very structures must be seen as dependent on history, on the encounter of humans with external nature, as it is here and now . . .
>
> (Lorenzer 1972, p. 7)

On this basis Lorenzer places his main emphasis on the generally socialising content in the early interaction processes of the child, not least the part of socialisation or personality formation that is embedded in the unconscious. He is thus mainly concerned with the earliest interaction between the child and its primary relation object in what he calls in a generalised form, the *mother-child-dyad.* Here the child forms its most fundamental subjective structures in its intimate interactions or exchange relations through accordances. Lorenzer points out that even here there will necessarily be frustrations. The mother will not be able to completely meet the child's needs, and frustrations are also necessary for the child to develop into a societal individual.

Later the field of interaction broadens, the child's structures develop and become differentiated, and the unconscious, sensuously spontaneous interaction forms are gradually supplemented by two further types of interaction forms: the linguistic symbolic interaction forms that are internalised into the conscious layer, and the sensuously symbolic interaction forms that lead to the creation of the so-called *protosymbols*, which can be characterised as broader and more open symbol formations which transmit the tensions between the conscious and the unconscious layers in relation to socially prescribed practice, and form the basis for the identity and the imagination.

However, in any stage of the development process there can also occur what Lorenzer calls *systematically broken practice*, i.e. repeated discordances, incomprehensible to the child, which can lead to the interaction forms in question being driven out of the linguistic level and becoming unconscious *clichés*, which 'make the subjects available at the service of an existing order (and) blocks potential discussions of the action norms that belong to the behaviour complex in question' (Lorenzer 1972, p. 143).

Socialisation is thus a process that will always embrace both development and limitation or damage, and will never be able to be the frictionless transfer of societal conditions to the individual that is the underlying basis in much of developmental psychology.

Today, the importance of Lorenzer's socialisation theory, itself, is probably rather limited. But his critical mode of thought has, without any doubt, inspired a number of his colleagues to produce a whole series of important contributions to the understanding of various important matters in connection with the interaction dimension of socialisation, and thus also learning, in modern capitalist society.

First to be mentioned are social psychologist Peter Brückner (1922–1982) with his highly critical book *The Social Psychology of Capitalism*, which drew attention to many repressive aspects of socialisation (Brückner 1972), and consciousness sociologist Oskar Negt, whose work on formation of experience and much more I return to in section 8.2. I also return later to social psychologist, Thomas Leithäuser, who both drew up the theory of 'everyday consciousness' and has taken interest in the life world in working life, first and foremost in section 9.3.

Other important names are Alfred Krovoza, who was particularly interested in the repression of sensuality and paid particular attention to the human resistance potential (Krovoza 1976), which made him a source of inspiration to the conception of resistance that is described here in section

9.5, as well as Regina Becker-Schmidt, who has especially worked on socialisation and ambivalence in low-skilled women, see section 9.4. Final mention goes to Thomas Ziehe with his understanding of cultural liberation and his interest in current youth and education problems, to which I have already made reference and will return several times, in particular in section 11.3.

There is, thus, no doubt of the importance of critical theory for the understanding expressed in many places in this book, and not least through its identification of the fact that the interaction processes that are part of learning can often be full of ambiguities and contradictions, and that many influences are deposited in the unconsciousness, *inter alia* if they subjectively are too much of a burden on conscious cognition. This is a very brief summary but, as mentioned, the various contributions will be taken up in the chapters and sections to which each of them belongs.

7.5 The heritage of the cultural historical tradition

I will now return to the Russian cultural historical school, which has always emphasised the viewing of learning from a societal perspective and thus, in principle, as relating coherently to the internal learning processes and interaction processes. Vygotsky in particular harboured ambitions to link the two aspects together:

> What Vygotsky sought was a comprehensive approach that would make possible description and explanation of higher psychological functions in terms acceptable to natural science. To Vygotsky, explanation meant a great deal. It included identification of the brain mechanisms underlying a particular function; it included a detailed explanation of their developmental history to establish the relation between simple and complex forms of what appeared to be the same behavior; and, importantly, it included specification of the societal context in which the behavior developed. Vygotsky's goals were extremely ambitious, perhaps unreasonably so. He did not achieve these goals (as he was well aware). But he did succeed in providing us with an astute and prescient analysis of modern psychology.
>
> (Cole and Scribner in Vygotsky 1978, pp. 5–6)

Vygotsky's in-depth studies of language, thought, learning and development were thus embedded in a materialistic societal frame of comprehension which, as far as the interaction dimension of learning is concerned, qualified his theories more decisively than other learning theory developments between the two World Wars, such as that of Piaget and the then predominant behaviouristic psychology in the USA. In a contemporary context, however, it emerges as a drawback of the Russian theories, particularly when they occur in an educational perspective, that their societal connection is so clearly linked to the Soviet-Marxist conception of society of that time. For although they contain many important and positive comprehensions, particularly of the significance of work and social community, there is, for good or ill, a huge distance from there to today's late-modern capitalistic market society – and it also seems problematic that communist society is, in principle, viewed as free from conflict.

The approach of the cultural historical school has, nevertheless, been continued, even outside Russia, in comprehensive studies using Leontjev's concept of human activity in particular as a pivotal point (Leontjev 1981 [1959]; see section 5.3). I especially regard Yrjö Engeström's work as a significant contemporary elaboration of the cultural historical tradition, while at the same time viewing it as a liberation from some of its ties to Soviet-Marxism. Although in my inclusion of Engeström's work, in Chapter 5, I related particularly to his transcendent conception of the internal learning processes, it should be borne in mind that this conception was developed within a fully prepared framework, in which the individual is in a community or society that has developed regulating norms, usable tools, both material and symbolic, and a societal division of labour (see Engeström 1987, pp. 73ff., 1996, pp. 131ff.). An important characteristic in Engeström is that he links the cultural historical tradition together with Bateson's concept of *double-bind* (Bateson 1972), for this brings a strong conception of conflict into the picture, contradicting the idealised communist view of harmony.

Another comprehensive elaboration of the cultural historical tradition can be found in the German so-called 'critical psychology' or 'Berlin school', which evolved into an independent psychological direction or position under the leadership of psychologist Klaus Holzkamp (1930–1995) (esp. Holzkamp 1972, 1983). I have previously quoted (in section 6.3) from Ute Holzkamp-Osterkamp's comprehensive work on motivational psychology, which has an important and established view on the relationship between knowledge and emotions. Klaus Holzkamp's own last important contribution was a comprehensive book on learning, which he basically views as a particular form of subjective action, and, therefore, deals with from the subjective perspective of the learner – in strong contradiction to the externally determined, dominating perspective of learning in school and education (Holzkamp 1995).

In contradiction to the cultural historical tradition and to Holzkamp's own earlier work in this book the concept of subjectivity has a central position. But this is a completely different conception of subjectivity than that developed under the auspices of the Frankfurt School by German researchers such as Lorenzer, Negt, Leithäuser and Becker-Schmidt, to whom Holzkamp makes no reference. While the Frankfurt School's concept of subjectivity in continuation of psychoanalysis is characterised by internal tensions and conflicts, Holzkamp's concept of subjectivity is rational and goal-directed. Holzkamp himself deals fairly briefly with this contradiction, and characterises psychoanalysis as an

> earlier subject-scientific thought tendency in the history of psychology. . . . Freud's theory is (and therein lies its potentially clarifying nature) – simply in making the contradictions and breaches comprehensible and (within the framework of what is possible) surmountable in striving for their realisation – irretrievably committed to human sense as the most important life value.
>
> (Holzkamp 1995, pp. 29 and 30)

And Holzkamp then quotes Freud:

> The voice of the intellect is a soft one, but it does not rest till it has gained a hearing. . . . In the long run nothing can withstand reason and experience.
>
> (Freud 1962 [1927], pp. 49 and 50)

The quotation is correct, but it is taken from a text in which Freud is dealing with religion, and it may well be something of a misrepresentation to use it in an attempt to place Freud somewhere in Holzkamp's conception of rationality – just as a view of Freud as standard-bearer for irrationality would be equally mistaken. Freud, and critical theory after him (which is quite different from critical psychology), was primarily oriented towards conflicts and contradictions, and the contradiction between Holzkamp's and critical theory's conceptions of subjectivity cannot be explained away. For outsiders, the contradictory relationship between the two German 'schools' seems highly unfruitful – but apart from this, Holzkamp's last book denotes for me an important step in the direction of understanding the significance of the subjective.

Finally, mention should be made of the continuation of the cultural historical approach which, since the end of the 1960s and with leading names such as Michael Cole, Barbara Rogoff, Sylvia Scribner (1923–1991) and James Wertsch, has taken place in the USA, *inter alia* in collaboration with Engeström. On the one hand it has been a matter of making, in particular, Vygotsky's work better known in the English-speaking part of the world and, on the other hand, continuation and application of the cultural historical approach, not least a special interest in the concept of 'the proximal zone of development' (for example, Scribner and Cole 1974; Cole and Scribner 1978; Wertsch 1981, 1985, 1998; Rogoff and Lave 1984; Rogoff and Wertsch 1984; Cole and Cole 1989; Cole 1996; Cole and Wertsch 1996; Rogoff 2003). As mentioned in section 5.3, Jerome Bruner has also had some connection with this group.

7.6 Communities of practice

However, the most important breakthrough in extension of the cultural historical tradition took place with Jean Lave and Etienne Wenger's previously mentioned work on 'situated learning' (Lave and Wenger 1991) and Etienne Wenger's work on 'communities of practice' (Wenger 1998), which draws to a considerable extent on the cultural historical tradition in combination with Lave's social anthropological and Wenger's broad psychological and information technology background.

In the context of the interaction dimension of learning, Lave and Wenger's book has been of decisive importance for the boom that has taken place since the 1990s in the understanding of the key position of this dimension in learning – even though theoretically their definition of the concept of 'situated learning' was ambiguous, because it was, at the same time, supposed to function as the focal point for promoting the values of apprenticeship learning in relation to traditional school teaching. On the face of it, the concept deals with all learning taking place in a specific situation, this situation being significant for the nature of the learning process and for its result. Thus Lave and Wenger write that the concept

> took on the proportions of a general theoretical perspective, the basis of claims about the relational character of knowledge and learning, about the negotiated character of meaning, and about the concerned (engaged, dilemma-driven) nature of learning activity for the people involved. That perspective meant that there is no activity which is not situated.
>
> (Lave and Wenger 1991, p. 33)

In this context Lave and Wenger make another very interesting point which further deepens the situation's general significance for learning, namely:

> that even so-called general knowledge only has power in specific circumstances. Generality is often associated with abstract represen-tations, with decontextualization. But abstract representations are meaningless unless they can be made specific to the situation at hand. Moreover, the formation or acquisition of an abstract principle is itself a specific event in specific circumstances. Knowing a general rule by itself in no way assures that any generality it may carry is enabled in the specific circumstances in which it is relevant.
>
> (Lave and Wenger 1991, pp. 33–34)

Thus according to Lave and Wenger it is not simply that the concrete situation influences the learning that occurs, but it also has significance for which existing learning results are activated. When the learning occurs in an interaction between existing structures and new impulses (see section 4.2), the environment and the learning situation influence not only the learner's perception of the new impulses, but also which existing structures are involved in the internal elaboration processes.

In my opinion, had Lave and Wenger kept to these positions, their concept of situated learning could have proved a clear and productive contribution to the understanding of learning. However, it seems as if they do not quite want to acknowledge these general points of view and elaborate on them, for they are following a different agenda. Their ultimate message is not that all learning is influenced by the situation in which it occurs, but that a specific type of situation has certain particular learning qualities, i.e. situations that can generally be termed *legitimate peripheral participation* and typically appear in connection with *apprenticeship*. I shall return to this subject in section 12.4.

However, the rather convoluted concept of legitimate peripheral participation would now seem to have faded into the background, also in Lave and Wenger themselves, and Wenger has first and foremost continued with a concept concerning 'communities of practice' as the crucial framework condition for learning, partly in his book of the same title (Wenger 1998), and partly in a number of later articles and books (in particular, Wenger and Snyder 2001; Wenger *et al.* 2002).

In *Communities of Practice*, Wenger set up what he terms a 'social theory of learning' (Wenger 1998, s. 4) – or what in the present context could be called a holistic theory of the interaction dimension of learning. He states quite clearly that it is precisely this dimension of learning on which he is focusing:

> There are many different kinds of learning theory. Each emphasizes different aspects of learning, and each is therefore useful for different purposes. To some extent these differences in emphasis reflect a deliberate focus on a slice of the multidimensional problem of learning, and to some extent they reflect more fundamental differences in assumptions about the nature of knowledge, knowing, and knowers, and consequently about what matters in learning.
>
> (Wenger 1998, pp. 3–4)

Wenger's conception that learning embraces various aspects or dimensions seems right in line with the basic view of this book, but while I attempt to specify and discuss the dimensions in relation to each other, Wenger gives priority to what I term the interaction dimension, and even though he also includes what in my terminology is called inner acquisition matters, this is placed under the social perspective, so much indeed that at times it seems that he has forgotten his introductory statement to the effect that other perspectives also exist.

Thus he also places the concept of 'learning' (not 'social learning') at the centre of the model that sums up his general understanding and approach (Figure 7.2):

Wenger himself gives the following explanation for the model:

> A social theory of learning must . . . integrate the components necessary to characterize social participation as a process of learning and knowing. These components . . . include the following:
>
> 1) Meaning: a way of talking about our (changing) ability – individually and collectively – to experience our life and the world as meaningful.
> 2) Practice: a way of talking about the shared historical and social resources, frameworks, and perspectives that can sustain mutual engagement in action.
> 3) Community: a way of talking about the social configurations in which our enterprises are defined as worth pursuing and our participation is recognizable as competence.
> 4) Identity: a way of talking about how learning changes who we are and creates personal histories of becoming in the context of our communities.
>
> Clearly, these elements are deeply interconnected and mutually defining. In fact, looking at [Figure 7.2], you could switch any of the four

Figure 7.2 Components in a social theory of learning (from Wenger 1998, p. 5)

peripheral components with learning, place it in the centre as the primary focus, and the figure would still make sense.

Therefore, when I use the concept of 'community of practice' in the title of this book, I really use it as a point of entry into a broader conceptual framework of which it is a constitutive element. The analytical power of the concept lies precisely in that it integrates the components of (the figure) while referring to a familiar experience.

(Wenger 1998, pp. 4–6)

The social dimension of learning is tied to community and practice, and creates meaning and identity, and therefore learning presupposes action and participation and converts them into experience and development. These key words and their positions in the model provide a valuable illustration of the significance of the community of practice for learning, which is elaborated through Wenger's further descriptions and finally converted into important consequences for the development of organisation and education.

The most important quality of the theory lies in its comprehensive and coherent understanding of the social level – while the psychological and societal levels are only brought in as extensions or examples. This is probably also partly why neither internal psychological nor societal conflicts have any important role to play in the theory. As a learning theory it expands the concept of social learning, but in relation to individual development, it lacks the perspective of conflict, and although there is a concept of experience, it is not in the same dialectic mode (and therefore developmental and conflict-oriented mode), as in the concept of experience developed in extension of the socialisation approach of critical theory. I will discuss this further in the next chapter.

In spite of the critical points and limitations mentioned, there can be no doubt that Lave and Wenger's work has represented a tremendous impulse for the understanding of the significance inherent in the social context of learning. Thus, it is my opinion in general that those who have inherited the cultural historical tradition have now worked themselves far further than the original Soviet Russian positions and have made important contributions to the understanding of the interaction dimension of learning.

7.7 Politically oriented approaches

Other approaches to the interaction dimension of learning are more directly politically oriented in that they refer to current social conditions and are focused on the way in which learning can contribute to solving urgent societal problems.

The classic and, probably, most extreme example of such an approach is to be found in the work of the previously mentioned Brazilian educational theorist and practitioner Paulo Freire, in particular in his books entitled *Pedagogy of the Oppressed* and *Cultural Action for Freedom* (Freire 1970, 1971), the first of which appeared in over 700,000 copies all over the world, making it probably the most read book on pedagogics ever.

Freire's pedagogical work was primarily oriented towards the simultaneous liberation of, and the teaching of reading skills to, poor rural labourers in Brazil, and later, broadly, of oppressed peoples in the third world, and his theory concerned pedagogics more than learning. Nevertheless, it contained several key points of learning theory. The most basic was about linking elementary reading instruction directly with discussions about political oppression through working with so-called 'generative themes':

> The starting point for organizing the program content of education or political action must be the present, existential, concrete situation, reflecting the aspirations of the people. Utilizing certain basic contradictions, we must pose this existential, concrete, present situation to the people as a problem which challenges them and requires a response – not just at the intellectual level, but at the level of action. . . . It is to the reality which mediates men, and to the perception of that reality held by educators and people, that we must go to find the program content of education. The investigation of what I have termed the people's 'thematic universe' – the complex of their 'generative themes' – inaugurates the dialogue of education as the practice of freedom.
>
> (Freire 1970, pp. 85 and 86)

The way is thus pointed to active, problem-oriented and action-directed learning around themes directly reflecting or exemplifying the participants' contradictory experiences of societal oppression, in contrast to the traditional 'filling up' form of teaching which Freire calls 'banking education' (see section 4.2).

Part of Freire's work was later taken up and continued in the USA, in particular by Henry Giroux and Stanley Aronowitz, with a series of critical books about the American school system, especially in relation to poor and oppressed groups. These included *Ideology, Culture, and the Process of Schooling* (Giroux 1981), *Education under Siege* (Aronowitz and Giroux 1985), *Schooling and the Struggle for Public Life* (Giroux 1988), *Postmodern Education* (Aronowitz and Giroux 1991) and *Pedagogy and the Politics of Hope* (Giroux 1997).

Of particular interest in the present context, however, is the book entitled *Theory and Resistance in Education – Towards a Pedagogy for the Opposition* (Giroux 1983), which first and foremost is about resistance against marginalisation and oppression *through* learning and education – which is something quite different from individual resistance *against* learning, which I deal with in section 9.5.

There are many parallels between Freire's approach and previously mentioned German consciousness sociologist Oskar Negt's concept about 'exemplary learning' (i.e. learning on the basis of representative examples) for capitalist industrial workers (Negt 1971 [1968]) – and one common element is, among others, the central importance of experience for learning, to which I return in the next chapter.

Here, however, as another European example of a politically oriented approach to the interaction dimension of learning I will discuss the work of Flemish Danny Wildemeersch, who works on youth and adult education from a social perspective and is particularly interested in learning perspectives in connection with grass-roots activities, social work and the like. Wildemeersch defines social learning as 'combined learning and problem-solving activities which take place within participatory systems such as groups, social networks, movements and collectivities, operating within "real life" contexts and thereby raising issues of social responsibility' (Wildemeersch 1999, p. 39).

Social learning thus occurs in *participatory systems*, which operate in a tension field between creativity, power and responsibility, and the learning takes place around four axes characterised as action, reflection, communication and negotiation. In the present context it is significant that Wildemeersch attempts to span both the external societal conditions and the internal psychological conditions.

Wildemeersch thus connects social learning with the processes that occur in dedicated forward-looking problem solving. This also includes a concept of *social responsibility*, which, in several contexts, Wildemeersch has been aiming at (Wildemeersch 1991, 1992; Jansen *et al.* 1998). This concept has not been precisely defined, but it is clearly more wide-reaching than the concept of 'responsibility for one's own learning' – as it spans right from the external societal responsibility regarded by many today as absolutely essential in a large number of contexts, both local and global, to the responsibility a participant may have in a goal-directed group project, and the personal responsibility for our own actions and our own lives.

In terms of learning, social responsibility forms a particularly significant relationship with reflexivity (Wildemeersch 1991, pp. 156ff.; see section 5.6). If reflexivity is not to end up in individualistic selfishness, lacking any social perspective, it must be connected with a sense of social obligation. Wildemeersch also uses expressions such as 'critical reflectivity' and 'aesthetic reflectivity', which imply a critical distance and a social connection, respectively (Wildemeersch 1998, pp. 98–99).

Social learning and social responsibility are thus for Wildemeersch a way to behave, which develops – or perhaps does not develop – societally as a part of socialisation, and comes to be seen in a new light in extension of late-modern developments which, in one respect, have put reflexivity on the agenda, and in another are handing more and more societal functions over to the market mechanism and to individuality.

When someone constantly has to make a choice between apparently boundless possibilities, and even has to choose his or her own life course and identity, there is no avoiding reflexivity, which settles everything in relation to oneself. In this way, learning through reflexivity becomes a necessity, however demanding it may be, and it becomes vitally important to qualify this form of learning (Wildemeersch 2000).

Wildemeersch has also worked together on these issues with Dutch Theo Jansen and Swiss Matthias Finger, in particular (see Wildemeersch *et al.* 1998; Jansen *et al.* 1998), and in his own work Finger has especially related the requirement concerning social responsibility to environmental policy and the environmental movements (Finger 1995; Finger and Asún 2001). In another important project about marginalised young people, Wildemeersch, together with, for example, Theo Jansen and British Susan Weil, has worked with the same angles of approach (Weil *et al.* 2004).

With respect to learning, this is a discussion with far-reaching consequences, for without the general development of a reflexivity that is always a match for the development of a market society, the in-built mechanisms within this development will lead to an ever-stronger impoverishment of the world's resources, both material and human. The basic qualification for balanced learning with both reflexivity and responsibility is that the learning content should be perceived to be meaningful with regard to oneself. This basic qualification is far from always fulfilled in institutional education, but is basically present in grass-roots activities and the like.

Thus Wildemeersch is active around the boundary between the critical and the pedagogical normative. Social learning is societally determined and for that very reason must be qualified. In terms of learning, this concerns experience, transmission and activity.

7.8 Social constructionism and postmodernism

Yet another view or school that relates to the interaction dimension of learning is 'social constructionism', (already mentioned several times previously) as typically represented by the American psychologist Kenneth Gergen (1994). The basis for the social constructionist conception is that 'the site of explanation for human action moves to the relational sphere. . . . Social constructionism traces the sources of human action to relationships and the very understanding of "individual functioning" to communal interchange' (Gergen 1994, pp. 69 and 68).

Social constructionism goes a decisive step further than the underlying view of the concept of social learning:

> For example, social learning theorists talk about the 'situation specificity' of behaviour. They suggest that our behaviour is dependent not upon

personality characteristics but upon the nature of the situations in which we find ourselves. Behaviour is therefore 'specific' to a particular situation. . . . What might it mean then, to say that personality is socially constructed? One way of looking at this is to think of personality . . . as existing not within people but between them. . . . Take some of the personality-type words we use to describe people: for example, friendly, caring, shy, self-conscious, charming, bad-tempered, thoughtless . . . words which would completely lose their meaning if the person described were living alone on a desert island. . . . The point is that we use these words as if they referred to entities existing within the person they describe, but once the person is removed from their relations with others the words become meaningless.

(Burr 1995, pp. 25, 26 and 27)

Social constructionists do not as such deny that learning processes occur internally in an individual. But they find it uninteresting, because the nature of these processes and the content of them are always determined by relations in the social field. They agree with Piaget and other constructivists that the world and society are not objective elements that can be acquired through learning processes. The surrounding world is perceived in both cases as something that is actively constructed. In a constructivist approach this construction occurs in the individual by means of meetings with the surrounding world and interactions with it. In a social constructionist approach the construction occurs socially as developments in the community.

In my understanding, however, the two approaches do not need to oppose each other. As already stated in Chapter 2, the way I view it is that social constructions occur in the communities that constantly interact with individual constructions in the internal learning processes. The social constructionists rightly point out the significance of the social field, but this can easily lead to the significance of the internal psychological processes in the individual being overlooked or underestimated. Friendliness is developed socially and only has meaning in a social context, yet it is individuals who acquire and practise friendliness.

I cannot, thus, accept the claim of 'pure' social constructionism that learning and other mental processes are only social, and not individually produced. In my opinion it is a mistake to regard it as an 'either/or': on the contrary, it is a 'both/and'. But it should also be mentioned that there are numerous more or less categorical positions concerning these matters, among them also different types of 'social construct*ivism*', some of which, at any rate, are more oriented towards accepting an individual element than pure social construct*ionism*.

Yet another school of understanding that is quite extreme with respect to the importance of the interaction dimension is so-called 'postmodernism', which in particular builds on the works of a number of French philosophers from the 1970s and onwards, including, for example, Jean-François Lyotard (1924–1998) and Michel Foucault (1926–1984), as well as linguist Jacques Derrida (1930–2004) and psychoanalyst Jacques Lacan (1901–1981). Although one can hardly speak of a definite, coherent understanding, the main features are that there are no eternal truths, 'the great narratives' are rejected, the world is constantly changing, everything must be understood locally and in its own time (for example, Lyotard 1984 [1979]).

I do not wish to elucidate further on postmodern culture and consciousness forms at this point, but would just like to sketch out a few main points of significance for learning conditions, starting with the English-Australian postmodernist education researcher Robin Usher (for example, Usher 1993, 1998, 2000; Usher et al. 1997).

Usher's central point is that people today do not have a coherent, authentic and rational self that can learn from experiences in a sensible way, autonomously and independently of emotional and social ties. Rather, the self is irrational, emotional, embedded in the body with all its needs, and stamped socially and societally.

The notion of the autonomous and rational self is a construction of an ideal, that evolved together with modern individualistic society and serves the interests of the authorities, particularly as a kind of target concept for discipline within the school/educational system using the systematic repression of emotional, bodily and social perspectives.

As I understand Usher, he regards the self that is operated with in psychology as an idealised false picture of personality formation, which many have perhaps tried to live up to, though very few have been able to in reality, for under the smooth surface there are always very different impulses moving. And in the postmodern period, which Usher perceives that we are in, this hopeless notion neither can, nor should be, maintained, for it is connected to the notion of a coherent world order, which cannot, nor ever could be, proven.

On the contrary, the world is divided, unconnected and constantly changing, and the self is correspondingly fragmented, unstable and enquiring, always on the move, never at peace, marked by the overflow of influences and apparent opportunities for choice, which pervades postmodern life.

It is characteristic that Usher's texts are usually limited to a deconstruction and criticism which, of course, is far more subtle and comprehensive than the above can cover (e.g. his scathing deconstruction of Habermas's concept concerning the ideal speech situation, Usher 2000). But Usher is also engaged in adult education and experience learning and from time to time in his texts one can find the rudiments of positive countermoves to the dissolution tendencies.

For example, he points to the different social movements and their importance as a political protest and possible corrective to modern societal governance, especially the possibility of influencing production through an

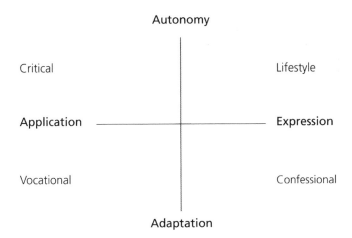

Figure 7.3 Usher et al.'s 'map' of experiential learning in the social practices of post-modernity (after Usher et al. 1997, p. 106)

alternative, e.g. 'green' pattern of consumption, to boycott actions against certain companies and goods, eco-tourism and a number of other forms of protest behaviour that range from wearing shabby clothes as far as self-destructive forms such as anorexia (Usher and Johnston 1996).

Finally, there is the education-oriented model developed by Usher together with British Ian Bryant and Rennie Johnston (Figure 7.3). It is construed with a starting point in a postmodern picture of society around two axes: the one passes between autonomy and adaptation, and the other between expression and application. This results in four spaces towards which educational and learning measures can be oriented, namely: the vocational (between adaptation and application); the confessional (between adaptation and expression); the lifestyle (between autonomy and expression); and the critical (between autonomy and application).

The figure is rather reminiscent of Kolb's learning model (section 5.2), and is first and foremost intended to state that there are many different forms of experiential learning that 'can function both to empower and control' (Usher et al. 1997, s. 118), liberating and adapting. What is meaningful can only be determined from the context, and it is reasonable that both learners and teachers can perceive what is going on.

7.9 Collective learning, collaborative learning and mass psychology

I have now examined what, in my opinion, are some of the most important suggestions concerning what is important in connection with the interaction dimension of learning. At the centre is the concept of 'social learning', not least in the international literature, and in most of the contributions I regard this as more or less tantamount to what I here have defined as the interaction dimension of learning or learning's social and societal dimension, i.e. the part of individual learning that concerns social interaction.

Sometimes, however, a concept about 'collective learning' appears, especially within the labour movement and learning in working life (as well as the concepts of 'organisational learning' and 'the learning organisation', to which I return in Chapter 12).

The understanding of the collective has always occupied a quite key position in the classical labour movement. Thus, in a summary of a long list of studies into worker consciousness in 1971, Danish psychologist Vilhelm Borg referred again and again to 'the collective consciousness of the working class' and similar expressions – e.g. in the following summing up of a Norwegian study (Lysgaard 1967):

> The development of the worker collective occurs through a problem-interpreting process and an organising process. . . . As the workers talk together and exchange viewpoints and experiences, they interpret the particular common situation. A collective consciousness develops . . . which is neither a kind of 'average' of the opinions or ideas of the individual workers nor does it need to exist as manifest ideas of the majority of the workers. . . . One of the most important functions of the worker collective is to preserve and elaborate this collective consciousness, which comes to act as a guide to the worker collective's organising process. The organising process contributes to the other aspect of development of the collective consciousness.
>
> (Borg 1971, p. 69)

With respect to learning in working life, Peter Senge, for example, writes twenty years later in the most central work on 'the learning organisation' that 'new and expansive patterns of thinking are nurtured, where collective aspiration is set free, and where people are continually learning how to learn together' (Senge 1990, p. 3).

The question is, however, what is actually inherent in this concept about the collective, and when and how it takes on any other meaning than that it is what some people do together. If there is to be any meaning in operating with a concept of collective learning as something specific, as distinct from the rather imprecise concept of 'social learning', that meaning must be that a group of people in specific circumstances can learn the same – which contradicts the basic assumption I made in section 4.2, that all learning occurs in the meeting between new impulses and previously established psychological structures, which are individual and different, meaning that the learning results will also be individual and different.

It would seem to be the case that under special circumstances a phenomenon can occur that distinguishes itself as something special. If this is to have any meaning, then as far as I can tell, three conditions must be met:

- first, the collective in question must be in a common situation;
- second, the participants in the sphere the learning concerns must have extensive common presuppositions; and
- third, the situation must be of such a common emotionally obsessed nature that there exists a clear basis for everyone to mobilise the necessary psychological energy for significant and, as a rule, accommodative, learning that concerns the common nature of the situation.

These conditions do not appear to have been systematically researched, but Borg states, with reference to the German political scientist Michael Vester, that opportunities for transcendent collective learning are facilitated by long strikes and the like (Borg 1971, p. 99; see Vester 1969). I would not deny that such possibilities can occur in the everyday of working life, but they are hardly present merely because a company strives to become a 'learning organisation' (see section 12.4).

As I see it there is a clear need for a concept concerning some people learning something together or in a community, but which does not need to live up to the far-reaching requirements normally inherent in the concept about collectivity. I would propose the concept 'collaborative learning' (i.e. cooperating learning), which one can observe in use now and then, especially in connection with computer-supported learning approaches (see section 12.5), where the concept of 'computer-supported collaborative learning' (CSCL) seems to be well established (for example, Dillenbourg 1999; Dirckinck-Holmfeld 2000). Already in 1990, Lone Dirckinck-Holmfeld showed that there is a great difference between learning processes in connection with computer-supported learning depending on the nature of the cooperation, and she introduced the concept of 'genuine collaboration' for cooperation where one genuinely enters a community to learn and develop something together (Dirckinck-Holmfeld 1990). I am thus proposing a terminology where:

- 'social learning' is employed in connection with the interaction dimension in individual learning;
- 'collaborative learning' is employed in connection with approaches where a group of people try to learn and develop something together;
- 'collective learning' is employed in the special contexts in which a group of people with wide-ranging uniform backgrounds in a field enter a learning context where the social situation contributes to them learning the same thing.

It should be added that such collective learning is not something exclusive to working life and the labour movement but, equally, can occur in connection with a right-wing authoritarian collectivity where the problem is not academically dealt with as collective learning (positive connotation) but as mass psychology (negative connotation). This was, first and foremost, considered by the Austrian psychoanalyst Wilhelm Reich in his book *The Mass Psychology of Fascism* (Reich 1969b [1933]), in which an authoritarian style of upbringing and the ego-weakness that accompanies it are identified as the psychological basis for the collective support for Nazism.

This problem was thoroughly considered at a later point by Theodor Adorno *et al.* in their work on 'the authoritarian personality' (Adorno *et al.* 1950; see section 7.4), and in a subsequent article, with direct reference to Freud's *Group Psychology and the Analysis of the Ego*, Adorno focuses on a form of collective narcissism as the definitive psychological basis for Nazism (Adorno 1972 [1951]; Freud 1959 [1921]). In these contexts the three conditions mentioned above seem to have been largely present – and Thomas Leithäuser has also stressed that authoritarianism must be perceived as a social phenomenon rather than an individual one (Leithäuser 1998).

Collective learning is thus not an unquestionably positive phenomenon, as it figures in the collective struggle of the working class. It can imply both a common consciousness and a common removal of personal responsibility. Currently, the concept is, perhaps, most relevant in religious contexts, and perhaps in connection with big musical or sports events, where the feelings of community that are repressed in our society's individualised everyday life are given a legitimate opportunity to flourish for a short while. The individualised society of today does not provide for collective learning, but for that very reason, there may be certain covert needs that push forward and are released on particular occasions.

7.10 Summary

All learning is situated, i.e. it takes place in a certain context of a social and societal nature which, through interaction with the learner(s) becomes an integrated part of the learning. In this way the learning comes to reflect the social and societal conditions for possibilities, and contributes to the participants' socialisation in relation to existing social conditions through processes that are often conflictual in character.

In practice, for the learner the interaction dimension of learning can often take many forms, e.g. typically perception, transmission, experience, imitation, activity, or participation, where what is important is that the more activity and engagement the learner involves in the interaction, the greater the learning possibilities are, not least with respect to the accommodative and, perhaps, transformative processes.

It is, therefore, important for learning that with respect to the more direct forms of interaction and the more general frames in the form of communities of practice and learning environments, the possibility exists for active participation and co-determination, involvement in subjectively relevant problematics, critical reflection and reflexivity and social responsibility.

Chapter 8

Learning as whole

This chapter deals with the interaction and totality of the three learning dimensions. With respect to the nature of learning, this takes place by means of a discussion of the concept of experience especially as treated by John Dewey and Oskar Negt. With respect to the learning that emerges from it, the focus is first the personality concept, next the modern competence concept and, finally, the identity concept. Different learning theories are then discussed that try to cover the whole broad field of learning as it has been defined and treated. The concluding section deals with different types of learning models.

8.1 Across the dimensions

Each of the three dimensions of learning has been treated exhaustively in the three preceding chapters. But it is, of course, important to maintain that learning is a totality. In this chapter, therefore, I try to gather the threads across the dimensions against the background of these chapters.

In the first place, and as something quite fundamental, from the model in Chapter 3 it must be pointed out that a holistic treatment of learning must always cover all three learning dimensions, and, from the typology in Chapter 4, that in general it is important that the four different learning types are activated where each of them is relevant, and in particular that appropriate interaction between the assimilative and accommodative and, in special cases, the transformative, processes is possible.

In addition, it was emphasised with respect to the content dimension of learning in Chapter 5 that a broad understanding of content is important, not just as knowledge and skills but also as, for example, understanding, meaning, overview, cultural and societal orientation, and self-awareness. Concerning the incentive dimension, it was emphasised in Chapter 6 in particular that the learner's motivation, emotions and volition are of key importance for learning. With respect to the interaction dimension, Chapter 7 focused on the participants' opportunities for activity, engagement, co-determination, involvement in subjectively relevant issues, critical reflection, reflexivity and social responsibility.

Most readers will probably find all of this reasonable. Nevertheless, there are many diverse matters that must be established in connection with a concrete learning situation, or planning or analysis of a course of learning, and it is thus important at this point to include some deliberations precisely to do with the totality in this broad and complex field.

8.2 Learning and experience

'From experience you shall learn' goes an old Danish folk expression, and there is no doubt that in everyday language, in both Danish and English, experience is reckoned to be better and more profound than 'ordinary learning', having another dimension of personal significance and involving personal commitment. But experience is also a central concept in learning theory, and in the following I will set out how and with which criteria this concept can be used as a common framework for understanding learning, which, in an important way, both covers and brings together the three dimensions I have discussed in detail in the preceding chapters.

I must immediately emphasise – as in section 5.2 – that I use the word 'experience' in a more demanding and qualified sense than it is given in everyday English, more so even than as used by Kolb in his book *Experiential Learning* (Kolb 1984) and many other researchers and debaters in this field. My use of the concepts 'experience' and 'experiential learning' goes beyond distinguishing between the immediate perception and the elaborated comprehension; it implies also that the process does not relate only to cognitive learning (as is, for example, the case in Kolb's work), but covers all three dimensions of learning.

It is this book's contention that all learning includes these dimensions to some degree, although the weighting can be rather unbalanced in some contexts. When I claim that experience is immediately understood as something other, and something more, than ordinary learning, I am, however, referring to a qualitative difference. On the other hand, it is not possible and not in accordance with the nature of learning, to make a sharp distinction between what is experience and what is 'ordinary' learning.

The concept of experience I am setting out here does not, therefore, solely concern the notion that all three dimensions are involved, for they are all in principle always involved, but all three dimensions must also be of subjective significance for the learner in the context. Experience has important elements of content and knowledge, i.e. we acquire or understand something that we perceive to be important for ourselves. Experience also has a considerable incentive element, i.e. we are committed motivationally and emotionally to the learning taking place. And finally, experience has an important social and societal element, i.e. we learn something that is not only of significance to us personally, but is something that also concerns the relationship between ourselves and the world we live in. Thus experience is set out as the central concept in the learning conception of this presentation: experience is characterised by incorporating the three dimensions spanned by the learning conception presented here in an important way.

It is, however, important to further qualify the experience concept, which I do in the following by referring to the two most important approaches that form the basis for the perception of the concept of experience as it is used in Danish pedagogy: first, the progressive approach developed in the USA in the early 1900s, particularly by the previously mentioned philosopher and pedagogue John Dewey. And, second, the approach of German sociologist Oskar Negt, also mentioned previously, who works in extension of the Critical Theory of the Frankfurt School and has played a large role as a theoretical reference for the development of experiential pedagogy in Denmark (see Webb and Nielsen 1996).

While the majority of Dewey's development of pedagogical practice and theory took place in the first decades of the twentieth century, he dealt with the concept of experience later in a short work entitled *Experience and Education* (Dewey 1965 [1938]) based on a series of summarised lectures. Dewey has a broad definition of the concept of experience in accordance with its everyday meaning. We experience things all the time, but what is important in pedagogical terms is – as I have also stated before – the quality of the experiences:

> to discriminate between experiences that are worthwhile educationally and those that are not. . . . Does not the principle of regard for individual freedom and for decency and kindliness of human relations come back in the end to the conviction that these things are tributary to a higher quality of experience on the part of a greater number than are methods of repression and coercion or force? . . . An experience arouses curiosity, strengthens initiative, and sets up desires and purposes that are sufficiently intense to carry a person over dead places in the future . . . (and not) operate so as to leave a person arrested on a low plane of development, in a way which limits capacity for growth.
>
> (Dewey 1965 [1938], pp. 33, 34, 38 and 37–38)

Thus, for Dewey, the criteria for what constitutes experiences are based in general humanism and a somewhat unclear growth concept and are thus on a more general level, although perhaps, nonetheless, not so different from my reference to the three learning dimensions. More concretely, Dewey, however, also stresses two integrated principles or dimensions as being central to upbringing, namely the principles of continuity and interaction.

The principle of continuity of experience means that every experience both takes up something from those which have gone before and modifies in some way the quality of those which come after. ... Interaction means [that] a transaction [is] taking place between an individual and what, at the same time, constitutes his environment.
(Dewey 1965 [1938], pp. 35 and 43)

Despite the reference to interaction, however, Dewey's concept of experience has often been criticised as individualistic and lacking a societal dimension. And it is precisely in the societal area that Negt's concept of experience exceeds Dewey's in decisive ways.

Negt's concept of experience is mainly dealt with in the book *Public Sphere and Experience* (Negt and Kluge 1993 [1972]), where it appears in a broad civilisation-critical context, which revolves round the question of the opportunities for the working class to experience their own situation and opportunities in our present society. The concept of experience is thus only directly defined through an oft-quoted and fairly intricate statement from the German philosopher Hegel (1770–1831): 'The dialectic process which consciousness executes on itself – on its knowledge as well as on its object – in the sense that out of it the new and true object arises, is precisely, what is termed experience' (Hegel 1967 [1807], p. 142).

With this reference Negt draws on a long philosophical tradition leading from Kant, through Hegel, to the Frankfurt School. But although the approaches are very different, the distance from Dewey is not, in my view, all that great as far as the concept of experience itself is concerned. What Hegel calls the dialectic process which consciousness executes on itself is the same as what Dewey is attempting to capture through his claim of continuity. And what Hegel calls the dialectical process on its knowledge as well as on its object is present in Dewey's claim of interaction.

This can also be seen as that which is dealt with in this book as, respectively, the internal psychological, and the external social and societal partial processes in learning – by which means the central point in Hegel's statement is that both these processes are dialectic in nature, i.e. they take the form of interplay or tension that may lead to a synthesis, an overlapping agreement. In the internal psychological processes, the dialectic lies between the psychological structures developed previously and influences from the environment (see the approaches of Piaget and Ausubel, section 4.2). In the external interaction processes, the dialectic lies in the interaction between the individual and the environment.

However, a general definition of the Negt approach to experience that is both more accessible and more complete can be found in the work of the Danish educational researcher Henning Salling Olesen:

Experience is the process whereby we as human beings, individually and collectively consciously master reality, and the ever-living understanding of this reality and our relation to it. Experiences in the plural exist, as in everyday language, but they are to be understood as partial products of this process. Experience is thus a subjective process as it is seen from the point of view of the person experiencing. It is also a collective process because when we experience as individuals we also do so through a socially structured consciousness. It is, finally, an active, critical and creative process where we both see and adapt. . . . This concept of experiences is inherited from the German sociologist Oskar Negt . . .

(Olesen 1989 [1985], p. 8)

It is interesting to note that despite the explicit reference to Negt, this definition could have been written, word for word, by Dewey, for this indirectly shows that the difference between Dewey's and Negt's conceptions of experience do not lie in the actual nature of the experience itself, but in the question of how the current societal structures actually affect the formation of the experience.

To quote Salling Olesen again, in the Negt conception it is all about the fact that 'reality is not immediately apparent' (Olesen 1981, p. 21), i.e. that there are central societal factors that cannot be immediately experienced, such as, for example, the relationship between utility value and exchange value, or the reduction of the workforce from a general human potential to being an item that can be bought and sold on the market. Although the central capitalistic structures are man-made and therefore may also be changed, they are experienced as natural, like a kind of 'second nature', and thus the entire experiential base is displaced.

In general, it is first and foremost important to maintain the totality of the concept of experience in relation to learning. The concept comprises all aspects of learning in principle, including internal psychological acquisition processes and social interactive processes, content-related aspects and incentive aspects, and all forms of learning and forms of interaction. But for learning to be described as experiential in the way this concept has been set up here, various specific qualitative criteria must be fulfilled.

First, the learning must be of considerable subjective significance with regard to the content, incentive and interaction learning dimensions.

Second, the learning must be part of a coherent process – there must be continuity, as Dewey puts it. Even if we focus exclusively on single experiences, it only makes sense to use the expression experiential learning when the single event can be understood in the context of earlier experiences and future opportunities for experience, for only through this can the single experience gain its significance. Any form of 'building block thinking' that fails to take this into consideration can be said to have misunderstood what the concept of experience is basically about. (Thus, we also encounter a difference in relation to the concept of learning as such, for in some cases it can be possible and meaningful to talk of learning as a more isolated phenomenon.)

Third, the interaction process between the individual and the surroundings must be of such a nature that the individual can be said to be a subject in the situation, i.e. that he or she is present and is self-aware. Whether that person behaves as such in that particular situation can obviously be hard to determine in practice. But in principle it is important to draw the line at situations in which the learner only plays a passive role and is uncommitted. It is not impossible to learn something in such a situation – there are plenty of examples in ordinary school teaching; but this kind of learning cannot be called experiential, for if you are not involved as a subject there will not actually be any mutual interaction process, but instead what is typically called a filling process – or 'banking' as Paulo Freire (1970) calls it.

Fourth, it is important that the formation of experience is always socially mediated. It does not occur in individual isolation, but of necessity requires a social context. Naturally this should not be understood as meaning that there cannot be occasions in which people gain their experiences alone, but for the very reason that it is a continuing process, the isolation is only momentary, and the context in which it takes place will always be socially marked.

Fifth, and finally, in Negt's conception at any rate, the influences from the environment that the interaction is concerned with must be such that they reflect or exemplify relevant societal, material and/or social structures. This is what lies in Negt's conception of 'the principle of exemplarity' or 'exemplary learning' (Negt 1971 [1968]; Christiansen 1999, pp. 60f.). Here, too, there can, in practice, naturally occur a limitation problem – a subject that I will not go into in more detail here, but will instead refer to fuller treatments of the form of project work (Illeris 1999).

In Denmark the concept of experience has come to play a central part in educational thinking since 'experiential pedagogy' crystallised after about 1980 as a kind of common term for a number of pedagogical endeavours and patterns of work that emphasise the formation of experience of the participants, understood as a total learning based on the requirements, problems and interests of the participants (see Webb and Nielsen 1996).

Throughout the 1970s there was a sparkling optimism and faith that new pedagogical creations would not only give pleasure to the participants and help them develop, giving them better qualifications more in tune with the times, but would also help to change society in a more liberating and democratic direction. A common slogan for a large part of these activities was that we should 'use the experiences of the participants as a starting point', and this particular statement was often understood as the maxim of experiential pedagogy. Another and slightly more open statement talked of 'connecting to the experiences of the participants', and in some cases it could be 'contributing to/preparing the formation of experience for the participants'.

In practice, however, the subject proved to be more complex – and on the basis of an analysis of three ambitious experiential pedagogical projects that were carried out around 1980 in primary schools, upper secondary schools, and basic vocational education, respectively, it could be quite clearly concluded that:

> ideal experiential pedagogical processes must be about the pupils' important, subjectively perceived problem areas, that are to be elaborated in a continuing experiential process based on their existing patterns of experience and governed by a forward-pointing action perspective.
>
> (Illeris 1984, p. 32)

Here it is probably the words 'problem areas' and 'action perspective' that are significant. The point was that looking back towards previous experiences is less interesting for pupils than looking forward towards new challenges and experiences. Therefore, the implementation of experiential pedagogy, in practice, had to build on fundamental principles of problem orientation, participant direction, exemplarity and solidarity – and when it was to take place within the framework of institutional education it could typically be done through the application of the pedagogical work pattern developed under the name project work (Illeris 1999).

At international level, since the 1970s the experience concept has been developed in English-speaking countries under the term 'Experiential Learning' and, in particular, Kolb's frequently mentioned book of this title published in 1984 led to widespread interest in the book, not least within the network called 'The International Consortium for Experiential Learning' (ICEL). This consortium was established in 1987 and every second or third year since it has convened large international conferences where at the beginning some of the key names were Australian David Boud, British Susan Weil and the previously mentioned Danny Wildemeersch (section 7.7) and Robin Usher (section 7.8).

Following the first conference, the book *Making Sense of Experiential Learning* (Weil and McGill 1989a) was published, and it quickly came to function as a kind of basic work for the network. In the introductory article, the editors characterise the network as the framework for four 'villages':

> Village One is concerned particularly with assessing and accrediting learning from life and work experience as the basis for creating new routes into higher education, employment and training opportunities, and professional bodies.

Village Two focuses on experiential learning as the basis for bringing about change in the structures, purposes and curricula of post-school education.

Village Three emphasizes experiential learning as the basis for group consciousness raising, community action and social change.

Village Four is concerned with personal growth and development and experiential learning approaches that increase self-awareness and group effectiveness.

(Weil and McGill 1989b, p. 3)

By means of this frame description and the village concept, Weil and McGill succeeded in creating a mode of understanding that could constitute a common platform for the variegated network in which there was room for the great differences, while, at the same time, all could find themselves. Moreover, with its starting point in the different fields of practice, the book clearly underlined the societal embedment of the network.

In another article in the same book David Boud pointed out three dimensions which, to varying degrees, are typical of all activities referring to the term Experiential Learning. These are a dimension concerning 'learner control', a dimension concerning the learner's 'involvement of self', and a dimension concerning 'correspondence of learning environment to real environment' (Boud 1989, p. 39).

Boud, moreover, pointed to four approaches to adult education where Experiential Learning especially has been in the picture as a way of liberating learning from traditional ties: first in connection with teaching technology rationalisations, especially in vocational education, with a view to avoiding superfluous activities – 'freedom from distraction'; second, in connection with self-directed learning processes related to American Malcolm Knowles's concept of 'andragogy' (Knowles 1970, 1973) – 'freedom as learners'; third in connection with student-centred education in the humanistic tradition inspired by Carl Rogers (Rogers 1969; see section 5.6) – 'freedom to learn'; fourth, and last, in connection with critical pedagogics and social action where, in the English-speaking countries, Paulo Freire is the great source of inspiration (Freire 1970; see section 7.7): 'freedom through learning' – (Boud 1989, pp. 40ff.).

Finally, in the same article Boud pointed out three teaching approaches within Experiential Learning, namely 'the individual-centred approach', 'the group-centred approach', and 'the project-centred approach' (Boud 1989, pp. 44ff.).

In so doing Boud placed the concept of Experiential Learning in its academic context and demonstrated its broad field of application. But, as in Weil and McGill, it is the concept and the activity of Experiential Learning which is placed in a societal and pedagogical context, while the understanding itself of what it is to experience, i.e. what lies behind the concept of 'experience', is not elaborated.

A more critical approach was launched by Danny Wildemeersch, who warned against the individualistic tendencies that can lie in the understanding of the concept, and underlined the significance of conversation and dialogue for learning gaining a social perspective (Wildemeersch 1989). British Avtar Brah and Jane Hoy also adopted a societal perspective and drew particular attention to the fact that Experiential Learning can easily become yet another contribution to favouring those who already are privileged at the expense of the less privileged (Brah and Hoy 1989).

Another couple of important collections of articles were published later (Wildemeersch and Jansen 1992; Boud *et al.* 1993), and while the network was moving in the direction of taking up learning conditions in the third world in particular, the concept of Experiential Learning has shifted from being something special to becoming, to a higher degree, an ordinary and generally accepted concept in international educational and learning-oriented literature.

8.3 Personal development

Another, broader concept for holistic learning is 'personal development' or 'personality development'. Unlike experience it cannot be related to a single event or a brief course but concerns the effect of the total learning in a certain context over a certain period of time.

There are many definitions of 'personality', such as 'the person as a whole having different skills, dispositions and qualities, emotions and motives' (Hansen *et al.* 1997, p. 295), and it is typical here that it is about the whole viewed in relation to the qualities, or what we call characteristics, that cut across different divisions such as the learning dimensions. If, for example, one says that a person is 'tolerant', it will normally imply that this tolerance applies across many or all spheres, although perhaps with varying strength. It is thus something that is difficult to specify and measure, but which, on the other hand, plays a major role in life.

In terms of learning there is the particular aspect of personality and personal qualities that they are to some extent anchored in certain individual genetic predispositions – such as what was at one time understood by temperament. These predispositions develop and form through life's influences, however, so some learning is also occurring, but, as mentioned, typically in the form of more general, long-lasting and, as a rule, demanding processes that imply considerable personal efforts and thus presuppose a significant degree of motivation. Put in everyday terms, you only change your personality or substantial parts of it if you perceive that there are good grounds for doing so.

In learning – and particularly institutionalised learning within the educational system and working life – personal development, in general, and the development of specific types of personal qualities, have since the 1960s increasingly become an area of substantial interest and study.

There has been a distinct development in what workplaces require of their staff, where the demand for professional qualifications has gradually been supplemented, and partly overshadowed, by the demand for 'generic' qualifications that precisely have the character of personal qualities. Today this is extremely obvious from job advertisements in the press and is also confirmed by the dominant attitudes of personnel managers.

In connection with a research project on general qualifications I was involved in analysing these matters in greater detail (Andersen *et al.* 1994, 1996), and in the course of this work the current personal qualification requirements were summarised in the following categories:

- Intellectual qualifications, that typically cover definitions such as rational, systematic and analytical thinking, sociological imagination, problem solving, change of perspective and skills in diagnostics, evaluation, planning etc. – centring on the individual's capacity for rational behaviour.
- Perception qualifications, concerning precise sense perception, typically including precision in observation and interpretation – centring on what is defined as sensibility in academic terms.
- Self-control qualifications, covering definitions such as responsibility, reliability, perseverance, accuracy, ability to concentrate, quality and service orientation – centring on the individual's inclinations and capacity to act in accordance with general instructions.
- Individuality qualifications, typically covering definitions such as independence, self-confidence and creativity – centring on the individual's ability to act alone, especially in unforeseen situations.
- Social qualifications, covering definitions such as co-operation and communication abilities, congeniality and sociability – centring on the individual's ability to interact with others.
- Motivational qualifications, covering a range of definitions such as initiative, dynamism, drive, openness, keenness to learn, adaptability etc. – centring on the individual's potential to keep up with and contribute to the 'development' (the much-used category 'flexibility' is often used as a group description for this sphere, but it also partially includes social qualifications).

(Illeris 1995, pp. 60–61)

What is characteristic of all these categories is that they cover all three learning dimensions but are weighted differently. In the motivational qualifications the incentive dimension is very important, for example, and the same is true of the self-control and individuality qualifications, although to a lesser degree. The main emphasis is on the content dimension in the intellectual qualifications and perception qualifications. The social qualifications clearly draw on the interaction dimension in particular.

With respect to the teaching and learning that can further the development of such personal qualifications, the project concluded that the academic and the general or personality elements in the practical organisation of education may be understood and treated as two aspects of the same thing:

> Briefly, education that is to strengthen general qualifications in a goal-directed way must be neither pure instruction, learning of skills or rote learning, nor pure personal development or therapy. It must on the contrary be organised in such a way that it combines a concrete, typical vocational or academic qualification with opportunities for expanding the participants' motivation to develop understanding, personality and identity.
>
> (Illeris *et al.* 1995, p. 188)

Altogether, development in society's qualification demands thus can be seen to prompt an educational effort for attempting the development of a very broad range of personal qualities by the organisation of teaching to combine a professional and a personality-oriented approach. In practice this typically occurs through problem-oriented and, to some extent, participant-directed projects with a concrete professional content that also involves, recalls and deals with relevant personal function spheres (Illeris *et al.* 1995; Andersen *et al.* 1996).

8.4 Competence

When it comes to what learning as a whole can result in, the classic concept in Germany and the Scandinavian countries has, as mentioned in section 5.1, been 'formation'. But, partly because of the endless discussions of what this concept really implies, and partly because it frequently has elitist overtones, during the 1970s and 1980s it became more common to speak of 'qualifications' and 'qualification'. The qualification concept is obviously more precise in relation to the concept of formation, but it is also more technocratic and, first and foremost, more vocationally oriented in its starting point and the way it is generally understood. Therefore, it was necessary to 'invent' and use the concept of 'general qualification' if a broader aim was to be included (see Andersen *et al.* 1994, 1996).

In recent years the concept of 'competence' has taken a central position – and this is not merely a chance or indifferent linguistic innovation. On the contrary, it could be said that this linguistic change takes the full consequence of the schism in the qualification concept outlined above. What I consider to be the most fully adequate Danish definition phrases it as follows:

> The concept of competence refers . . . to a person's being qualified in a broader sense. It is not merely that a person masters a professional area, but also that the person can apply this professional knowledge – and more than that, apply it in relation to the requirements inherent in a situation which perhaps in addition is uncertain and unpredictable. Thus competence also includes the person's assessments and attitudes, and ability to draw on a considerable part of his/her more personal qualifications.
>
> (Jørgensen 1999, p. 4)

Competence is thus a unifying concept that integrates everything it takes in order to perform a given situation or context. The concrete qualifications are incorporated in the competence rooted in personality, and one may generally also talk of the competence of organisations and nations.

Where the concept of qualifications historically has its point of departure in requirements for specific knowledge and skills, and to an increasing degree has been used for pointing out that this knowledge and these skills have underlying links and roots in personality, the perception in the concept of competence has, so to speak, been turned upside down. In this concept, the point of departure lies at the personal level in relation to certain contexts, and the more specific qualifications are something that can be drawn in and contribute to realisation of the competence. Where the concept of qualifications took its point of departure in the individual elements, the individual qualifications, and has developed towards a more unified perception, the concept of competence starts with a unity, e.g. the type of person or organisation it takes to solve a task or fulfil a job, and on the basis of this points out any possible different qualifications necessary.

It is thus characteristic that the concept of competence does not, like the concept of qualifications, have its roots in industrial sociology, but in organisational psychology and modern management thinking. It has thus acquired a dimension of 'smartness' which makes it easier to 'sell' politically, but also makes it tend toward a superficiality which, in this context, seems to characterise large parts of the management orientation (see Argyris 2000); it has thus been called a 'prostitute' concept rooted in an economic view of man by the Danish philosopher, Jens Erik Kristensen (Kristensen 2001).

However, at the same time it is difficult to deny that it captures something central in the current situation of learning and qualification. It is ultimately concerned with how a person, an organisation or a nation is able to handle a relevant, but often unforeseen and unpredictable problematic situation, because we know with certainty that late-modern development constantly generates new and unknown problems, and the ability to respond openly and in an appropriate way to new problematic situations is crucial in determining who will manage in the globalised market society.

However, great problems have also developed concerning the definition and application of the competence concept. This is primarily because a number of national and supranational bodies have taken over the concept and sought to implement it as a management tool. Wide-ranging work has been initiated to define a number of competences that the various education programmes should aim at and to make these measurable in order to make it possible to judge whether the efforts succeed (see Illeris 2004). I will not go further in my criticism of these matters here. At present it seems that the problems involved in such 'technocratisation of competence' have been so great that the project has been shelved, in Denmark at least.

But I do find it important to point out that the concept of competence also contains some extremely positive openings for making a contribution to a general or holistically oriented understanding of the far-reaching perspectives and requirements embedded in the current discussion about learning. This was already pointed out in connection with the model development in section 3.2, where the competence concept in relation to the learning dimensions in general was presented as a combination of functionality, sensitivity and sociality.

I find it important – together with the definition of competence quoted above (Jørgensen 1999) – to maintain such a broad, holistic understanding of competence both on the general level and in relation to certain areas of action. A parallelism with the understanding of learning is thus indicated, which I regard as being an important theoretical point because it makes possible overall thinking and treatment of learning as process, and competence as something aimed at in this process. This is particularly important vis-à-vis a concept of competence which is rapidly becoming the horse dragging a carriage of narrow economically oriented control interests that deprive the concept of the liberating potential springing from the place of the competences as relevant contemporary mediators between the societal challenges and individual ways of managing them.

The concept of competence can thus be used as a point of departure for a more nuanced understanding of what learning efforts today are about – with a view to reaching a theoretically based and practically tested proposal concerning how up-to-date competence development can be realised for different people in accordance with their possibilities and needs, both within and outside of institutionalised education programmes. Such an approach has, in my opinion, far better and more well founded possibilities for contributing to real competence development, at the individual level as well as the societal level, than the measuring and comparing approach that has been mentioned above. However, it will to a much higher degree be oriented towards experiments and initiatives at practice level than the top-down control approach inherent in the measuring models.

Quite concretely it is about the fact that competence development may be promoted in environments where learning takes place in connection with a (retrospective) actualisation of relevant experience and contexts, that (at the same time) interplay between relevant activities and interpretation of these activities in a theoretical conceptual framework, and a (prospective) reflection and perspective, i.e. a pervasive perspective in relation to the participants' life or biography, linked with a meaning and conception-oriented reflection and a steady alternation between the individual and the social levels within the framework of a community (see Illeris 2004).

8.5 Learning and identity

If one wants to examine the overall results of learning, it is, however, not enough to look at competence development. For learning to be maintained in the whole of the breadth encompassed by this book, there must also be focus on the connection, and thereby the understanding and application value, that what is learned has for the learner. There are a number of different concepts with a somewhat different perspective that could be relevant to take up here.

I have already looked at the concept of 'the self' several times, in section 4.6 and especially in section 5.6, where it concerned the self as the content object of learning. I also mentioned here that this concept has been disputed – but under all circumstances it has the character of a mental instance concerned with the individual's experience of themselves, i.e. one 'looks at' or experiences oneself from the inside.

Another concept in the area is 'personality', which, among other things, has given the name to the psychological discipline of 'personality psychology'. It is characteristic here, however, that the individual is 'looked at' or characterised from the outside; for example, different qualities are attributed to the individual which eventually can be registered by means of different (personality) tests.

There is, in addition, the more recent concept of 'habitus', developed by French sociologist Pierre Bourdieu (1930–2002). This concept implies that the cultural and societal conditions with which the individual has been confronted are deposited as stable inner dispositions which, to a high degree, influence the individual's mode of thought, emotion and action and thus become the focal point of the imprint of the social background (see Bourdieu and Passéron 1977 [1970]; Bourdieu 1998 [1994]).

All three concepts could even be useful in connection with the personality development which learning as a whole can result in, and in recent years not least the habitus concept has appeared in a great deal of pedagogically oriented literature (e.g. Hodkinson *et al.* 2004). Nevertheless, I prefer here to take my point of departure in the somewhat older concept of 'identity', because I regard it as being the most holistic concept that expressly ranges over both the individual and the social level.

The identity conception that today is regarded as classical was primarily drawn up by the German-American psychoanalyst Erik H. Erikson, especially in his book entitled *Identity, Youth and Crisis* (Erikson 1968). Erikson belonged to the post-war 'neo-Freudians', who distanced themselves from what they regarded as deterministic characteristics in Freud, were more oriented towards societal conditions, and also attributed increased significance to the ego in relation to the drives, i.e. that, to a higher degree than in Freud's understanding, the individual has the possibility of controlling his or her own life.

The word identity, itself, refers to the Latin *idem*, which means 'the same' and has to do with the experience of being the same or recognisable both to oneself and others in changing situations. This also points to the duality in the identity, so central to Erikson's concept, namely, that one is an individual creation, a biological life while simultaneously being a social and societal being, in the last analysis without any individual possibility for existence. Therefore, identity is always an individual biographical identity, an experience of a coherent individuality and a coherent life course, at the same time as being a social, societal identity, an experience of a certain position in the social community.

In this way there is a striking parallelism between Erikson's concept of identity and the concept of learning outlined in this book. In both cases, there are two linked characteristics which always coexist and work together. Corresponding to Erikson's individual side of identity, and the personal experience of coherence in Erikson, is the individual acquisition process in learning that takes place within the framework of structures which, in the final analysis, are made possible by means of the enormously complicated biological development of the human brain and central nervous system. And corresponding to Erikson's social side of identity and the experience of how one is experienced by others is the social interaction process of learning, which takes place within the framework of the societally developed structures of the surroundings. Thus, from the point of view of learning, identity development can be understood as the individually specific essence of total learning, i.e. as the coherent development of meaning, functionality, sensitivity and sociality, and in the learning figure its core area can be placed around the meeting between the two double arrows that illustrate the two simultaneous processes of learning (Figure 8.1).

At the same time, Erikson's concept of the youth stage and the development of identity is part of an overall concept of the course of a human life as a series of life stages, where each stage culminates in a crisis, the solution to which is a prerequisite for a successful life in the next stage. Erikson outlines a total of eight stages, the fifth of which is adolescence,

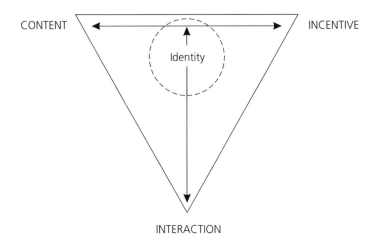

CONTENT   INCENTIVE

Identity

INTERACTION

Figure 8.1 The position of identity in the structure of learning

which is centred around identity development that can end in a more or less stable and coherent identity formation or become side-tracked and end in identity confusion, producing great problems in adult life.

Erikson characterises his stages theory as 'epigenic', which means that the stages have been developed throughout the phylogenetic history of human beings. They are thus part of our genetic heredity in the way that the central problem in each individual stage is already nascent in the earlier stages and is carried into the later stages as a potential for further development. Thus identity formation is not merely something taking place in the youth stage. It reaches far back into early childhood and can continue throughout the whole of life, but its crucial moments lie in the identity crisis of youth.

It should also be mentioned that Erikson's identity theory has been strongly criticised for being merely a refined adjustment theory because successful identity formation appears as the individual's adjustment to the norms of the group and the society, while more than momentary resistance to the norms is stamped as being identity confusion.

If we return to the youth phase in our present postmodern society, it is clear that a type of identity process still exists, that young people, in one way or the other, are trying to discover who they are and want to be, personally and socially. But both the notions of a more or less fixed identity as the goal of the process, and identity confusion as the frightening counter picture, must be relativised today. When one of society's most central and direct requirements of its members is that we must always be flexible and ready for change, a fixed, stable identity becomes problematic. In addition, when older members of society are often criticised and rejected by the labour market because they are inflexible and unwilling, this has precisely to do with the fact that over the years they have built up stable identities and self-understandings which they cannot, or will not, change.

Flexibility and confusion of identity are, naturally, not the same, but on the other hand such notions of identity as in Erikson or which in classical psychology of personality are formulated in ideals such as 'the mature personality' (Allport 1967) – today, may be experienced almost as a reminiscence of the pictures of patriarchal, white, well-educated, complacent father figures who, in the flickering changeability of late modernity would have severe problems with the demand for flexibility.

Thus, it is clear that Erikson's identity theory and the entire classical conception of identity development can only form a point of departure today. It has become increasingly visible that these concepts presuppose a society with a degree of stability and common norms and forms of consciousness that no longer exist.

The first important signs of this development were registered by American psychoanalysts as early as the 1960s. They were described in more detail, first and foremost, by Heinz Kohut (1913–1981) (1971) and Otto Kernberg (1975) as 'narcissistic personality disturbances' and 'pathological narcissism', respectively, and in Europe by the German psychologist and youth researcher Thomas Ziehe in his work entitled *Puberty and Narcissism* (Ziehe 1975).

The starting point of all this was that new types of psychological problems were becoming dominant in the clinical picture emerging in psychoanalytical practice. In contrast to the classical anxiety neuroses, these symptoms were more diffuse and typically were, for example, a lack of self-esteem, feelings of emptiness, a feeling of not really existing, a lack of pleasure in work and of initiative, and an increased tendency towards routine behaviour. In relation to more classical neuroses and psychotic states, it was characteristic that by and large the patients had maintained a coherent self. They were not threatened by self-dissolution, regression or extreme mental fragmentation, but primarily by lacking ego stability, a need to reflect themselves and to gain self-esteem through others, and a fear of losing contact with themselves psychologically. Therefore, their existence was dominated by an urge to avoid getting into situations where the unstable self could be threatened.

Theoretically an attempt was made to capture these symptoms by a revision of the Freudian conception of narcissism as the inadequate phase-out of the self-centredness of the period of early childhood, presenting an obstacle to pleasurable relations with others. On the contrary, the new narcissists seek out and utilise others as self objects. They need others in order to build themselves up; they are not sought out for their qualities as independent objects but are involved as compensation for the lack of psychological structure, for the experience of an inner emptiness and an inadequate sense of reality.

The most pronounced reaction to these descriptions was culturally pessimistic, moralistic decline thinking and condemnation most strongly expressed by the American Christopher Lasch (1923–1994) in his book, *The Culture of Narcissism* (Lasch 1978). In contrast to this, not least Thomas Ziehe tried to describe the situation as a reasonable reaction to a number of new trends in society in the direction of the break-up of the nuclear family, the intensification of work, and the explosion of compensatory consumption and compensatory satisfactions. On the basis of this conception, Ziehe pointed to a number of liberating possibilities in societal and cultural development and to the changes in the forms of upbringing and education as a way forward (Ziehe 1975; Ziehe and Stubenrauch 1982).

However, the most consistent and extreme challenge to the traditional perception of identity was developed during the 1990s within the psychological mode of perception self-designated as social constructionism, which was discussed in section 7.8. This mode of perception is fundamentally based on the premise that mental processes and phenomena are developed in social interaction. In this perspective the extent to which one can speak at all of a fixed identity or an authentic self becomes doubtful, because when the social situations and contexts change, identity and the self must also do so. Identity takes on an incoherent, situation-determined form with the character of a number of different social roles which the individual assumes or slides into, as a worker, parent, road-user etc., and the roles do not have to have any inner cohesion. The late-modern person is just as split as the world in which he or she lives.

In his most widely read book, Gergen uses the term 'the saturated self' (Gergen 1991). This is a self or an identity that is constantly exposed to influences that are so many and varied that the self or identity cannot contain them, at any rate not in any coherent or holistic understanding.

The question, however, is whether such an extreme dissolution of identity is a reasonable description. At any rate, other current ways of perceiving the situation are also to be found, which, while being aware of the dissolution trends, also note that there still exists, and must exist, a type of inner mental coherence in the individual.

One of these perceptions focuses on the life story or the individual biography as that which holds the individual together mentally and which thus can be said to form a type of identity (e.g. Alheit 1994; Antikainen *et al.* 1996; Dominicé 2000; see section 5.6). What is central here is that the self-understanding of the late-modern person is held together by his/her perception or narration of his/her life story. The narration is neither a precise nor a truthful account of the actual life course but precisely the history of the life course that the person in question has developed, the constant interpretation and attribution of significance one assigns to events and contexts which one subjectively finds important for the life course and the current situation – in the same way as the identity is a more or less coherent entity which, however, constantly develops and is reinterpreted.

The British sociologist Anthony Giddens (especially Giddens 1991) has a somewhat different perception. While Giddens also refers to the life story as an important element in self-understanding, he places the major emphasis on what he calls 'self-identity' which he defines as 'a reflexively organised endeavour' (Giddens 1991, p. 5) that includes the maintenance and revision of a coherent life story and of reflexively structured life planning and lifestyle 'in terms of flows of social and psychological information about possible ways of life' (Giddens 1991, p. 14). What is most important in Giddens is thus that the identity is the result of constant reflexive processes where one constructs and reconstructs one's self perception in the light of impulses from one's surroundings. It is this reflexivity and changeability that is typical of modern self-identity in contrast to the more fixed identity of earlier times.

In contrast to social constructionism, the life story and the reflexivity oriented perceptions are characterised by the fact that the late-modern trends towards dissolution and fragmentation of the identity of the individual are countered by different means that can create a certain inner coherence and continuity. This implies that somewhere 'deep inside' there must be a mental instance, a self or a core identity, from which this resistance or counter-move can derive. Daniel Stern (1995), the American child psychologist, is of the opinion that already during the first years of life, the child normally develops a 'core self' with crucial significance for further personality development. None of the other theoreticians mentioned above deal directly with such a concept, but Giddens's concept of 'ontological security' implies a fundamental personal confidence, acquired early, as the foundation which, in the final instance, self-identity presupposes and upon which it builds (Giddens 1991, pp. 35ff.).

From the point of view of learning there is every reason to pay attention to the necessity of such a core identity – or maintaining the ontological security, to use Giddens's terminology. This is so, in the first place, because total identity fragmentation or situation identity appears to be an impossible and exaggerated consequence of the dissolution trends of late-modernity. This would imply a return to medieval mental structures without any real individuality, while it is almost the opposite that is the case, namely, that the individuals of late-modernity are drowning in the struggle to maintain their individuality in the face of constant, unpredictable external pressure. In the second place, this is so because it implies that what must be learned and maintained is precisely the duality of both a core identity and extreme flexibility, which must not have the nature of identity confusion but, rather, that of constant reconstruction.

A perception of a core identity surrounded by a layer of more flexible structures also harmonises with the concept of learning described in this book, partly because it acknowledges both the social and the individual sides of the mental processes, and partly because it allows room for both stable patterns and structures and on-going changes through influences and learning, cognitively, emotionally and socially.

I do not think that there is any clash between the perception of a core identity and the biographical approach, but only different points of view as the core identity typically includes an essence of the life story and, at the same time, also an essence of the notions of the individual concerning the future. However, from the point of view of education, in this connection it is important to realise that the life story approach can easily come to emphasise the retrospective view because the life story is, of necessity, retrospective. When this is the case, the focus is unilaterally on the background for further development while the dynamic, progressive factors that can provide the development with power and direction lie in current problems and future perspectives. In his biographicity concept, Peter Alheit is also endeavouring to cross this barrier by noting the interaction between the life story and the current challenges. The initiative does not lie in the questions about 'Who am I?' and 'Where do I come from?', but in questions such as 'What could be better for me?' and 'Where do I want to go?'.

On the other hand, it seems unrealistic to imagine total fragmentation or a lack of a stable identity. All the experience that the individual has had throughout childhood and youth, with respect to the way in which she or he functions and is regarded in a wide range of different contexts, cannot but leave generalised traces about who one is and how one is regarded by others. Even if one feels uncertain and unstable, these can also be elements of an identity. Total emptiness or the lack of authenticity also involve total incapacity and, in the last instance, mental breakdown. (It is, moreover, also worth noting that the most extreme perception of identity dissolution was developed in the USA where modernity development has gone furthest, while all the more moderate perceptions have been developed in Europe.)

8.6 Holistic learning theories

Following the examination above of various holistic perspectives on learning centred around the concepts of experience, competence and identity, it could be asked whether learning theories exist that span such a totality.

I have already examined and referred to a great number of different theories and learning theoreticians, and tried to point out their strong and weak sides along the way. Viewed in relation to the holistic perspective, for example, it is clear that Piaget consciously avoids this perspective by expressly concentrating on cognition and content, while Freud and other psychoanalytically oriented approaches correspondingly concentrate on the incentive dimension. I have also pointed out that while the cultural historical school and its heirs span both the content and the interaction dimensions, they only rarely include the incentive dimension, and, similarly, that those who build on critical theory focus on the incentive and interaction dimensions but only sporadically involve the content dimension (see section 14.2).

However, in the material reviewed there are at any rate two theoreticians who would seem to be more balanced with respect to the three dimensions, namely, American Etienne Wenger and British Peter Jarvis. To this may be added a theory put forward by American Robert Kegan, which I have not yet included. In this section I will briefly discuss these three approaches in relation to the holistic perspective, and conclude with some remarks on the system theory approach which, almost by definition, aims at being holistic.

Wenger's learning model is reproduced in section 7.6 (Wenger 1998, p. 5). In this, learning is embedded between four conditions: meaning, practice, community and identity. Meaning relates to the content dimension in the same way as I have applied this concept above in section 8.3. It is rather clear that practice and community concern the interaction dimension and refer here to a practical and a consciousness level, respectively. Identity concerns all three learning dimensions as treated in section 8.4, and thus under this the incentive dimension also.

Wenger himself takes the model as a starting point for an analysis of communities of practice as frames for learning, and in this way he includes all three learning dimensions. He has also a lengthy note in his first chapter in which he relates to a wide range of other learning theories. But it is clear that with his special orientation towards learning in communities of practice, Wenger prioritises the interaction dimension, and he himself calls his theory 'a social theory of learning'.

Wenger's theory could thus have been developed as a general learning theory including all three dimensions of learning in a balanced way. But he has chosen to focus on the interaction dimension and then include the two other dimensions from here. This orientation has become more pronounced in his later texts where it is precisely the design and functions of the communities of practice that he does further work on (e.g. Wenger and Snyder 2001; Wenger et al. 2002).

Jarvis's point of departure was at first sociological and specifically concerned with adult education. However, philosophical and psychological orientations have been increasingly included in his extensive production since the 1980s, and his two most recent books are entitled *Human Learning – An Holistic Approach* (Jarvis and Parker 2005), and *Towards a Comprehensive Theory of Human Learning* (Jarvis 2006). Moreover, when this book is published, Jarvis's book *Globalisation, Lifelong Learning and the Learning Society* (Jarvis, 2007) will be available, updating his views on the connections between contemporary global developments and their consequences for the conditions of learning and education.

There is thus no doubt that from a declared sociological- and education-oriented position Jarvis (Jarvis 1987) has moved towards a more general, holistic orientation which he terms existentialist, i.e. his point of departure is in man's existence or 'being', which he swiftly expands to 'being-in-the-world' and further to 'being-in-the-world-with-others'. In so doing he develops a dialectic between the person and the environment corresponding to the foundation on which I am working in this book (Jarvis 2006, pp. 13–16).

Throughout the whole of Jarvis's extensive production, his relation to the interaction dimension, and its societal level in particular, has occupied a prominent position, and led among other things to his great interest in lifelong learning as a concept and as a political agenda (although he has become more and more sceptical about the economic orientation which increasingly dominates this agenda – see Jarvis 2002).

But Jarvis has, at the same time, come close to the acquisition process by drawing up a learning model that he launched in 1987 and has since revised on several occasions. The point of departure for this model was a feeling that Kolb's model (section 5.2) was, perhaps, important and interesting but it was far too simple. Jarvis, therefore, asked a large number of course participants to describe how they experienced their inner learning process. He subsequently analysed the descriptions and summarised them in a complicated model with many options and exits. I reproduce the original version of the model here (Figure 8.2), because the later versions have become more streamlined, and in my opinion the first version with the soft contours best reflects the somewhat messy and complex diversity that is at issue.

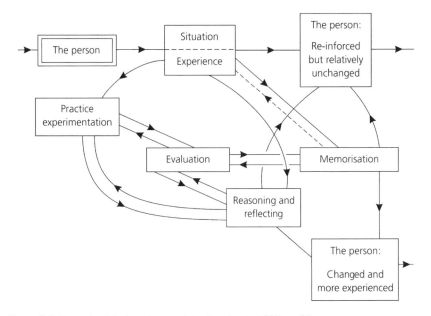

Figure 8.2 Peter Jarvis's learning model, after Jarvis 1987, p. 25

What is remarkable about the model is, first, that in contrast to so many other learning models, Kolb's among others, it shows that learning processes can take many different and winding paths, even when they are reproduced in a simplified form. Second, it shows that the processes can also have many different outcomes, which Jarvis summarises in the text in three main types: non-learning, non-reflective learning and reflective learning (Jarvis 1987, pp. 133ff.).

In his most recent book Jarvis also takes up the idea of the three learning dimensions (Jarvis 2006, p. 24), but in relation to the terms I have used, he proposes that what I now call 'the interaction dimension' should be changed to 'the action dimension'. Development has taken us in the same direction and the only difference seems to be that while Jarvis's proposal is viewed from the learner's position, it is he or she who acts, by using the term interaction I am trying to orient myself towards the relation between learner and the environment.

On a more general level it is clear that while Jarvis refers to philosophical discussions and sources to a far greater extent than I do, I go into more depth with psychology, both when it refers to learning and non-learning. Nonetheless, there is to me no doubt that Jarvis is the learning researcher who comes closest to the holistic perspective that I am also trying to reach in this book.

The third learning researcher I take up is Harvard professor Robert Kegan. His approach to learning can best be characterised as consciousness theoretical and, more specifically, he himself terms it 'constructive-developmental'.

In his two major works, *The Evolving Self* (Kegan 1982) and *In Over Our Heads* (Kegan 1994) Kegan works broadly with personal development. He establishes a number of levels of cognition or orders of consciousness which one can go through, and describes the transitions between them as transformations (thus employing this concept a little differently and more generally than Mezirow, and he speaks of 'transformational learning' as a lifelong phenomenon or process – in contrast to Mezirow's 'transformative learning', which refers to certain processes concerned with certain transformations).

It is thus a matter of a continued series of transformations throughout the whole course of life and, in Kegan's opinion, one is better able to understand and encourage such transformations when one has knowledge of the earlier processes and the future options towards which the person in question is oriented. What characterises these transformations, according to Kegan, is that what before was the subject of cognition becomes the object through the transformation – i.e. that by which one was previously controlled now becomes something one controls oneself. On this basis Kegan sets up a five-step scheme (Figure 8.3).

		SUBJECT	OBJECT	UNDERLYING STRUCTURE
		PERCEPTIONS Fantasy SOCIAL PERCEPTIONS/ IMPULSES	Movement Sensation	Single point/immediate/atomistic
		CONCRETE *Actuality* Data, cause-and-effect POINT OF VIEW Role-concept Simple reciprocity (tit-for-tat) ENDURING DISPOSITIONS Needs, preferences Self-concept	Perceptions Social perceptions Impulses	Durable category 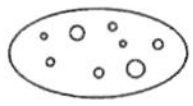
The Socialized Mind	TRADITIONALISM	ABSTRACTIONS Ideality Inference, generalization Hypothesis, proposition Ideals, values **MUTUALITY/INTERPERSONALISM** **Role consciousness** **Mutual reciprocity** *INNER STATES* *Subjectivity, self-consciousness*	Concrete Point of view Enduring dispositions Needs, preferences	Cross-categorical Trans-categorical 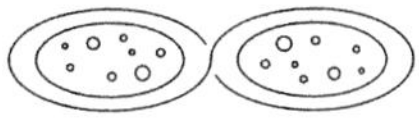
The Self-Authoring Mind	MODERNISM	ABSTRACT SYSTEMS Ideology Formulation, authorization Relations between abstractions **INSTITUTION** **Relationship-regulating forms** **Multiple-role consciousness** *SELF-AUTHORSHIP* *Self-regulation, self-formation* *Identity, autonomy, individuation*	Abstractions Mutuality Interpersonalism Inner states Subjectivity Self-consciousness	System/complex 
The Self-Transforming Mind	POST-MODERNISM	DIALECTICAL Trans-ideological/post-ideological Testing formulation, paradox Contradiction, oppositeness **INTER-INSTITUTIONAL** **Relationship between forms** **Interpenetration of self and other** *SELF-TRANSFORMATION* *Interpenetration of selves* *Inter-individuation*	Abstract system ideology Institution relationship- regulating forms Self-authorship Self-regulation Self-formation	Trans-system Trans-complex 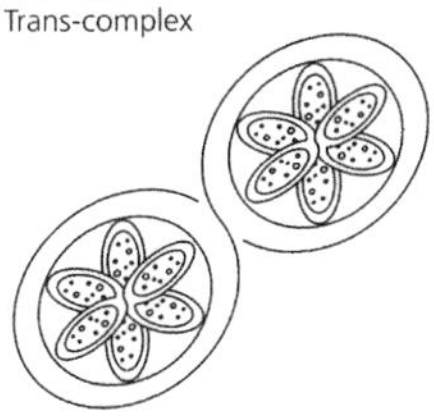

LINES OF DEVELOPMENT	
K	COGNITIVE
E	**INTERPERSONAL**
Y	*INTRAPERSONAL*

Figure 8.3 Kegan's five-step scheme (adapted from Kegan 1994, pp. 314–315 and Kegan 2000, pp. 62–63)

On step 1, the small child is controlled by unique perceptions and impulses while it develops its movements and sensations.

On step 2, from about the age of two years, a transformation has taken place so that the child has formed bigger and more varied categories covering more elements, for example, it distinguishes between what belongs to others and what belongs to itself, between what it wants itself and what others want it to do (Kegan 1994, p. 22). On this basis it can control its own perceptions and impulses while it is simultaneously controlled by the events, role-concepts and dispositions that apply.

On step 3, which arrives at the age of six, the child begins to be capable of cutting across the single categories. It can now control events, viewpoints and preferences and is controlled by more abstract generalisations, values, relations to others, role-consciousness and self-awareness. On the societal level Kegan calls this step 'traditionalism'. Inherent in this is that this was the highest step one usually achieved in the Western European countries before the breakthrough of modernity with the Enlightenment, capitalism and industrialisation in the eighteenth and nineteenth centuries (Kegan 1994, p. 10).

On step 4, which today one can reach during the teenage years, one has the possibility of understanding and mastering more extensive and complex systems. Thereby one can, oneself, control the more abstract matters such as generalisations, values, relations with others, role consciousness and self-awareness, and in this one is controlled by abstract systems such as ideologies, institutions and identity. On the societal level Kegan speaks here of 'modernism'.

Finally, on step 5 the possibility presents itself of exceeding the systems, liberating oneself from fixed ideologies, institutions and identities and achieving a general, dialectical order of consciousness where, on the basis of one's interpretations of the environment, one can make decisions about formulations, paradoxes, contradictions and relationships with other people and oneself. Kegan understands this order as 'postmodernism' and thus as a level which has only become generally accessible with postmodernity's liberation of the individual from a number of institutional ties since the 1970s.

Kegan has thus proposed an extremely comprehensive construction. In its point of departure it is based on inspiration from both Piaget and Freud (Kegan 1994, p. 9), but unlike them he does not conclude with the possible transition to modernity's anticipated adult status (the self-authoring mind – step 4): on the one hand, the possibility exists for going further (to step 5) and, on the other hand, many have problems in even reaching as far as step 4.

From the point of view of learning, it is important that Kegan quite clearly includes all three dimensions of learning (which he terms the Logical-Cognitive Domain, the Social-Cognitive Domain, and the Intrapersonal-

Affective Domain – Kegan 1994, pp. 30–31). But on the other hand, among other things, in continuation of Mezirow and Brookfield, his position can also be viewed as the completion of the content-oriented approach where it becomes clear that content cannot be fully understood without including the incentive and the interaction dimensions.

With respect to types of learning, Kegan also covers the whole register, and even though he alters the formulation a little, it is clear that transformative processes occur at the transitions between the levels; processes that include reconstructions in all three learning dimensions.

There are thus a few learning researchers who, in different ways and from completely different angles, have reached holistic understandings that are reminiscent of those I present in this book. This may be taken as confirmation of the fact that there must be a certain meaning in what I have arrived at and it can also be seen as a happy opportunity for the possibility of continuing to develop more adequate and varied understandings.

The situation is, in my opinion, somewhat different when it comes to the system theoretical approaches that seek to lift the understanding of learning up to a general, abstract level by relating it to some general guidelines for how different systems can function, including human beings and their learning. Gregory Bateson's learning typology is a rather simple theory that is system theoretical in nature, as referred to in section 4.1 (Bateson 1972), while a more widespread and more complex system theoretical approach is to be found in Niklas Luhmann. This is briefly mentioned in section 5.6 (Luhmann 1995 [1984]).

I am by no means implying that such approaches and theories are wrong, and I have often experienced that some people find they have great explanatory value. However, I will not go further into these approaches because I personally find them too distanced in relation to the everyday level of learning that is at issue. I find it difficult to recognise living persons with their endeavours and problems, their emotions and relations in the abstract categories and reflections. For this reason I can only refer interested readers to the authors themselves if they wish to obtain more information about such theories.

8.7 Learning models and courses of learning

Yet another approach to the totality of learning is to look at some of the learning models that have been drawn up from different perspectives, a number of which have already been discussed in various contexts. There are three types of model: sequence models, stage models and structure models.

A very simple sequence model relating directly to Piaget's theory of learning, was developed in Denmark by Jens Bjerg *et al.* (including Thomas Nissen) as a kind of wave or exchange model, that shows in an idealised

assimilative processes

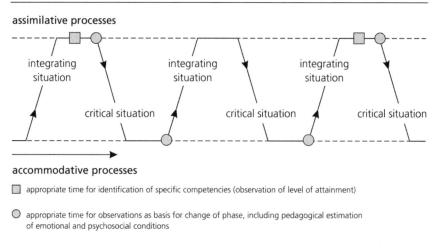

accommodative processes

☐   appropriate time for identification of specific competencies (observation of level of attainment)

◯   appropriate time for observations as basis for change of phase, including pedagogical estimation
of emotional and psychosocial conditions

Figure 8.4 The interaction between assimilative and accommodative learning (Bjerg 1976,
p. 45)

form the interaction between assimilative and accommodative learning
processes (Figure 8.4).

The model shows how a learning sequence shifts from (predominantly)
assimilative processes through a critical situation to (predominantly)
accommodative processes, back through an integrating situation to
(predominantly) assimilative processes, and so on – and it also indicates
points of time in a sequence of this kind that can be ideal for pedagogical
observations of attainment levels and observations of phase changes,
respectively. This model is, of course, very much simplified – as a model
always has to be – but is also a good illustration of this book's conception
of ordinary everyday learning sequences.

A better-known model which, in principle, illustrates the same idea, is
that of the American social and organisational psychologist Chris Argyris,
for 'single-loop' and 'double-loop' learning in organisational and management development (Figure 8.5) (Argyris 1992).

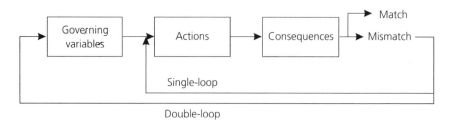

Figure 8.5 Single-loop and double-loop learning (Argyris 1992, p. 8)

Argyris is concerned with learning in organisations (see section 12.4). Organisations exist to fulfil certain specific goals, and they do this through actions. These actions can lead to the expected consequences, so a 'match' is obtained, or the consequences can be inconsistent with what was expected, resulting in a 'mismatch'. In cases of mismatch it might be possible to then attempt another solution within the same frame of reference, making this a single loop in terms of learning, or, alternatively, it might be possible to attempt to pass beyond this framework, these 'governing variables', making this a double loop.

On the one hand, Argyris's model is special because it is so closely linked to organisations; the actions can, for example, be ascribed to individuals or the organisation itself, and the only learning that is of interest is that which leads to altered practice in the organisation. On the other hand, there are clear parallels between this model and the fundamental conceptions of Piaget, Bateson and Mezirow, that there is a considerable distinction between learning that builds on existing presuppositions, and learning that involves changes to, or transcendence of, these presuppositions – and Argyris's model has the obvious advantage of being easy to understand and being linked to a specific practice context. However, it must be said that Argyris's model lacks a more explicit theoretical root, although it is clear that he (just like David Kolb and Donald Schön) draws on a conception basis that predominantly relates to Kurt Lewin and Gestalt psychology.

Kolb's learning cycle (section 5.2) and other circle models can also be understood as a type of sequence model, and when the circle models repeat themselves at increasingly higher levels, they become spiral models, as Kolb also demonstrates in his discussion of Dewey's learning understanding (Kolb 1984, p. 23). A typical example of a spiral model can be found in American Jerome Bruner's proposal for 'the spiral curriculum' (Bruner 1960, pp. 13, 33 and 52ff.). This was based on his challenging thesis that 'any subject can be taught effectively in some intellectually honest form to any child at any stage of development' (Bruner 1960, p. 33).

The challenge is 'just' to find forms of presentation and examples that correspond to the child's stage of development – and so it becomes a spiral learning process in which the same points are returned to in new ways in step with the child's development.

All of these circle and spiral models have the disadvantage that they indicate a 'smooth', evenly progressive sequence – in contrast to the uneven sequence of reality with jumps in learning that are accommodative in nature, as illustrated in Bjerg's and Argyris's models. They also have the unfortunate tendency to indicate that it is the same type of sequence that repeats itself the whole time.

However, another type of spiral model is English adult education researcher Tom Schuller's triple helix for development throughout the course of life (Schuller 1998). The model is inspired by the biochemical structure in a DNA molecule, and shows as a simplified model how Schuller views biological, psychological and social development as three independent and yet intertwined sequences which, together, reflect the life course of the individual (Figure 8.6A). In reality, however, development does not take place in so simple and harmonious a manner as this idealised model might suggest, and there are fluctuations and tempo variations for each of the development strands, so an illustration of a life as it is lived might look like that shown in Figure 8.6B.

On the basis of the approach in this book it would be more appropriate to convert this model into a quadruple helix by dividing psychological development into a content strand and an incentive strand, at any rate from the age of about six.

However, the most refined sequence model is, without doubt, Jarvis's model. This was discussed in the previous section and in all its complexity it gives an excellent and less idealised or standardised impression of how learning sequences take place in reality.

From the understanding that a learning sequence can include important qualitative jumps, it is not far to the development of various forms of phase, stage or step models for different types of learning and development sequences.

With respect to stage models, it is naturally obvious to refer first to Piaget's and Freud's well-known stage theories of cognitive and psychosexual development in childhood, respectively, even though neither of them has been translated into graphic models. The same is true of, for example, the Dreyfus brothers' five-step model for the development of

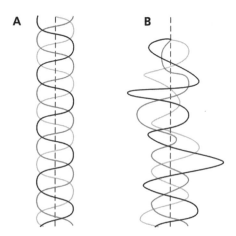

Figure 8.6 Tom Schuller's triple helix. The idealised model (A) and the 'reality' model (B). The biological, psychological and social development of a life course (Schuller 1998, pp. 32–33)

'human intuition and expertise' (Dreyfus and Dreyfus 1986). In an attempt to describe how human intelligence is superior to any computer in certain vital points, there is a description of how we pass through stages such as novice and advanced beginner, then competence and proficiency to reach the stage of expertise. This does not consist, as it would in a computer, of us quickly and logically surveying and analysing vast amounts of information, but instead means that we find ourselves in a comprehensive experience within a field, enabling us to intuitively find relevant possible solutions in a problem situation – a conception that also fits with the description of experts' means of functioning that the aforementioned Donald Schön achieved through empirical studies (Schön 1983; see sections 5.2 and 5.5).

However, the Dreyfus brothers' model does not clearly specify what the criteria are for the various phase transitions, and therefore this model does not fulfil the requirements for a psychological stage model which, with reference to Piaget, Danish life span researcher Johan Fjord Jensen (1928–2005) has advanced in five overall principles: that the stages shall be sequential, i.e. they must come in a specific order and build on one another so that no stage can be skipped; they must be universal, i.e. they must apply to everyone, regardless of time and place; they must be complex in the sense that the later stages include the earlier in an increasingly complex order; they must each comprise a period with structural equilibrium so that they include all relevant elements in a common structure that lasts until the next phase transition; and finally they must be qualitatively different (Jensen 1993, p. 91).

These extensive requirements are largely met by the two great stages theories of psychology, that is, Piaget's and Freud's, and by some of the different stage theories of modern life age psychology for the whole of the life course, including, not least, Erik H. Erikson's stage model as mentioned in section 8.4. I confine myself here to presenting Fjord Jensen's own refined stage model, which has the form of a double life arch (Figure 8.7).

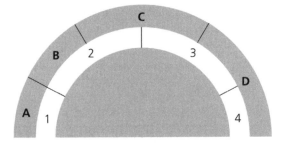

Figure 8.7 The double life arch. Social life ages: (A) childhood; (B) youth; (C) adulthood; (D) old age. Interpretive life ages: (1) childhood; (2) first adulthood; (3) second adulthood; (4) old age (Jensen 1993, p. 182)

The point of the model is that in adult life there are two types of stages that typically appear displaced: the social life ages and the interpretive life ages:

> With one part of life and consciousness, the person belongs to society, but with the other he belongs to himself. From one viewpoint he is on a life course that is regulated by the structures of that age culture, with its own social-biological milestones and age-related rituals. In belonging to this, the person becomes part of a social age culture with its own life ages. From another viewpoint he is on a life course which he regulates himself with his own interpretations. As such he is driven by personal needs of development and expression.
>
> (Jensen 1993, p. 182)

Looking at this approach in relation to Tom Schuller's triple helix, there emerges an image of biological and social development intertwined in a single cadence of stages, while psychological development – which can perhaps be separated into a cognitive and an incentive strand – follows a second cadence of stages.

Another and quite different way of viewing the course of life is that of David Kolb, who perceives it as having three main stages generally characterised by an ever closer connection of the four learning modes (see section 5.2) into an integrated total (Figure 8.8).

The first stage, which covers childhood to puberty, is characterised by *acquisition*, and the self is still undifferentiated and embedded in the environment – this stage can also be divided into sub-stages in accordance with Piaget's theory. The second stage, up to what Fjord Jensen calls the life turn, which can occur at a variety of ages (see section 11.5), is characterised by *specialisation* (on the basis of Kolb's description I would prefer to call it qualification – in relation to career, family and society) – the self is content- or case-oriented, and absorbed in interaction with the surrounding world. Finally, there is the third stage, which according to Kolb not everyone reaches, characterised by *integration* – the self takes on the nature of a process; one relates to one's own life course and the role one plays in relation to the surrounding world (see Kegan's step 5, section 8.5).

The final type is the structure models. Here it is natural to first mention the triangular model that was developed in Chapter 3 and continued in different ways in sections 7.1 and 8.3, respectively. But Wenger's model, which was reproduced in section 7.6, is also a structure model, and the same applies to Heron's model in section 6.5. In addition I have mentioned Gagné's model of learning types in section 4.1 and Maslow' well-known needs or motive hierarchy in section 6.6, both of which have the character of structure models.

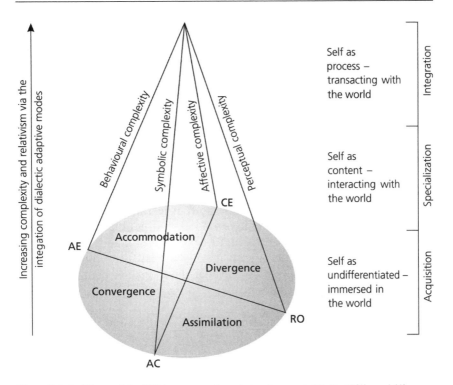

Figure 8.8 Kolb's model of lifelong growth and development (Kolb 1984, p. 141)

Such models replicate a number of matters and categories within the area with which they deal and the connections between these, but they lack a time dimension and must, therefore, be understood as a kind of map illustrating a certain view of a field and providing the reader with an overview. There is, thus, a kind of 'free choice' when this type of model is set up, but one should be aware that the graphic presentations have a stronger effect than the text on many readers, and one should be careful about proportions, choice of sharp or soft forms and the like, and the model must be clearly explained in the text.

Overall there are reasons for being cautious with models and, for example, carefully considering if they are aiming at illustrating that 'this is always the case' or that 'this is typically how it can be', in particular if they contain a certain order or prioritisation. The triangular model of this book actually contains a claim that its two processes and three dimensions are part of every learning process, but it has nothing to say about the strength of these different components. This means that the extent to which the individual components apply in a certain process can vary. In contrast to this, I have already pointed out several times that Kolb's learning circle, and partly also Heron's model, implies an order of different elements in learning that conflict with the brain's flexible mode of operation and can, therefore, at best be regarded as illustrations of a typical sequence. Similarly, Maslow's hierarchy of needs cannot claim to illustrate more than what is typical – it is a simple matter to find examples where the prioritisation of the various needs is different.

Models can be very useful illustrations but they always simplify the diversity of reality, and in many cases they can be seductive, precisely because they reduce this diversity.

8.8 Summary

The three dimensions of learning and the four learning types are summed up in the totality of learning. This can be carried out on the basis of different perspectives and concepts, and I have chosen here to focus on the concept of experience as an important holistic expression for the process of learning, and the concepts of personal development, competence and identity, respectively, as corresponding expressions for what is learned or developed.

The majority of learning theories relate for the most part to certain sides or elements of learning, but there are some theories that include the totality to a high degree. There are also numerous learning models dealing with certain perspectives on learning and which can be divided into sequence models, stage models and structure models. However, it is true of all models that one must be careful not to regard them as more than illustrations which, in many cases, reduce the diversity of reality.

Chapter 9

Barriers to learning

Relevant learning theory is not just a matter of what happens when one learns something. It is just as important to be interested in what happens when intended learning does not take place, or when one learns something other than what was intended. Barriers to learning can appear in all three dimensions of learning and will often relate to two or all three dimensions at the same time. In relation to the content dimension, this mostly concerns such circumstances as, for instance, a lack of concentration in the learner, inadequate explanation, misunderstandings etc., summarised here under the concept of mis-learning. In the incentive dimension, it is largely a matter of different types of mental defence against learning. A special form of defence has the character of ambivalence, i.e. that at one and the same time one wants to and does not want to learn something or other. Finally, especially in relation to the interaction dimension, resistance to learning can arise when pressure is experienced in the direction of learning that one finds personally unacceptable. Resistance to learning can, at the same time, be a strong impulse for launching alternative learning.

9.1 When the intended learning does not occur

It is practically a matter of course that learning psychology has chiefly been concerned with what happens when someone learns something. But in many contexts it is just as important to be interested in what happens when somebody does not learn something in situations that could give rise to important learning, or when somebody learns something other than what they or others have intended. However, it is far from always the case that the impulses and influences met by the individual in his/her interaction with the environment are transformed into an internal psychological acquisition process – and especially in education and other contexts that form the setting for a specific kind of learning, it is clearly a problem when this learning does not occur, or perhaps occurs only partially or in a distorted form.

One of the few learning theorists to have considered this subject in detail is Peter Jarvis to whom I have already referred several times (especially sections 7.3 and 8.6). Jarvis divides 'non-learning' into three categories: *presumption* implies that one already thinks one has an understanding of something and, therefore, does not register new learning opportunities. *Non-consideration* implies that one might register new opportunities, but does not relate to them, perhaps through being too busy or too nervous of what they might lead to. *Rejection* means that on a more conscious level, one does not want to learn something new in a particular context (Jarvis 1987, s. 133ff., and several other texts).

Jarvis's categories thus cover three degrees or levels of consciousness in non-learning and introduce an important line of approach. However, the levels are defined only through short general descriptions without distinct criteria. I will, therefore, content myself here with taking them as a source of inspiration, and instead use a distinction that relates to the three learning dimensions to a certain extent. This concerns what I generally term *mis-learning*, which very largely relates to the content dimension; what I generally call *defence against learning*, mostly in relation to the incentive dimension; and what I call *resistance to learning*, mostly in relation to the interaction dimension.

It should, however, immediately be stressed that in practice it can frequently be difficult to distinguish directly between these different forms, in particular where defence and resistance are concerned, and that they can naturally also appear simultaneously and be more or less integrated. But, as will appear from the following, there are considerable differences in principle and thereby also differences in what the three main forms can lead to and how one can relate to them from the point of view of pedagogics and education.

9.2 Mislearning

Mislearning is about learning that does not correspond to what was intended or what was communicated as to content. In many situations there will, thus, be simple mislearning, i.e. somehow or other there will be what we, in ordinary terms, call a misunderstanding, or perhaps a failure of concentration, leading the individual to not quite understand or grasp what is going on, or, in an educational situation, what was meant to be learnt.

Mislearning is easiest to relate to in spheres where it can clearly be established what is right and what is wrong. I have found a very ordinary example of this in the work of American psychologist Robert Mager, who has worked on programmed learning. Having the task of developing a programmed course in elementary electronics, he found through a pre-liminary testing of the students that although they all claimed to know nothing about electronics, they all had a fair amount of knowledge and understanding of the subject, of which a certain amount was mis-knowledge and misunderstanding (Mager 1961). They had all learnt something about electronics, without having learnt it formally – and some of what they had learnt was wrong.

However, this example only concerns the most tangible and easily con-firmed mislearnings, which are relatively easy to correct – that is, if they are detected. They can certainly be serious, for if one assimilates further information on a mistaken basis, the misunderstanding will naturally become more pervasive. In a subject such as mathematics, for example, it is easy to see how a single mislearning can lead on to another, so that extensive and intricate contradictory structures of correct and mistaken understand-ings build up, which can contribute strongly to the student in question ultimately giving up, having learnt mainly that 'I just can't understand maths'.

If one looks at other subjects or spheres, however, it quickly becomes more complicated; for example, what is mislearning in the context of the interpretation of a text where many different interpretations are possible? And in the personal sphere, there is an infinite number of development possibilities, all with far-reaching consequences for the individual. None of the possibilities can be asserted to be the correct one, but some possibilities can be understood as wrong or problematic if they later lead to serious difficulties for the person in question.

In education mislearning must naturally be avoided as much as possible, but it is only in limited situations that it is possible to make unambiguous distinctions between error and non-error. And if, for example, the pupils are always told what is right and what is wrong, what they may and may not do and so on, they are unable to develop a sense of judgement, or independence or responsibility – this cannot really be called mislearning, but the learning is distinctly misplaced in relation to the environment the pupils have to relate to.

Where errors are unambiguous, one can, of course, attempt to avoid them, and correct them when they do occur. But, otherwise, it is just as important to remember that something different is always learned, because learning, as previously emphasised, always concerns something new being linked to what was already in place – and that which is already in place differs from person to person. Empathy, dialogue and tolerance are needed in most cases. Progress, both for the individual and more generally, can be something that happens when something is understood in a different way from normal.

9.3 Defence against learning

While mislearning is mostly connected with the content dimension of learning, mainly in connection with the incentive dimension, mental defence against learning can take place in the way that learning is prevented or distorted by largely unconscious mental mechanisms serving to protect the individual against learning which, for one reason or the other, can be threatening, limiting or in some other way places a strain on maintaining mental balance. In some cases the defence can be physically embedded in the form of what the Austrian psychoanalyst Wilhelm Reich defined as a body armour or character armour (Reich 1969a [1933]; see section 2.3).

The concept of psychological defence mechanisms is closely linked to Freud and appeared very early on as a key concept in the development of psychoanalytical theory (Freud 1940 [1894]). The classic example is *repression* as a defence against unacceptable drive impulses, psychological conflicts and recognition of traumatic experiences, but eventually Freud also referred to many other mechanisms of defence such as *regression*, *projection* and *isolation*, and, in the classic book on the topic, his daughter Anna Freud (1895–1982) enumerates a long list of different types of mechanisms of defence (Freud 1942 [1936], pp. 45ff.).

Later, the previously mentioned German social-psychologist Thomas Leithäuser, in connection with the development of the theory of everyday consciousness – to which I will return later in this section – identified other types of mechanisms of defence that regularly occur in current learning contexts, examples being: *reduction* ('Of course I know this' – of something new and actually unknown); *harmonisation* (emphasising unimportant common traits in conflicting conditions); *displacement* ('Not my department'); *levelling* ('This is really no problem'); or *personification* and *scapegoat mechanisms* (Leithäuser and Volmerg 1977, here reproduced from Andersen *et al.* 1993, p. 24).

In terms of learning, the mechanisms of defence can, first and foremost, entail a *rejection*, i.e. one simply will not let the impulses in question into the consciousness; for one reason or another, one will not accept them or become involved with them, and one ignores them, so naturally no learning takes place. And where the rejection is subjectively important and perhaps has to be repeated several times, it can take on the nature of a *blocking*, i.e. it appears automatically and heavily, and perhaps assumes neurotic features such as a *phobia*, often involving strong anxiety reactions.

However, more common than blocking or phobia is the reaction, in some ways more refined, that can be termed a *distortion*, i.e. the unacceptable impulse is not perceived as it is, but is distorted into something acceptable. In this connection a particular phenomenon that Piaget calls *distorted assimilation* should be mentioned; this is the notion that children assimilate to their wishes and fantasies instead of to reality (see Furth 1987, p. 38).

Distorted assimilations of this kind will, for the most part, be corrected later without any major problems, but another form of distorted assimilation occurs very widely in both children and adults, when one comes across situations or impulses that are incompatible with the cognitive structures already developed. In such cases one ought, according to Piaget's theory, to undertake an accommodation that can bring the cognitive structures into agreement with reality. But very often there is, instead, a rejection, or one distorts the impulses to make them fit the existing structures in order to 'manage' them by means of assimilative processes which – as pointed out earlier (section 4.5) – demand less energy and are less troublesome than accommodations.

This kind of distorted assimilation typically occurs in connection with what we call prejudice. Prejudice entails a mistaken understanding having been built up concerning a particular subject which it would cost a great deal for the individual to give up. Therefore, the individual systematically distorts any impulses that contradict it.

In an educational context such a defence mechanism can contribute strongly to some participants rejecting the teaching. In general, defence is probably the psychological mechanism that most contributes to learning not taking place or becoming different, and, as a rule, a high degree of security, permissiveness and motivation is required to get over this defence, for to a certain extent it is needed for the maintenance of self-worth and identity. But at the same time, overcoming defence is often the most decisive factor for achieving a progressive learning, both academic and personal.

All of this has to do with the fact that some decisive changes have occurred in this whole field since Freud discovered the defence mechanisms during his clinical work at the beginning of the twentieth century. Where, at that time, it was a case of something developed by the individual in relation to burdensome and unbearable individual conditions and experiences, modern society has created some more general defence mechanisms that we all have to develop in order to maintain our mental balance in the face of a world that is mentally overwhelming for the individual in many ways.

These general defence mechanisms typically manifest themselves in relation to three main forms of stress and strain. First, with respect to the volume of new influences and impressions to which we are all exposed and which we deal with by developing what Thomas Leithäuser has called an 'everyday consciousness'. Second, in modern society there is a steady flow of changes in all possible areas which partly are captured by everyday consciousness, but in some cases also bring a more extensive 'identity defence' to the fore. And, finally, it applies to the difficulties in maintaining an experience of being able to grasp and control one's own existence in relation to the so-called 'risk society' (Beck 1992 [1986]; see section 5.6). We can try to handle this either by means of defensive accommodations (see section 4.5) or, more generally, through the development of a stronger identity and contextual understanding that can enable us to better understand, grasp, and in some cases also handle, the problematic situations we encounter. In the following I will examine each of these three types of mental defence a little more closely in relation to learning.

With respect to defence against the huge number of influences and impulses we are constantly exposed to, as I have already mentioned we launch a special type of mental defence that is part of what Leithäuser has called our *everyday consciousness* (Leithäuser 1976; see also section 7.4).

Leithäuser bases his argument on the notion that everyday life – i.e. everything lying outside of working life – has become independent, fragmented and impoverished, because the productive sphere is dominant, and all other aspects of life are eventually ordered in accordance with its economic rationality.

Everyday life, today, is characterised as consisting of a long succession of separate situations, that apparently all have their own meaning, but are perceived as unconnected because the underlying common denominator, i.e. that everything will submit to capitalistic economic rationality, is not immediately apparent. For each of the various types of situations we must adopt various roles, as wage earner, as parent, as consumer, as road-user, as resident, as television viewer, as voter etc. And just as the situations are unconnected, neither does there need to be any reciprocal connection between the various roles.

What is common to all these various fragments is time structure. Our lives are increasingly ruled by the clock. What is important here is, of course, the division wage labour makes between work time and 'leisure' time. Within wage labour time is structured in varying degrees by breaks and meetings and so on – and within the education system by the timetable; this also accustoms children to accept an externally imposed time structure without any connection to the content of the activities that are being structured. Our leisure time is correspondingly more and more subject to time structures – just think of what significance television programmes now have for the internal structure of our home lives.

In order to deal with this unconnected diversity, modern man makes use of a number of routines that mean need is repressed, postponed and made to conform to the time structure. Need repression and postponement naturally occur in every society; this is a basic precondition for the formation of a society. But with the all-embracing time structures that have developed in modern society, this situation has reached a point where a highly developed internal constraint is demanded of every single member of society in order that it can function.

The routines also free us from the necessity of keeping ourselves open and candid in every one of the innumerable situations we come across in our everyday life. That would quite simply be practically and psychologically overwhelming – and we are able to distance ourselves from all the atrocities that appear every day on our television screens, or the irresistible offers from the supermarkets angling for our limited funds.

On the other hand, modern mass-communication provides a torrent of potential interpretations and possible meanings, which are just as unconnected as the time structure, but are well able to form strong emotional links between confused everyday events and the repressed dreams and ideas, and all the angst and disarray that is a consequence of repression.

Corresponding to the practical routines we must also, therefore, rationalise our consciousness, and this typically occurs through the development of an everyday consciousness that has taken over the place where, previously, coherent religions or other ideologies structured our conception of the diversity of our everyday lives. But just as everyday life has been fragmented into a continuous succession of situations, everyday consciousness is not a coherent conception like the ideologies, but is, rather, characterised by fragmentation, stereotypes and unmediated contradictions (see similarities and differences in relation to the identity understanding of social constructionism, section 8.4).

In connection with learning, it is of particular interest how everyday consciousness evolves in the individual as a psychological structure. Leithäuser describes this by means of the concept of theme-horizon-schemes – i.e. mental schemes or structures that maintain a specific theme within a specific horizon, limited by an everyday situation. By means of these schemes we are able to routinely interpret the themes we come across in the many detached situations of our everyday lives, without actually reflecting on them or forming an independent opinion of them. This is a form of 'filtering', which we can practise in a semi-automatic way, i.e. largely unconsciously but still in such a way that we can disengage the automatics and make a more conscious selection.

In this current context it is worth noting that the two modes of function for the theme-horizon-schemes named by Leithäuser correspond, to a great extent, to my earlier deliberations on the Piagetian theory: an event that could give rise to disturbances is either rejected, i.e. the impulse is defined away and not adopted into the psychological structures; or the impulse is disqualified within the field of consciousness to a non-observation or non-perception by being distorted so that it fits into the previously established structures, in the relevant theme-horizon-scheme.

In this way we avoid relating to the huge stream of new impulses to which we are all subject in today's society. We need to do this in order not to be overwhelmed, but at the same time transcendent learning is thus obstructed. This can only take place through a so-called thematisation, i.e. an accommodation that transcends everyday consciousness. Thus such thematisations are fundamentally essential because society is so complex, and the important financial and power structures so impenetrable, that the individual has no immediate possibility of forming a coherent understanding of how things work.

However, the thematisations require psychological energy. In the Piaget-oriented conception it will concern offensive accommodations that lead to existing theme-horizon-schemes being reconstructed as schemes of a less limiting nature. In a Freud-oriented conception, everyday consciousness has the nature of a generalised mechanism of defence and, just like other mechanisms of defence, it has both positive and negative aspects, and defensive and offensive features.

The positive aspect consists primarily of the fact that we would be completely unable to cope with our lives without such a defence; we would be overwhelmed and soon end up in a mental hospital (which quite a few of us actually do, anyway). The negative aspect concerns the fact that part of our life fulfilment is confined in routines, impoverishment, falsity and prejudice. The defensive aspect deals with the notion that we use distortions when the surrounding world becomes too much for us. The offensive aspect is the ability to convert defence into a counterattack; in situations where the challenge becomes too insistent and we are able to mobilise a certain reserve of energy, we can take up the challenge and do something about the situation, internally on our own behalf, or externally through individual or collective actions. I return to this in section 9.5 on resistance.

At the same time as modern society exposes us to a flow of influences that is so overwhelming that we have to develop a semi-automatic defence that filters a great deal out, society also exposes us to constant changes in all possible areas, and with a frequency that far exceeds our capacity to relate to them and adopt them. Therefore, the everyday consciousness we develop also includes a defence against changes, which partly frees us to relate to what we semi-automatically define as outside our field of interest, and partly distorts other changes to make them fit within the frames of our pre-understandings.

But all the time there are also changes affecting ourselves and our situation to such an extent that we, so to speak, cannot avoid them. In our working lives, our private lives and within our fields of interest, today we are constantly exposed to changes that are of important significance for the way we live our lives, our possibilities and our patterns of understanding – because the societal structures are constantly changed to keep up with the 'development' that consists precisely of all these changes.

On the one hand, all of this gives rise to lots of learning that can contribute to developing and enriching us, but it can simultaneously constitute a powerful strain that we always have to keep up with changes and alter our existence and ourselves in accordance with them. In some cases this becomes too much; the defence mechanisms of everyday consciousness cannot keep up and we have to mobilise a stronger defence to retain a tolerable mental balance.

In such cases we make use of what could be called an *identity defence*, because this is a type of defence potentially developed together with the identity and which serves to protect it. As a general psychological phenomenon, the development of personal identity is linked to the individualisation that followed with the transition from the old feudal society to modern industrialised and capitalist society throughout the eighteenth and nineteenth centuries. It consists of the experience of oneself as a unique individual and the experience of how one is experienced by others.

As discussed in more detail in section 8.4, in late-modernity the 'classic' form of relatively stable identity is, however, on the way to being replaced by a more flexible form of identity with a relatively limited 'core identity' supplemented by a layer of more changeable sub-identities. It is, nevertheless, characteristic of most adults in our society that their 'adulthood' psychologically is connected with a relatively firm and stable identity, typically embedded in education and occupation, family relations and perhaps also in, for example, political or religious convictions.

Such an identity is developed over the course of a number of years and, simultaneously, an identity defence is established in the form of mental barriers that can catch the influences that may threaten the established identity. In adults such identity defence typically finds expression in learning and education situations aimed at readjustment, re-training or personal development.

For example, if one has had a certain job for years and has experienced oneself as well functioning and well qualified in this context, and one then suddenly becomes unemployed, not because one is not good enough but because the company is downsizing, production is being moved to another country, the work is being automated etc., one finds oneself in a situation where against one's will one has to both demolish the existing identity and build up a new one, i.e. one is faced with a demand concerning a learning process of a transformative nature. Something similar can be the case in connection with, for instance, a divorce, the death of somebody close to one, or other sudden changes in the foundation of life.

A great number of the participants in adult education today have this type of background in many different forms, and, to the degree that the situation has not been fully acknowledged and accepted by the persons in question, there will be identity defence, which frequently – and especially in the case of the slightly older participants – can prove a massive obstacle to the intended learning processes.

But the condition also exists, although in less massive forms, among many other young and adult participants who have not fully accepted that the education in which they are participating is suitable or necessary for them. In fact, they more or less experience it as 'having been placed' there by, for example, the public employment service or the social authorities. Thus, identity defence can, in general, be characterised as the most profound and usually also the strongest defence mechanism against learning which, as a rule, is intended by others but not, or only partly, accepted by the person in question.

Yet another type of defence against learning can occur when, in general or in a specific situation, one feels helpless or without influence on the conditions that have necessitated a course of learning that one otherwise would not have entered into.

In this connection, it is important that it is the *experience* of an unreasonable situation that is at issue, quite irrespective of what various others might think. In what could be called 'tradition directed' societies, fitting in with or adapting to the current traditions and norms will seldom be experienced as unreasonable, even though it may be viewed as both unreasonable and inappropriate when seen from the outside. But in modern societies that define themselves as democratic, most people – not least the young – expect to be able to decide for themselves what they are going to learn and not learn, and when this is not the case it is experienced as an injustice.

Precisely in the context of transition to the modern knowledge society, this problem would seem to be taking on new and greater dimensions. In a globalised world the educational level of the population is assumed to be a key parameter for the economic growth and competitiveness of countries. This brings with it a need on the part of the state for as many people as possible to be educated as much as possible at the same time as choosing the education programmes regarded as most appropriate in this connection. All of this is neatly phrased in the expression 'lifelong learning', which was originally launched in the tradition of public enlightenment as a message saying that everybody should have the possibility of learning as much as they want to, but is now well on the way to developing into a requirement of members of society instead of an offer (for example, Field 2002; Jarvis 2002; Coffield 2003; Illeris 2003b).

However, this requirement is swiftly proving to conflict with the education wishes and needs of both young and older adults, so regulation is necessary because society naturally cannot make available the education of anyone at all for anything at all, even if the persons in question themselves pay the costs fully or partially. There are, for example, limits to the number of television hosts, actors and designers that could be needed, and, at the same time, we need enough labour for a number of service industries and for the necessary production.

Where the boundaries are drawn and who defines the rules of the game for all of this is, however, entirely a political question. Even though all possible attempts are made to obtain 'objective' analyses and prognoses, there is a huge range in the criteria that can be applied, and for the individual this can very quickly become something that is experienced as an unreasonable break with the democratic right to make one's own decisions.

In such cases the immediate defence reaction will very often be in the nature of what I earlier called a defensive accommodation (section 4.5) – i.e. that the individual learns in a transgressive manner that the authorities she or he is facing are unreasonable, insensitive, dictatorial, undemocratic or the like, and the person very rarely benefits from this. In the final analysis this is, of course, a clear conflict of interests. But an easier solution could probably be found in many concrete cases if both parties were prepared for this.

The authorities could make more of an effort to limit control to what is absolutely necessary while providing honest explanations. But there is, first and foremost, a need for time for far more empathetic counselling processes. In my research experience this would considerably reduce both conflicts and defence (e.g. Illeris 2003b).

The individuals in question need to adopt more realistic and flexible attitudes, i.e. have greater insight into their own qualifications and interests in relation to the societal realities, and a more conscious approach to being able to navigate in a way that is both flexible and goal-directed on this basis. But such attitudes do not come out of the blue, and, therefore, the problem easily rebounds on society in the form of a need for better incentives to develop these attitudes up through childhood and youth.

Experiencing helplessness is debilitating for the individual, and if this applies to many, it also applies to society. Mental defence is both natural and necessary, but it is a stressful situation which, unfortunately, occurs far more often than should be the case in an affluent and democratic society.

9.4 Ambivalence

In continuation of the three typical types of defence I examined in the above, I will now proceed to the more complex mental reaction called ambivalence, which, in relation to learning, concerns the fact that at one and the same time, the individual both wants and does not want to become engaged in a course of learning. This is a way of relating that seems to be appearing with increasing frequency in connection with the pressure to involve oneself in learning – something many experience in modern society.

The issue of ambivalence in relation to learning was taken up first in women's research, not least by German Regina Becker-Schmidt, whose point of departure is critical theory (see section 7.4) and who has focused on industry in particular. She takes a starting point in the contradictions that influence the existence of many women: 'The learning content, which is what our considerations of social learning are all about, is linked to women's reality, to the conflicts in female lives, which the societal organisation of gender relations necessarily result in' (Becker-Schmidt 1987, p. 9).

Basically it concerns the contradiction between wage work and reproduction in the private sphere, including motherhood. But even within each
of these fields, the situation of women is full of contradictions, for the role
of women in relation to society is full of ambiguities: femininity is both
idealised and undervalued at one and the same time; it is women who deal
with most of the practical and social problems of everyday life, but societally
they are not valued, either in terms of wage or status, and socially they
have to put up with scorn and humiliation.

Psychologically these basic contradictory conditions are converted into
ambivalence. In the context of learning it concerns, in general, how people
learn to live with the contradictions and conflicts of reality, and the
development of the capacity to deal with both external and internal conflicts
and keep an open mind towards ambiguity. Two key concepts in this context
are ambivalence defence and ambivalence tolerance. People have to learn
to live with ambivalence, to recognise it and develop a psychological
resistance to it:

> Ambivalence therefore has its response on both internal and external
> fragmentation. Our psychological reality is just as controlled by
> conflicting desires as the social reality is pervaded by contradic-
> tions. In both cases 'mixed feelings' express subjective and objective
> conflicts. . . . When we question ourselves, face conflicts and endure,
> that is 'ambivalence tolerance'; when we shrink from them, that is
> 'ambivalence defence'.
>
> (Becker-Schmidt 1987, p. 8)

Learning in these contexts thus implies acknowledging ambivalence and
its causes. This can happen through reality testing, i.e. putting experiences
into context in time and space, to emotionally 'feel' and to logically 'think
about' (see sections 5.6 and 5.5). One can try to transcend the customary
patterns, accept dislike by moving into the unknown, give names to the
contradictions and the ambivalence – this develops ambivalence tolerance.
It requires willpower and energy and the motive to make these efforts may
lie in a notion that it could be better, not to understand as such that the
contradictions could be solved, but that they could be handled better if
you acknowledge them, also thereby gaining the opportunity to understand
and accept ambivalence (Becker-Schmidt 1987, pp. 62ff.).

Although considerable differences may exist between women's social
situation in the Germany of the 1980s and conditions in many countries
today, in general Becker-Schmidt's deliberations and concepts concerning
ambivalence have not become less topical. The fundamental gender inequal-
ities still exist, and the societal contradictions and thus the ambivalences,
have also become more urgent in a number of other important areas. In
relation to learning this applies especially to the situation for the young,

the low-skilled and the unemployed, and perhaps most of all to those with a foreign ethnic background.

With respect to the young, first and foremost the steadily increasing requirements concerning learning and education have been coupled with an individualisation which, on the one hand, apparently opens the possibility of individual choice between a mass of learning opportunities and, on the other hand, makes it the responsibility of the young people themselves to choose what is absolutely right and to realise it successfully. This has proved to be a very demanding situation for many youngsters. It draws out the period of youth and implies for many an infinity of doubt, insecurity and defeat (for example, Ziehe 1989, 2004; Beck and Beck-Gernsheim 2002; Illeris 2003a; Weil *et al.* 2004).

On the labour market, it is primarily the weakest, the low-skilled and the unemployed who feel the ambivalence between the massive requirements for qualification and an uncertain and merciless labour market. The pressure to engage oneself in 'lifelong learning' is constantly balanced against the risk of being 'left behind', with resultant social and economic marginalisation and doubt as to whether one can manage it and if it leads to anything. To a growing extent, adult education is populated by people who have poor self-esteem and inadequate or obsolete qualifications and who feel they have been 'placed' there. They often find it difficult to see how they are going to 'pull themselves together' (for example, Illeris 2003b).

Finally, for many immigrants and refugees and their descendants the situation is often even more contradictory, balancing between the norms and traditions they brought with them and demands to readjust under strained social and economic conditions. Furthermore, many are both young and do not have much schooling, and they might also be women, at the same time as having a foreign ethnic background.

All of these cases provide fertile soil for profound ambivalences in connection with learning, which is clearly a necessity but which for the individual can simultaneously be associated with far-reaching unwillingness and uncertainty. In Becker-Schmidt's precise terms, this becomes a solid 'ambivalence defence' that one cannot avoid but only learn to deal with by means of a corresponding 'ambivalence tolerance'.

9.5 Resistance to learning

Even though one does not have to be within institutionalised education programmes for very long before one experiences participants who resist the intended learning, this does not seem to be something that has been taken up to any great extent by educational and learning research. On the contrary, one could get the impression that there is a form of collective repression among school and education personnel in refusal to face this fact.

Resistance appears in the literature exclusively as a psychoanalytical concept concerning clients' resistance against cooperating with the therapist (see Olsen and Køppe 1981, pp. 254ff.), or otherwise as education as a part of a resistance struggle or struggle for freedom as in Paulo Freire or his American successor Henry Giroux (see Giroux 1983). More generally, one finds a discussion about societal and political resistance in certain Marxist-oriented social theoreticians and historians of ideas, but this is not related to learning and education. Nonetheless, I have found numerous examples of resistance to learning and education in my own empirical and theoretical research (see Illeris 1981, pp. 63ff., 2002, pp. 80ff.).

In concrete situations it can often be difficult to distinguish between resistance and defence against learning, and they can coexist, but there is a deep, fundamental difference that consists in the fact that defence is something that is built up before the situation in which it is expressed, a preparedness that is at one's disposal, while resistance is something that is mobilised in certain situations where the individual is faced with something that she or he either cannot, or will not, accept.

In order to fully understand the nature of resistance, it is useful to return to the discussion concerning Freud's understanding of drives in section 6.2. In Freud's opinion mental energy originates in different life drives, basically the drive to uphold one's life and develop one's potentials, and to ensure the continuation of the species. He later also introduced the concept of a death drive which was supposed to be capable of explaining aggressive and destructive tendencies that Freud met with in his patients to a very high degree. I rejected this, however, referring precisely to the fact that these tendencies must be understood as defence and resistance. But while Freud concerned himself with, and researched, the defence mechanisms to a wide extent, he was not aware of what in Freudian terminology could be called the fundamental resistance drive, but which I will here call human beings' *resistance potential*.

In everyone's life course and development there are always obstacles and resistance that cannot just be overcome and accommodated, but which, on the contrary, seem to act as a brake on development and life fulfilment. In cognitive terms, it could be conditions that seem incomprehensible and unreasonable; in affective terms, it might be frustrations or relational conditions which, in some cases, can assume dimensions as dramatic as the violent emotional processes involved in the Oedipal situation described by Freud.

Limitation of life fulfilment is thus an existential condition that no one escapes. In early childhood the limits are typically imposed by parents and/or other close carers, but later it increasingly becomes a case of societally organised regulation through institutions and structures that limit or directly repress opportunities for life fulfilment that the society in question does not find acceptable.

In terms of learning and development, what happens is that when a small child comes up against an insurmountable obstacle that limits his or her life fulfilment, he or she reacts with a form of psychological resistance that manifests itself as anger, fury or aggression. The potential for life fulfilment always also contains the potential for resistance to conditions that limit that life fulfilment – and throughout the pre-school years a separation of the two potentials gradually takes place.

Freud's Oedipal drama can be seen as a particular variant of this process, characterised by the fact that limitations on life fulfilment in bourgeois society in Freud's day were strongly concentrated on the sexual sphere, which therefore came to take a central position in the process. But the Oedipal drama can also serve as an example of how the resistance potential can fail against the realities of the surrounding world, and how that can bring submission, repression and so on that can lead to psychological problems and disease.

Generally speaking, the resistance potential is ultimately biologically embedded in humans as part of the human equipment in the struggle for survival, and the learning processes that get their energy from the resistance potential will typically be of a predominantly accommodative nature as well as being strongly emotionally obsessed. This has to do with the over-coming of considerable obstacles for life fulfilment, and it will typically involve a reorganisation of both cognitive structures and emotional patterns.

On the psychological-structural level it is a case of external resistance being countered by an inner psychological response that can set off an accommodative learning process, possibly leading to qualitatively new knowledge or a personal development of an offensive or defensive nature. If you cannot get the one you love, you have to either accept it – and in so doing, perhaps, accept that you do not have the requisite qualities – or else you develop some defensive justifications to explain it away.

In practice it is, of course, impossible to clearly distinguish between the potential for life fulfilment and the potential for resistance to conditions that stand in the way of this life fulfilment. It is more like two aspects of a survival potential corresponding to the polarisation that is, again, found in Freud as the conflict between the pleasure principle and the reality principle, or between libido and aggression.

The energy basis for learning thus lies in this double potential, and not only in the desire for life fulfilment. All learning requires psychological energy, and this energy comes from either the desire for life fulfilment, the desire for resistance, or a combination of the two, and both potentials can ultimately be traced back to the fundamental basis for managing in the biological struggle for survival.

In learning-related practice, the resistance potential is expressed, as previously mentioned, first and foremost in situations where one is faced with something one, for one reason or another, regards as so unacceptable that one either cannot, or will not, put up with it. It can occur, more generally, if one finds oneself in contexts one experiences oneself as being in conflict with, e.g. a more or less unwanted school or training course, a specific subject, a specific teacher or the social situation in the class or team.

Activation of the resistance potential does not have a general blocking effect on learning, but it is rarely the originally intended learning that occurs. On the contrary, there will often be defensive accommodative processes occurring – e.g. pupils who end up learning that they just cannot understand maths, viewing the teacher or other pupils as their enemies and attributing all kinds of negative qualities to them, or more broadly, that school and education stink, or are at any rate nothing the person concerned can get anything out of. In adult education we often come across participants with this negative kind of attitude towards education, which developed during their years in school, and which has to be overcome if there is to be a meaningful educational process. In particular cases and in single situations that are especially provocative, resistance can also take the form of more or less uncontrolled aggression, and there can also be interaction between defence and resistance, which can make the situation even more complicated, not least for the learners themselves.

However, resistance can also lead to accommodations of a more offensive nature with far reaching results, partly because the resistance potential can be a very strong incentive which, in a constructive process, can unite with the life fulfilment potential in an effort to find and develop alternatives to those conditions perceived as unacceptable. This will often happen in situations where one is 'ready to go', i.e. one is engaged and mentally focused, and, therefore, mental resistance can also encourage learning to a high degree and even be the motive force in a very far-reaching and transgressive learning process.

In institutional education, participants' resistance is almost always viewed on the face of it as something negative by the teachers and other representatives of institutions. It is at best troublesome, but can also easily undermine planned activities and cause them to go off course, and, in a broader perspective, it can also cause similar problems for the framework, milieu and self-comprehension of the institution.

Nevertheless, it is often in connection with resistance, or at least elements of resistance, that the most important transcendent learning occurs. Personal development in particular, which is currently accorded such significance in education, often occurs through a process characterised by resistance. And it must not be forgotten that resistance is a central element in a democratic society, for part of the way democracy functions is that public resistance should be able to restrain or correct those in power. In society as a whole, in education, at work and in other spheres of everyday life, resistance can be what leads to conditions changing and developing in step with new circumstances and new needs.

Seen from a learning perspective, resistance contains a great potential that can, however, be difficult to deal with in institutional education. Pedagogically, it concerns, on the one hand, creating a space for learning and situations that can allow room for participants' resistance and, on the other, acknowledging resistance as a legitimate form of expression as well as giving it both the challenge that is its natural precondition and the support that can promote important learning.

This might sound very positive, but in ordinary education it can be tremendously demanding to relate to the participants' resistance, and institutional frameworks can impose limits that make it extremely difficult to carry out a constructive resistance process – the resistance might well, for example, be directed at those very institutional frameworks, or it could be supported by social indignation and frustrations with restricting conditions, which in the educational environment can be hard to relate to, even if the resistance is perceived as altogether justified.

All the same it should not be forgotten that in many cases education forms the only context where participants have a realistic opportunity to allow their resistance to unfold and to adapt it in a constructive and progressive manner, and that this can be the source of the most far-reaching potential for learning. On the other hand, frustrated resistance will typically be converted into defence and blockings that can hinder further learning.

The entire discussion on the social sorting process that is constantly demonstrated in the school and educational system, has a lot to do with certain types of resistance that are perceived as acceptable and legitimate in the institutions, while others are not, and this difference typically follows certain social distinctions – school is very often organised and functions on the premises of the already privileged members of society. There is nothing new in this, and the problem cannot be solved simply on a pedagogical level, but there will always be situations where the pupils' resistance can be dealt with in a more or less constructive way.

Active resistance to learning is usually established already in early childhood in situations in which one must, of necessity, learn to limit and control one's behaviour and activities, but it is probably otherwise something that mostly belongs to the period of youth and can typically play a very important role in the identity development that has its central point in this period. By means of resistance, for example, decisive development and recognition of one's own opinions, potentials and limitations can take place.

Active resistance is not so frequent in adult education but, on the other hand, it is typically less experimental in nature and it is clearer, sometimes adamant. The adult, perhaps precisely through challenging learning processes in the years of youth, may have landed on some standpoints, convictions and patterns of reaction that form elements in a more consistent identity. In this way the borderline between resistance and defence can be even finer, but in general the point of departure for resistance is more conscious and well-thought-out, while to a very large extent defence functions automatically. Therefore, in principle, new learning can also be a direct part of resistance, while defence must be broken down or transgressed for significant new learning to take place.

What, on the other hand, is far more widespread in adult education programmes is a more passive form of resistance that can express itself in many different ways that may be extremely irritating and inappropriate in a teaching context. The Danish psychologists Peter Berliner and Jens Berthelsen have given the term 'passive aggression' to the phenomenon, and pointed out that it contains 'a protest and an energy to want something else' (Berliner and Berthelsen 1989). This is, again, different from defence, which precisely does not want anything else. But active resistance is held in check; the situation is not found important enough to warrant open protest or one may feel powerless in advance and then the resistance finds various indirect modes of expression. The consistent reaction is, naturally, to stop and to depart from the education programme. But in many cases this would lead to some completely unacceptable and unmanageable consequences, and one simply 'gets off' mentally and is indifferent. Nonetheless, one often cannot help making irritated and irritating comments and creating discord, more or less demonstratively.

In this context it is important to maintain that passive resistance also actually contains important learning potential, and it can help to ease the situation and contribute to important learning processes if the resistance can be made to come forward openly. On the other hand, this often presupposes that the teacher and other participants can see through and identify the situation as a form of passive resistance and have the courage and energy to face a possible confrontation.

9.6 Summary

Barriers to learning can lead to possible learning being rejected or to something being learned that is different from what was intended by the learner or others. Three main types of barrier can be distinguished which, in the present book, are treated as mislearning, defence against learning, and resistance to learning, respectively. A special form of defence can be in the nature of ambivalence, i.e. that at one and the same time the learner both wants to and does not want to learn something.

Mislearning that results from inadequate prior qualifications, a lack of concentration, misunderstandings or inappropriate communication takes place on a large scale, but in most cases it is of relatively limited significance and can usually be corrected if this proves necessary. We all walk around with a lot of wrong knowledge and misunderstandings as a result of mislearning.

Defence against learning is a necessity in our modern knowledge society, partly because the learning possibilities far exceed what the individual can manage. A distinction can be made between three main categories of defence against learning. The concept of everyday consciousness contains a semi-automatic, selective defence against the volume of learning impulses we meet in our everyday lives. Everyday consciousness also implies a mental defence against the constant stream of changes we are faced with, but in more serious cases where the changes mean important undesired changes in the life situation of the individual, a more extensive and deeper identity defence can be mobilised. Finally, defence against the experience of power-lessness can occur. It can take the form of defensive accommodations directed against the power-holding authorities who are experienced as unreasonable, or more constructive reactions in the form of development of a more coherent understanding and mode of relating.

Ambivalence in relation to learning occurs in particular in groups of people involved in courses of learning that may be societally required and important for the persons in question but which they would rather have been able to avoid. Today this typically concerns young people who find it difficult to orient themselves and adjust to the education programmes, low-skilled and unemployed persons who need up-grading, and ethnic groups who are more or less forced into courses of education.

Resistance to learning is mobilised in contexts and situations that are experienced as unacceptable. All people develop a resistance potential that can be activated in the face of unacceptable situations and which, among other things, also can be an important motive force for learning, which will then typically take other paths than the generally recognised and intended ones but can be an important part of personal and societal development.

Chapter 10

Learning, dispositions and preconditions

This chapter deals with a number of the most important internal and external preconditions of significance for the learning possibilities of the individual person. These are the areas of intelligence and abilities, learning style, gender, and what is called 'social heredity', i.e. the results of the social and economic conditions under which the individual grew up. There is a great deal of disagreement in all these areas about the effect they have on learning and how important they are. These matters will be discussed on a general level as far as it is possible to get into each of the topics.

10.1 Heredity, environment and dispositions

Up to now this book has dealt with different topics around how learning and non-learning take place. I now move on to discuss various types of conditions that can be of significance for learning. In the first place these are different kinds of general preconditions or dispositions in the learner, which I take up in this chapter. The following two chapters deal with learning and life course and different types of learning contexts.

The first question I discuss is the classic issue of heredity versus environment, or nature versus nurture. This topic is traditionally dealt with in connection with learning as a question about how large a part of our learning possibilities is fixed in advance through our genetic or hereditary equipment, and how much room for manoeuvre exists for all the influences and contexts we are exposed to throughout our lives, i.e. for environmental influences in the widest sense of this concept.

It is well known that the relation between the significance of hereditary and environmental conditions is different with regard to various characteristics. The colour of our eyes is exclusively dependent on the genes we inherit from our parents, our height and build are also largely determined by heredity but can, nevertheless, to a certain extent, depend on, for example, our nutrition and the uses to which we put our bodies. On the other hand, different forms of behaviour are developed to a higher degree on the basis of our environment or culture. There are thus large differences in the significance of heredity and environment, respectively, in different areas, and in many cases there are, in addition, especially critical periods during childhood when there is special sensitivity to environmental influences. For example, we are extremely open to conditions that develop our use of language at the age of eighteen months to two years.

The most common method for establishing the significance of the relative importance of hereditary and environmental conditions on different areas is studies of identical twins who always have identical genes but who can grow up under more or less different conditions.

However, modern brain research has convincingly shown that the development of these conditions in the individual is far more complex and diverse than revealed by the studies of twins. Already from the embryo stage there is enormously subtle interaction between the inherited dispositions that lie in the genes, the inner environment in the single individual, and influences from the outer environment. English brain researchers Marc Solms and Oliver Turnbull write as follows:

> The overwhelming vast topic of nature-nurture influences on the brain has the potential to include everything that neuroscience knows about the development sequence. . . . Genetic and environmental influences on behaviour are *absolutely inextricable*, and genetic influences are therefore anything but immutable. In fact, genes would be a terrible handicap if they were not accessible to environmental influences . . . Nature and nurture are in a dynamic interplay from the earliest moments of development.
>
> (Solms and Turnbull 2002, pp. 217 and 218)

It is also the case that the complexity of this interaction is embedded as far down as in the single electrochemical circuit of the brain that controls our behaviour and thoughts. Well-known American brain researcher Joseph LeDoux, who has, in particular, worked with these circuits and the functions in the so-called synapses that mediate the circuits' numerous transitions between different brain cells, writes that:

> the synaptic connections that ultimately determine what a circuit will do and how it will do it are wired up epigenetically, that is, by interactions between genes and environment (including both the internal and external environment). . . . To the extent that psychological characteristics are mediated by synapses in the brain, the psychological and synaptic levels are intimately related.
>
> (LeDoux 2002, p. 82)

In their book *The Brain and the Inner World*, Solms and Turnbull exemplify this complicated interaction through sexual development (Solms and Turnbull 2002, pp. 223ff.). Spontaneously, a person's gender is clearly enough genetically determined through the sex chromosomes that are either type XX (female) or XY (male). However, during the first three months the development of the foetus is identical in the two genders. At some point after that, a substance is secreted from a sequence of genes in the male foetus's Y chromosome that influences the rudimentary sexual organs so that the foetus develops testicles where it otherwise would develop ovaries. This is the genetic foundation of the gender difference, but it is actually possible to alter it by artificially (i.e. by means of outer influence) introducing this substance into the female foetus or preventing its secretion by the male foetus.

Soon after this the male foetus begins to produce the male hormone testosterone, which by developing a special enzyme called 5-alfa-reductase can change testosterone into dihydrotestosterone which influences a number of the body's organ systems so that they develop differently than in the female foetus. If, for one reason or another, not enough of this substance is developed, the foetus will develop in a masculine direction to a limited degree only, and if there is very little, it will develop in a feminine direction even though it has testicles and each cell contains a Y chromosome – a phenomenon that, *inter alia*, has been seen in a number of athletes who are women by gender but have developed in a masculine direction with respect to build and strength.

In a subsequent phase of the development of the male foetus a new enzyme is produced called aromatase. This enzyme changes testosterone into the female hormone oestrogen, which is necessary for the brain to develop into a male brain (I return to the implications of this in section 10.4) and thereby causes the individual to function and experience himself as a boy, and later a man, in behaviour and mentally. However, if this process is not completed for one reason or another, the result is a male body with some degree of female psyche and sexuality.

As all the processes mentioned are susceptible to environmental influence, sexual development is an example of the extremely fine balances that can exist between hereditary and environmental factors, which determine the actual development, and, if the balance deviates even a little from what is genetically programmed, in this case it can result in a number of major or minor sexual deviations. For example, there are indications that if the mother is stressed during the crucial critical periods for the above-mentioned processes, this can lead to problems for sexual development. One study shows that there is an above average share of homosexuals among men born in Germany during or just after the Second World War. This could be connected with their mothers having had above average exposure to stress (Solms and Turnbull 2002, p. 233). But this cannot be proved and one should be careful of drawing far-reaching conclusions in these very complex areas.

However, this example of some key details in connection with sexual development can serve as an illustration or indication of the close and complicated interaction, also applying to learning possibilities, between hereditary and environmental factors. The more generally dominant understanding within brain research today is that the mental preconditions a person has at their disposal at a given time have the character of *dispositions* – for instance, in relation to learning in different areas and to the dimensions of learning. These dispositions have come about in a close and inseparable interaction between hereditary and environmental factors, and they can also change and further develop through such continued interaction. The weight or share of the two types of factors in a certain area can, to a certain extent, be determined in general on the basis of studies of twins, but it is both impossible and mistaken to make such a separation in the single individual. It is not a competition between heredity and environment that determines development, but precisely their interaction. Therefore, in principle, there is always a possibility of new developments, but not merely any type of development whatever.

Two general conclusions pertaining to learning can be drawn from this. The first is that human beings as a species, in all cases in which no decided mis-developments have taken place, inherit colossal and colossally complicated learning possibilities, far exceeding what all other creatures have at their disposal. The second is that the concrete learning possibilities for the individual comprise a great number of dispositions in different areas that are under continuous development in close interaction with genetic and environmental factors.

10.2 Intelligence, abilities and smartness

There can hardly be any doubt that the area that has been at the centre of the debate about heredity and environment in relation to learning possibilities for the last century is what we call intelligence and concerns our general abilities to learn and think and to understand and solve problems.

However, approaching a closer definition of what intelligence actually is remains a great problem. This is because the definitions are either very general and imprecise, precisely in the direction of our general possibilities in various rather unclearly identified areas, or else the definition becomes operational, i.e. some formulation or other which, in the final analysis, leads to the circular argument that intelligence is what we measure by means of intelligence tests.

To this can only be said that intelligence tests have actually proved to be quite good at predicting how an individual will manage at school and other types of formalised education, and this is exactly the main purpose for which they were developed. But at the same time they have, to a high degree, been understood as a kind of objective for talents, prudence or functionality – whatever these terms mean – even though they have not proved very good at showing anything about the way in which the individual will manage in contexts outside of the education system. This, of course, has to do with the fact that what different intelligence tests contain is different tasks that reflect the types of common sense and understanding that traditionally are at the heart of education programmes, for example, in areas such as working with figures, logical thought, language skills and spatial orientation.

The first intelligence test was developed by the Frenchmen Alfred Binet (1857–1911) and Théodore Simon (1873–1961) in 1905 at the request of the Parisian school authorities, who needed a tool to identify pupils in need of remedial teaching. It contained a number of tasks in the areas mentioned, at different ages and with scales that could translate the results into an intelligence quotient. The test was subsequently translated, standardised and further developed and has thus been very widely disseminated.

The Binet-Simon test was, first and foremost, the solution to a practical problem, while two main types of approach developed concerning the theoretical aspect. On the one side is the largely European G factor view, which was devised by British Charles Spearman (1863–1945) in particular and supported by studies that have shown that when children score high in one (classic) area of intelligence, the possibility of them also achieving a high score in other areas is increased (Spearman 1923). On the other side, is the largely American view, the so-called 'factor analytical' approach, according to which intelligence consists of a number of independent areas or factors. The most refined expression of this view is a three-dimensional intelligence model with a total of 120 factors launched in 1967 by the American intelligence and creativity researcher Joy P. Guilford (1967), who has already been mentioned in connection with Kolb's learning cycle (section 5.2).

The theory and the debate concerning intelligence was, however, fundamentally altered later through the theory of multiple intelligences first presented by American psychologist Howard Gardner in 1983, and which he has subsequently continued, developed and varied (see in particular Gardner 1983, 1991, 1993).

Very briefly, it is Gardner's theory that there are a limited number of interdependent intelligences. He originally reckoned with the following seven:

- Linguistic Intelligence
- Musical Intelligence
- Logical-Mathematical Intelligence
- Spatial Intelligence

- Bodily-Kinaesthetic Intelligence
- Interpersonal Intelligence (understanding of and contact with others)
- Intrapersonal Intelligence (understanding of and contact with oneself)

(Gardner 1983)

He later added another two intelligences:

- Naturalist Intelligence (understanding of and contact with nature)
- Existential Intelligence (which Gardner regards as being partly different from the other intelligences)

(Gardner 1991)

Gardner's original definition of intelligence was 'the ability to solve problems or to create products that are valued within one or more cultural settings' (Gardner 1993), but later he changed the definition to 'a biopsychological potential to process information that can be activated in a cultural setting to solve problems or create products that are of value in a culture' (Gardner 1999, pp. 33–34). What is important in this change lies in the switch from the word 'ability' to the word 'potential', because it makes clear that intelligence is not something that can be measured. Hereby, Gardner clearly distances himself from every type of intelligence test.

Gardner also sets up a number of requirements that must be met if one is to speak of an independent intelligence, but these requirements are not precise and it is not necessary that they all be met, which means that there is also a considerable degree of estimating here. Even though Gardner pays great attention to arguing for the individual intelligences, it is thus not so much the nine intelligences selected as Gardner's way of understanding the intelligence concept and the pedagogical consequences he arrives at that have been important for the very high degree of breakthrough his theory has achieved.

What is most decisive and innovative is, perhaps, that Gardner pluralises the concept of intelligence. He speaks of several intelligences and not of factors as sub-elements of one intelligence. In so doing he lets the air out of the one-dimensional, branding and at times also elitist-oriented thinking that has otherwise stuck to the intelligence concept and the calculation of intelligence quotients. According to Gardner we are all to one degree or another well equipped with some intelligences and less well equipped with others. The pedagogical task is to find out where the individual has his or her strong and weak sides and take the consequences of this. The school should be a place where there is room enough to cultivate the intelligences that the individual child is good at, and provide it with support to be capable of managing reasonably well in the other areas.

At the same time Gardner operates with a limited, clear and relatively easily comprehended number of intelligences that correspond somewhat to the immediate, popular understanding – and, at any rate, are far away from Guilford's very complicated 120 intelligence factors. In this way Gardner helps to de-mystify the concept, which doubtless has also contributed to the impact of his theory.

Finally, Gardner very clearly transcends the boundaries of cognitive orientation, which has formed the basis of the understanding of intelligence ever since Binet. To Gardner intelligence is not just a matter of being 'brighter' (in relation to the requirements of the school – and this was precisely Binet's task), but it deals much more broadly with being able to manage, and traditional cognitive intelligence is not sufficient for this. It has also to do with empathising with oneself and others and with aesthetic and bodily functions. Gardner's intelligence concept is thus not so far away from the understanding of what it all is about in contemporary society, which is contained in the modern competence concept (see section 8.4). With the interpersonal and intrapersonal intelligences the concept also covers the whole of the learning field set out in the learning triangle of this book.

But Gardner's understanding can also be criticised, even from different angles. For example, Daniel Goleman, who launched the concept of 'emotional intelligence' (see section 6.4) and fully acknowledges that Gardner has been a major source of inspiration for him, writes:

> While there is ample room in Gardner's descriptions of the personal intelligences for insight into the play of emotions and mastery of the managing them, Gardner and those who work with him have not pursued in great detail the role of feeling in these intelligences, focusing more on cognitions *about* feeling. This focus, perhaps unintentionally, leaves unexplored the rich sea of emotions that makes the inner life and relationships so complex, so compelling, and so often puzzling. . . . Gardner's emphasis on the cognitive elements in the personal intelligences reflects the zeitgeist of psychology that has shaped his views.
>
> (Goleman 1995, p. 40)

I am inclined to agree with Goleman. Even though Gardner has been very successful in wresting himself free of the one-sided cultivation of cognition, and even though he has been highly successful in transcending the oppressive element in the intelligence concept, nevertheless, there is a clear tendency in his work that the cognitive is more important than the bodily, emotional and interactive areas.

A couple of attempts to achieve more balance are inherent in the surprising shift in angle pointed out in two very different but nonetheless parallel ways by Danish psychologist Mogens Hansen and Russian-American brain researcher Elkhonon Goldberg. Mogens Hansen writes:

> There are, however, good reasons for including attention or ability to concentrate in the group (of intelligences, KI.) Will-directed attention is a necessary basis for learning. Without targeted attention, i.e. will-directed, focused and enduring attention, one learns nothing. . . . Will-directed attention is part of the directing function of the brain and the consciousness, called the executive function, which is used for the self-regulation of actions on the basis of intentionality (intentions, will), planning and decisions. . . . It is therefore reasonable to speak of intelligence no. 1. Those who do not learn anything are the same as those who have never learned to control their own attention.
>
> (Hansen 2005, pp. 28–29)

It should be noted that the role Mogens Hansen attributes to attention is parallel to the way in which I discussed the mediating role of attention between motivation and learning in section 7.1. It is through the intensity of the attention we devote to a situation or elements in a situation that we most directly convert learning motivation into concrete learning.

Elkhonon Goldberg's angle of approach is different, but his conclusion points in the same direction. He expresses surprise at some people being evaluated by others as being 'smart' while others are evaluated as 'dumb'. But those regarded as smart can be bad at a lot of things and, in contrast, the dumb ones can have many strong sides:

> Peculiarly, a certain degree of independence exists between this global dimension of human mind and the more narrow special traits. . . . What are the brain structures whose individual variations determine these global traits? . . . Regardless of how the cognitive construct of general intelligence is defined, I am not aware of the existence of any distinct, single brain characteristic, shown to account for such a G factor. . . . But what about the S factor (S for 'smart')? I believe that, unlike the G factor, the S factor does exist. . . . In the 'multiple intelligence' scheme of things, it is the executive intelligence that we intuitively recognize as 'being smart', the S factor – the 'executive talent' – shapes our perception of a person as a persona, and not just a carrier of a certain cognitive trait.
>
> (Goldberg 2001, pp. 104–106)

And 'the executive intelligence' is the working memory in the frontal lobe of the brain (see section 2.4), in which Goldberg has specialised, and his book deals with the same thing that Mogens Hansen describes as 'the executive function, which is used for the self-regulation of actions on the basis of intentionality (intentions, will), planning and decisions' – intelligence no. 1, attention.

Yes, but have Hansen and Goldberg not introduced the G factor again, just in a different way? The answer is both yes and no. Goldberg's S factor is not an ability or potential in the same way as in Gardner's intelligences, but a general function that coordinates and controls the different abilities and potentials, integrates the content and the incentive, and includes relevant sub-elements from the long-term memory, a function that cannot be measured but can be developed through use. That is to say that the S factor is crosscutting like the G factor, but it has the character of a function.

It is rather obvious that people have different dispositions in different areas, and in the above it was established that these dispositions constantly develop in an inseparable interaction between hereditary and environmental elements. If we can maintain and perhaps develop Gardner's understanding of the diverse intelligences or abilities, combined with an understanding of the flexible and executive function of the working memory, in my opinion we will have come closer to the actual situation than the traditional understanding of intelligence was able to do, and we will also have a basis for recognising people's differences in all their diversity without, as in traditional intelligence research, running into grading, cultivating elites and branding each other. We all have our various strengths and weaknesses and some people are also in general 'smarter' or 'dumber' than others, but the one-dimensional intelligence understanding is far too blunt an instrument, and through our activities it is also possible to develop our abilities in the areas in which we engage.

10.3 Learning style

Another way of relating to the differences between people in connection with learning has found expression the concept of 'learning style'. The concept emerged in the USA during the 1970s as part of an attempt to find other explanations of individual learning differences than those discussed in terms of intelligence or abilities (e.g. Cronbach and Snow 1977). The idea is that people can learn in many ways, but for the single learner there are some special individual conditions that promote learning. Each of us has his or her own learning style.

However, no generally accepted definition of the concept has been reached, not to speak of a generally accepted theory on the area (see, for example, Merriam and Caffarella 1999, p. 209), and severe criticism has been raised (e.g. Coffield et al. 2004). A further complication is that there exists considerable overlap with the concepts of cognitive style (e.g. Hiemstra and Sisco 1990) and thinking style (Sternberg 1996). In the following I will briefly discuss some of the most prominent discussions in the area and conclude with a few brief general comments.

One of the best known approaches to the concept of learning style is that launched by David Kolb in close connection with his learning cycle and learning model, discussed in more detail in section 5.2 (see also Kolb 1984, Chapter 4). Basically, Kolb's understanding is that different people, to different degrees, orient themselves in their learning towards each of the four modes in the learning cycle – concrete experience, reflective observation, abstract conceptualisation, and active experimentation. By measuring these orientations through special tests an individual profile or learning style emerges that can be drawn into the learning circle, for example, as shown in Figure 10.1.

The example shows a female social worker's learning style, which has a clear emphasis in the top left section of the learning circle, i.e. in the space for accommodative knowledge (see Figure 5, section 5.2), and she

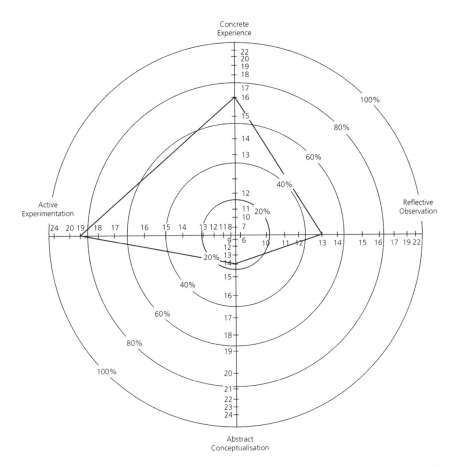

Figure 10.1 Example learning-style profile – female social worker (after Kolb 1984, p. 70)

is, therefore, categorised as an accommodative learner or an 'accommodator': she is typically creative and her learning is intuitive. Correspondingly, on the basis of their learning style others can be categorised as divergent, assimilative or convergent learners, or they can be close to the borderline between two of the categories. The divergent learner typically has good imaginative abilities and is good at seeing a case from several perspectives. The assimilative learner is typically good at concepts and theories, while the convergent learner is typically good at deductive thinking and problem solving. The learning style profile can thus provide a picture of where the individual has his or her strong sides, and one can then select one's areas and structure one's teaching appropriately on this basis.

But Kolb goes a step further with the practical consequences. If one draws up a learning profile for people in different education programmes and occupations, it emerges that on average they have their learning focal point in different places. For example, students in the fields of psychology, political science and history have, on average, a largely assimilative learning style, students of engineering and nursing a largely convergent learning style, students of commerce a largely accommodative learning style, and students in the fields of mathematics, chemistry and physics have, on average, a learning style that is close to the borderline between the assimilative and the convergent (Kolb 1984, p. 86). According to Kolb, such measurements can be used in connection with student counselling and structuring of the studies – but it can also be viewed as yet another example of Kolb's mastery in putting everything in its place in his system and thereby quite firmly limiting and systematising human diversity.

A quite different approach to learning styles is that which has led to the formulation of the test called the 'Myers-Briggs Type Indicator' (Myers 1980), where the focus is on personality differences. The dimensions measured are extroversion/introversion, sensing/intuition, thinking/feeling and judgement/perception (Myers 1980, p. 9) – and on this basis a profile emerges with four personality traits, e.g. extroversion, sensing, thinking, judgement. It is also emphasised that it is the learner him or herself who must be aware of his/her profile and organise his/her learning on this basis.

However, the broadest understanding of the concept of learning style is, without doubt, that at which Americans Rita and Kenneth Dunn have arrived through a practice-oriented approach. It simply includes all matters of relevance for learning and on this basis, by means of different observations, measurements and analyses, a total of 21 different factors are set up of significance for a person's learning style within the following categories: environmental (sound, light, temperature, design), emotional (motivation, persistence, responsibility, structure), sociological (self, pair, peers, team, adult, varied), physical (perceptual, intake, time, mobility), and finally psychological matters (global/analytic, hemisphericity, impulsive/reflective) (Dunn and Dunn 1978; Dunn 1996). There is no actual theoretical foundation and, as can be seen, a very complex orientation has emerged from it. But on the basis of the 21 categories a number of experiments have been conducted and guidelines have been drawn up in relation to teaching children, young people and adults (Dunn and Dunn 1992, 1993; Dunn and Griggs 2003).

Finally, mention should be made of the approach to learning styles focusing on the fact that there are differences between people with respect to the sensory impressions that appeal most to their learning. Originally a distinction was only made between those who learn best on the basis of linguistic expressions that come auditively through the hearing or visually through reading, the numerically oriented where figures are at the centre (again either auditively or visually) and the auditive-visual-kinaesthetically oriented, who learn best through experiences and by touching and manipulating things. This approach was later elaborated by Swede Lena Boström, who more clearly distinguishes between visual auditive, tactile and kinaesthetic learning styles.

More generally it can be said that the concept concerning learning styles viewed in relation to the intelligence concept, first and foremost, focuses on the fact that people are different and learn in different ways. This avoids the ranking that has had such a strong position in connection with the intelligence orientation – because basically the claim is that no learning style is better than any other, but in each case it is a matter of finding the way that is best suited to learning. In this way the approach is rather parallel to Gardner's understanding of intelligence. Moreover, the concept concerning learning styles seems, to an even higher degree than the intelligence concept, to lead to the learning situation having to be adapted to some fixed characteristics of the learners and thus to overlook the fact that the learners can change and develop on the basis of the challenges they meet or are faced with.

In addition to this, the thinking in learning styles has a tendency to lead further into deliberations and instructions concerning study technique. If one learns in this way or that way, one must simply acknowledge it and do that or this. This opens up a wide field including the most detailed instructions about how to sit, the type of lighting one should use, how frequently one should take a break, how to take notes etc., as well as what could be called late-modern learning forms through so-called 'didactic toys' (i.e. toys aiming at targeted learning) for young children, exciting games with or without computers for older children, young people and adults, and even role plays where participants can learn by experimenting with their own and others' identities (for example, Montola and Stenros 2004).

10.4 Learning and gender

Gender differences with respect to learning can be treated on three different levels. First, on the bodily or physiological level, where not least gender differences in the structure and function of the brain play a key role. Second, on the psychological level, on the way in which the two sexes relate to, and experience, different forms of learning in different ways. And third, on the sociological level on the societal potential and need for learning that exist for each of the sexes.

When it comes to the physiological level, it is obvious that girls/women on average mature more quickly and that boys/men on average become bigger and stronger. This means that girls can learn a great deal earlier than boys, and that men can perform more than women in areas requiring physical strength. These are, of course, important differences, but simultaneously something we are inclined to take completely for granted and which, therefore, are not discussed to any great extent.

However, it becomes considerably more complicated when it comes to the brain physiological gender differences. In the first place, on average, men's brains are bigger and have more cells than women's, also in relation to body weight – but it is unclear whether this has any consequences for learning. There are also a number of gender differences in the brain that are linked to the sexual functions but probably do not have anything to do with learning (Solms and Turnbull 2002, pp. 223ff.).

But there are, furthermore, other and more special differences, and it would also be strange if this were not the case, because when the two genders – like many animal species – have different functions in a number of areas, corresponding, different dispositions are only to be expected. These dispositions have been developed through the selection processes that for millions of years have favoured those who were best at managing their functions and thus at surviving and reproducing (see Baron-Cohen 2003, pp. 117ff.).

It has been discussed that there are certain differences with respect to the two hemispheres of the brain, which are different in the two sexes. The main difference is that the left half of the brain, which performs a number of language functions among other things, is more developed in women, while the right half, performing, among other things, a number of logical and spatial functions, is more developed in men. More recent research has, however, shown that things are not quite so simple, in particular because different parts of the language function can be developed and located differently. The situation is rather that the language functions in girls/women are placed in both halves of the brain to a higher degree, while the greater development of spatial perception in the right half of the brain of boys/men has 'repressed' more language functions to the left half. Furthermore, it may be especially the language functions that have to do with linguistic understanding and empathy, and not the grammatical aspects of language, which girls/women are better at (see Baron-Cohen 2003, pp. 105ff.).

Another matter that can be important in this context is that the connections between the two hemispheres of the brain are more extensive in women than in men, which facilitates greater integration between the functions of the two hemispheres. Correspondingly, men's brains have a better connection between the front and back areas of each hemisphere and, therefore, greater functional integration in this dimension that could cover the connection between the working memory and the centres supplying the cognitive and emotional input it works with. Elkhonon Goldberg is of the opinion that it may be this difference in the integration potential that is most decisive for the typical differences between the sexes with respect to their mode of functioning. It must, however, be stressed once more that these are 'typical' or 'average' matters that do not necessarily apply to the single individual (Goldberg 2001, pp. 96ff.).

This leads Goldberg to the assumption that the general mental difference between the sexes can be understood as a difference in what he calls 'cognitive style' (a concept that is somewhat reminiscent of learning style as discussed above, but is more broadly defined to include cognitive function modes as such), so that women are more inclined to make 'context independent' decisions based on general impressions, while men rather make 'context dependent' decisions related to the specific situation. Goldberg emphasises that, first, this is merely an assumption based on a number of different experiments and deliberations and, second, that it is only a tendency. Both sexes make both types of decisions, and the individual need not be in accord with what is typical of the sex. In addition he thinks that 'the optimal decision-making strategy' is probably arrived at by a dynamic balance between the two types of decisions (Goldberg 2001, pp. 88ff.).

In his book entitled *The Essential Difference* English brain researcher Simon Baron-Cohen goes, however, a considerable step further when he launches the thesis that: 'The female brain is predominantly hard-wired for empathy. The male brain is predominantly hard-wired for understanding and building systems' (Baron-Cohen 2003, p. 1).

Here it is not just a matter of a cognitive style, but a general orientation that plays the role of starting point for brain function as such. Empathy covers everything that has to do with relations to others, including mutual understanding, communication, interaction and language. And system orientation covers a sense of systematic features in all possible and imaginable contexts.

The background to Baron-Cohen having developed this thesis is that for many years he has worked with autistic people who are typically characterised by one-sided, and often highly developed, insight into a rather narrow mathematical or technical area combined with little or no interest in social contact. He regards this as an extremely developed male brain, which corresponds to the fact that 90 per cent of all autistics are boys and men. Baron-Cohen then discusses what the corresponding female deviation could be – a person with 'system blindness' and 'hyper empathy' – without, however, reaching any clear conclusion (Baron-Cohen 2003, pp. 170ff.).

Baron-Cohen also, naturally, stresses on almost every page that this is a tendency or a generalisation that does not apply to the single individual. On the contrary, a woman can very well have a male-oriented brain and vice versa. But on the level of statistics this will be a distribution, which he illustrates by the figure for the gender distribution of systemising shown in Figure 10.2 (a similar but reversed figure could be drawn for the distribution of empathy).

From the point of view of learning, in my opinion both Goldberg and Baron-Cohen touch on something important when they point to some characteristic general tendencies in the brain's gender differences. I find it convincing that there are some tendencies for gender differences with respect to learning and that they, among other things, move in the directions pointed out. But precisely with their characteristically male systemising brains, I find that both Goldberg and, especially, Baron-Cohen go too far in wanting to arrive at a single characteristic feature – and thereby a signal word or label – for something that is so extremely diverse and complex. Their many reservations also indicate that in one way or another they are aware that they are on thin ice.

At the same time, on the general level I find Baron-Cohen's illustration quite persuasive both in relation to the distribution he himself is preoccupied with and in relation to many other distributions when we speak of differences between groups in psychological areas. There will almost always be a minority of extreme examples in different directions and a large overlapping majority in the middle, where several features appear in one or other form of mutual interaction.

With these deliberations, together with Goldberg and Baron-Cohen I have also already moved from the brain physiological over to the psychological level, where it is a matter of gender differences with respect to how one relates to and experiences different types of learning.

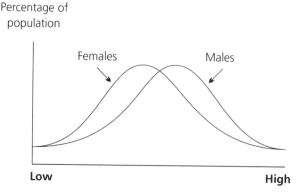

Figure 10.2 Male and female scores in systemising (Baron-Cohen 2003, p. 85)

A sphere of learning that is of particular significance in this context is gender socialisation in childhood and youth. Many theories have been put forward on how this development occurs in an interaction between the given biological factors and the current societal factors. Here I will very briefly reproduce the main points of a conception developed by American psychoanalytically oriented sociologist Nancy Chodorow (1978) and further elaborated by the two Scandinavian women researchers, Harriet Bjerrum Nielsen and Monica Rudberg, partly by comparison with a large empirical project carried out in the USA in the 1960s, which was headed by psychologist Margaret Mahler (1897–1983) (Mahler *et al.* 1975; Nielsen and Rudberg 1994 [1991]).

The basis for this conception is that the first process of separation and individuation is almost always played out between the child and its mother or another woman. This means that a boy's gender identity is fundamentally built on an experience of difference, and a girl's on an experience of similarity. When, in the course of the second year of life, the boy starts to experience separation from his mother, they are both more prepared for this separation because of the gender difference: being a big boy means being separated from mother. A mother's relationship with a girl, however, centres on similarity, making the separation process more reluctant and ambivalent.

When the boy later discovers the difference between the genders, he can come back to his mother and experience a form of intimacy with someone of the opposite gender. The girl, on the other hand, has an earlier orientation towards confidentiality and intimacy; when she discovers the gender difference in relation to her father, she sees a new way to autonomy via an intimate relationship based on difference.

This fundamental difference has a great influence on children throughout the rest of their childhood. Both genders tend to practise gender roles. This takes place best among playmates of the same gender, so during this period children are usually divided by gender. Sexuality is not absent, but it is miscommunicated. Boys have to show off, for they believe that the way to intimacy is through autonomy. Girls become absorbed in their appearance and their friendships, for they believe that the way to autonomy is through intimacy. Thus the two genders take distinctly different paths in their childhood development, and for both genders, some of these factors are sharpened through late-modern society's limitless and overwhelming stream of indirectly mediated influences, both epistemic and emotional.

This psychoanalytically oriented description of gender socialisation is, however, characterised by taking both the nature-given gender and the existing societally developed gender roles as a point of departure. In opposition to this there is, today, a social constructivist orientation that does not think that gender differences with regard to matters such as behaviour, consciousness and learning can be understood so simply, but that gender behaviour and gender consciousness are something that develops as constructions or compositions in the cultural interaction, and instead of a bipolarity between two genders are oriented towards very differentiated, complex and overlapping forms that appear in this area in late-modern society (for example, Butler 1993, 2004).

In general, it must be clear that gender-related matters develop in closely integrated interaction between dispositions and influences, and that they are important for learning to a high degree. Whether one takes a starting point in the nature-given gender or in the culturally disseminated constructions, it is also clear that in our society there exist extremely varied and complex patterns in forms of both behaviour and consciousness in this area, and thus also in the forms of learning. I also find here that Baron-Cohen's model can function as a usable summary with a large common area with broad overlapping possibilities for both genders and some more gender-specific border areas – but it is, naturally, a far cry from such a general view to the diversity of concrete expressions that are part of this complex field.

In the specific area of learning there is extensive material concerning calculations and discussions about gender differences, for example, typically in connection with applications for different education programmes. But, on the other hand, there are not very many more theoretically oriented contributions in the area. Within the American feminist traditions, however, there are two important books written by women researchers Mary Belenky, Blythe Clinchy, Nancy Goldberger and Jill Tarule, namely, *Women's Ways of Knowing* (Belenky *et al.* 1986), based on an extensive interview study, and *Knowledge, Difference, and Power* (Goldberger *et al.* 1996), in which the many reactions to the first book are discussed.

In the first of these books women's perspectives on knowledge are listed in the following five main categories:

1   Silence – a position in which women experience themselves as mindless and voiceless and subjects to the whims of external authority. (They are passive, feel incompetent, and are defined by others.)
2   Received knowledge – a perspective from which women conceive of themselves as capable of receiving, even reproducing, knowledge from the all-knowing external authorities but not capable of creating knowledge on their own. (They listen to the voices of others; their world is literal and concrete, good or bad.)
3   Subjective knowledge – a perspective from which truth and knowledge are conceived of as personal, private and subjectively known or intuited. (The locus of truth shifts to the self; intuition is valued over logic and abstraction; here women begin to gain a voice. Half the women in the study were in this category.)

4 Procedural knowledge – a position in which women are invested in learning and applying objective procedures for obtaining and communicating knowledge. (This position takes two forms: separate knowing – the self is separate from the object of discourse, making it possible to doubt and reason; and connected knowing – there is intimacy and equality between the self and the object of discourse, based on empathetic understanding.)

5 Constructed knowledge – a position in which women view all knowledge as contextual, experience themselves as creators of knowledge, and value both subjective and objective strategies for knowing. (This stage is characterized by the development of an authentic voice.)

(Quoted after a summary in Merriam and Caffarella 1999, pp. 146–147)

This is an important statement both because it has something to say on women's different forms of knowledge on an empirical basis and because, as a whole, it reveals that the acquisition of knowledge can take many different forms, and thus also, from the point of view of gender and in general, distance itself from an understanding of knowledge in the sense of something that is, or should be, objective, logical and cohesive. But one could also ask whether the very dimension from dependence to independence that characterises the statement could not also be utilised to describe men's forms of learning.

The material available in this area is, however, even more limited, but as a counterweight to the article by Belenky *et al.* reference can be made to an article by American cognition researcher John R. Anderson, in which he characterises the cognitive style to which Euro-American men in the USA are oriented as context-independent, analytical and non-affective while, for example, American men of African or Native American origin and many Euro-American women in the USA practise a more context-dependent, relational, holistic, and affective style (Anderson 1988).

The conclusion must be along the lines that, in the dominant Euro-American cultures at any rate, there are obvious tendencies towards general gender differences in the way in which learning is practised, but that considerable differences also exist within both genders and one must make significant reservations when talking about female and male forms of learning.

At the level of society it is well known that there are big differences at school and in education programmes with respect to the subject of educational directions mainly preferred by the two sexes, and the learning preferences that this reflects. In addition, the situation in Denmark today is that there are, in general, more women than men in the education system, and at the same time concerned voices are heard to express that the primary and lower secondary school has become 'feminised' – there are more female than male teachers, the teaching appeals more to the girls than the boys, and more boys than girls 'give up' or are referred to remedial teaching. Moreover, the modern teaching forms with project work and the like in many parts of the education system seem to appeal more to the female than the male students.

There are, thus, indications that, at present, approaches to learning and education that appeal more to women than to men have achieved such dominance in some places that boys and men, in general, have greater difficulties in the school and education system, and that, in general, women are on the way to achieving a better level of education than men. To this can be said, however, that men outside the education system are maintaining their privileged position in a large number of contexts typically concerning status, pay and influence. Irrespective of how much talk there is about the importance of education in society, gender would seem to mean more than education in a large number of key areas.

On the whole, matters to do with gender and learning appear to be a reflection of the fact that there is a tendency in the area of learning towards some gender-related differences that are in line with other gender differences on the levels of consciousness and behaviour. On the societal level, on the other hand, there are some other differences that are part of the way in which society in general relates differently to the sexes. Thus, with respect to gender differences learning is no different from the broader patterns of which it is a part – and if anything is to be changed, it would seem that it cannot be done only by relating to learning but must become part of some developments to do with the situation of the sexes more generally.

10.5 Social background and ethnicity

During the last decades of the twentieth century the concept of 'social heredity' became widely accepted in Denmark as a term for the ancient phenomenon that individuals' social background – rather than, for example, some form of intelligence or the like – is statistically the most powerful factor of significance for the position in the social hierarchy that is achieved by the individual, a phenomenon that is also well known in many other countries (for example, Coleman *et al.* 1966; Jencks *et al.* 1972; Bowles and Gintis 1976).

In Scandinavia the concept itself comes from a book published in 1969 by Swedish psychiatrist Gustav Jonsson (1907–1994), who worked with young criminals (Jonsson 1969). It was precisely at the time when the welfare societies were really undergoing development in Northern Europe that scholarly interest in these matters came into focus at international level and, more or less simultaneously, a number of more qualitative contributions were published to the understanding of the way in which social heredity shows through in practice. English sociolinguist Basil Bernstein (1924–2000) found significant and profound differences in language between the language codes of the working and the middle class ('restricted' and 'elaborated' code, Bernstein 1971), while the so-called 'Birmingham School' in England uncovered the significance of various matters to do with sub-cultures and consciousness among the young, *inter alia* in the key book by Paul Willis entitled *Learning to Labour: How Working Class Kids get Working Class Jobs* (Willis 1977), which was a detailed account of class-specific work socialisation. Finally, mention should be made of French sociologists Pierre Bourdieu and Claude Passéron's more general book on social reproduction (Bourdieu and Passéron 1977 [1970]).

In many European countries in the wake of all this came several political initiatives aiming, for example, at getting rid of social imbalance and reducing the proportion of young people who do not complete any education after primary and lower secondary school. But, in general, it has not proved even remotely possible to live up to the ambitious targets of creating 'equality through education' through the measures of education policy that there was political will to utilise. Already at the beginning of the 1970s Danish education researcher and sociologist Erik Jørgen Hansen argued strongly that obtaining 'equality of chances' would not be enough. The children of the affluent will always be able to exploit equal chances better than the less privileged, and only by openly favouring the weaker groups could the target be approached (Hansen 1972).

In addition, in the course of the last 10 to 15 years two large-scale, problematic challenges concerning societal education and learning opportunities have appeared on the scene.

The one concerns the whole issue about adult education programmes raised internationally through the slogan of 'lifelong learning' – and where we once again are confronted on a massive scale by the so-called 'Matthew effect' that 'for whoever has to him shall be given and he shall be caused to be in abundance' (Matthew 13:12), i.e. that those who already are the best educated participate in adult education programmes to a considerably greater extent than those with brief schooling (see Illeris 2004).

The second concerns all the education problems linked to the integration of immigrants and refugees, including language teaching, general education and vocationally oriented education and training. This is a problem complex ranging far beyond education, but where special educational efforts that can satisfy these groups' many and different needs nevertheless must, of necessity, be a key element in any attempt to create better integration.

I will not go further into these wide-ranging issues that are peripheral to the theme of this book. But it is, naturally, extremely important to maintain that the question of possibilities for, and interest in, participating in institutionalised education is very comprehensive and diverse and that social, cultural and ethnic factors in this area are at least as significant as questions to do with individual abilities, gender and other personal matters.

10.6 Summary

The individual person's capacity for learning is of a general biological, social cultural and ethnic nature as well as being individual and personal. It is also characteristic that the many different factors involved are interwoven in a huge, unclear pattern.

On the individual level, there is the 'classic' issue to do with intelligence and skills, where there are various competing theories and a discussion which, at times, is passionate. On the one hand, it is clear that different people in a complex interaction between hereditary and environmental matters have developed different dispositions for different kinds of learning, but, on the other hand, it must also be maintained that these dispositions can always be altered and developed. Moreover, again on the level of statistics, there would seem to exist some gender-related learning differences. And finally, attempts have been made to identify some general differences in learning style, even though the picture is very unclear in this area.

On the general level, first and foremost, it has been very convincingly shown that so-called 'social heredity', despite a great number of political measures designed to counteract it, still makes a powerful impact on the way in which the groups who educationally, socially, economically and culturally have the best prerequisites also, in general, both quantitatively and qualitatively, obtain or become involved in most education, and attain higher levels in the education system. It does not appear possible to break or decisively reduce this connection by means of the education policy measures for which political will has existed up to now. But it is emphasised that even though these conditions show clearly in the statistics, they do not automatically apply for the individual.

Chapter 11

Learning and life course

Just as different people have different learning possibilities, there are also considerable age differences in how learning is managed and progresses. Cognitive maturation, social and societal situation and some very different motivation structures have an important influence on the learning-related changes that take place in the course of a life. This chapter describes what is characteristic of learning in each of the four main life ages: childhood, youth, adulthood and mature adulthood. Finally, there is a discussion of what is characteristic of this development as a whole.

11.1 Lifespan psychology

While the previous chapter focused on different features of different people and groups of people of possible importance for learning – skills, learning style, gender, social background and ethnicity – this chapter will concern what characterises learning at the different stages in the course of life. It is important to maintain here the relation to all of the three dimensions of learning, because even if there is a certain degree of maturing with respect to the learning capacity for content, it can, to at least the same extent, be emotional, motivational, social and societal conditions that change with age and create different learning possibilities and conditions.

In the following my point of departure will be in the special research area that has been termed lifespan psychology (for example, Baltes and Schaie 1973; Sugarman 2001), because more clearly than biographical research (see section 5.6) it relates to the age aspect in the development of the life course.

In lifespan psychology the focus is not on the individual person as such, but primarily on the identification and demarcation of various life ages and their characteristics – and from this it becomes quite clear that people in different life ages generally have essentially different motivational structures and different perspectives on learning and education.

Lifespan psychology really began in the 1930s as an extension of child and developmental psychology into that of adult life (Bühler 1933, 1968). Already at this point there were considerations of different phase divisions for the life course and, later, there have been many attempts to divide life up into a number of life ages based on various criteria, including Erikson's eight-stage staircase model, Kolb's three-stage conical model and Fjord Jensen's four-stage displaced double life arch model, all of which were discussed in detail earlier (sections 8.4 and 8.6).

There is a widespread conception in lifespan psychology that the various life ages typically have attached to them various orientations or 'tasks', which partially determine the learning motivation; also that the life ages are separated by periods of major or minor crisis, in which the prevailing orientation is brought to an end and replaced by a new one.

I do not want to go into detail here about the various concrete phase or stage divisions. It seems obvious to me that although there might be differences in determining the exact transition points and other phase distinctions, nevertheless there is broad agreement on four main phases of interest with respect to learning, namely, childhood, youth, adulthood and mature adulthood. (I use here Giddens's term (1993) 'mature adulthood' – in place of 'old age' – because the latter concept easily brings to mind ideas of weakness. In many cases there is, in fact, a fifth phase after mature adulthood, in which there is a weakening of the cognitive functions and thus of the capacity for learning. Naturally, this may be important and interesting to work on – What is the nature of this weakness? What slips out and what is retained? How can the person relate to that? etc. – but it is beyond the perspective of this book.)

In my view, these four phases, in relation to learning, can today be characterised as follows:

Childhood lasts from birth to the onset of puberty, which occurs these days around the age of 11–13 (previously it was at a later point). In terms of learning, childhood centres on the child developing and capturing its world.

Youth lasts from puberty until the preconditions for a more or less stable adulthood are established, typically through relatively permanent relationships with partners and work, or perhaps a consciousness of not wanting to enter into such relationships. It is a characteristic of present-day society that the period of youth is longer than it has ever previously been, and has a very fluid transition to adulthood; it is quite within the bounds of normality for it to finish anywhere between the ages of about 20 and 35. The end of it will often be incomplete, with a degree of connection to the youth phase being carried over into adulthood. In terms of learning, youth centres on the development of a personal identity – although social constructionists and postmodernists claim that this is not possible in our existing society (see section 7.8).

Adulthood lasts from the end of the youth period until the 'life turn' – a concept which has been fully discussed in Danish by Fjord Jensen (1993) implying that the end of life has been perceived on the distant horizon, and the person is beginning to accept this and relate to it. The actual moment of the life turn and thus the transition from the first part of adulthood to mature adulthood is extremely fluid within the period stretching between the ages of about 45 to 65. There are also considerable differences between the genders in the nature of this transition. In terms of learning, the main orientation in adulthood is broadly towards the management of the life course and its challenges, typically centring on family and work, and, more broadly, on interests, lifestyle and attitudes.

Mature adulthood lasts until death, or in terms of learning, perhaps only until mental weakness begins to take hold to a considerable extent, see above. In learning terms, mature adulthood – if energy and other circumstances permit it – is typically oriented towards bringing about meaning and harmony in life and of being satisfied with a personal form of 'life wisdom' as a kind of summarising understanding of existence and the course of life.

In the following four sections I will look more closely at learning motivation and opportunities for learning in these four life ages, drawing on material from lifespan psychology as well as from sources and experiences that more directly concern the individual life ages. Then, in conclusion, I will try to point out certain trends that run through the life ages and link them together to a degree.

11.2 Children want to capture their world

The overall characteristic of children's learning is that, in line with their development, they are absorbed in capturing the world by which they see themselves surrounded and of which they are a part. In child psychology there are comprehensive descriptions of the many different facets and stages in this capturing process, including, for example, Freud's division into phases, Erikson's developmental ages and Piaget's stage theory. Here I will only point out certain overriding factors that determine some of the general conditions for the process.

In learning terms, it is naturally important that the cognitive learning capacity develops gradually throughout childhood – this is what Piaget's stage theory is about. When Bruner asserted that any subject can be taught in some intellectually honest form to any child at any stage of development (Bruner 1960; see section 8.6), this does not mean that children of any age can learn anything – but the reverse: that teaching must be appropriate to the children's age and presuppositions.

In addition it is an important factor that children basically expect to be guided by their parents and other adults as to what and how they should learn. As babies their only connection with the surrounding world is through the mother and other adults, and the first 'capture' involves establishing the separation between themselves and the surrounding world. The child is, from the start, subject to the control of adults and can only gradually free itself from it – Alfred Lorenzer and Daniel Stern in particular have, in my view, produced important descriptions of this process (especially Lorenzer 1972; see section 7.5; Stern 1985; see sections 4.7 and 8.4).

In childcare institutions and in the early years at school, children are still obliged to unfold and develop within a framework set by adults. They must, of necessity, accept this as a basic condition, even though naturally they can resist when they feel that they are being restricted or they are unable to understand what is going on – and this resistance is also a highly significant factor in development and learning (see my treatment of the concept of resistance in section 9.5). However, children are typically ready to accept explanations that tell them that learning something may be good or important for them later even if they cannot grasp it right now.

Nevertheless, the development of our late-modern society has brought about certain trends for change that apply to some of these basic factors affecting learning in childhood. These have been clearly identified by Thomas Ziehe (Ziehe and Stubenrauch 1982), but also appear in many other places.

In general, cultural liberation gives children plenty of opportunities for activities, relations and impulses which previously lay beyond their reach, while at the same time, the disintegration of traditions and norms weakens or removes a number of fixed points and structures from which children could previously take their bearings. Like young people and adults, children today perceive a number of potential choices from an early age – of which some are real and many others are only apparent – while previously there was a much higher degree of certainty, for good or ill.

The mass media play a special role here. More than parents or other adults, they give children the opportunity to experience – or often almost force on to them – a mass of impulses, including things such as catastrophes, violence and sex; experiences to which they have not previously had access, and which can have strong emotional influences on them, as well as introducing these things in advance of the formation of personal experience, making it more complicated for them to later acquire their own experiences in these spheres.

Another important factor is that developments in some spheres of society can happen so fast that adults have difficulty keeping up, while children can leap, so to speak, straight into the development at its present stage, which in some areas makes them able to overtake adults. This typically occurs in the field of information technology, where teachers and parents often find that some of the children know more than they do themselves.

From a learning perspective, it is generally important to remember that childhood as a life age is basically influenced by the huge acquisition process of integrating and relating to the whole of the complex material, social and societal environment. This requires a broad spectrum of protracted constructive processes that the child is disposed to carry out, trusting in adults and being supported by them. Childhood is typically a period of primarily gentle, gradual and stable assimilative learning processes, even though these processes have tended to become more complex and contradictory. Examples of the processes that are gone through are motor and linguistic development, acquisition of symbol management (including reading, writing and arithmetic), and knowledge of the surrounding world and its rules, structures and means of function.

It is not so strange that Piaget, who performed exhaustive studies of some of these processes, gained a perception of the assimilative processes as central to learning, for in the years of childhood and in the cognitive sphere, the assimilative processes are, indeed, extremely comprehensive. It is also these factors school is traditionally based on, and this is part of the reason why school is organised the way it is.

In connection with these assimilative processes, there also occur a number of accommodations, which are typically of the limited and correctional nature that Piaget paid attention to – directed towards getting the acquisition process back on track again when it has gone astray. However, in other spheres there are large and decisive accommodations in childhood learning – particularly in the spheres connected to identity development, including the development of gender roles (corresponding to Piaget's conception of the decisive role of accommodations in the individuation process, see section 4.2). These factors are elaborated and strengthened in the next life age, that of youth.

11.3 Young people want to construct their identities

Youth has not always been perceived as existing as a life age in its own right. Historically the concept of youth developed together with capitalism and industrialisation: 'The adolescent was invented at the same time as the steam-engine. The practical architect of the latter was Watt in 1765, of the former Rousseau in 1762' (Musgrove 1965, p. 33).

Swiss-French philosopher Jean-Jacques Rousseau (1712–1778) published his famous book 'Emile' in 1762, putting child-centred pedagogy on the agenda. At that time, a need was growing in the bourgeoisie for an extended schooling or period of upbringing in which the next generation could acquire the knowledge they would need, as well as suitable behaviour – and at the same time Rousseau agitated for a child's right to be a child until that point.

In the beginning, the concept of youth was limited to a few years, but gradually it became a longer period and the notion of youth increasingly spread beyond the middle classes:

> The definition of the adolescent implied a theory of the rate of progress towards maturity. This rate was to be retarded (or allowed to find its hypothetically 'natural' level) in order to insert between childhood and adulthood a discrete and distinctive phase of human growth and development.
>
> (Musgrove 1965, p. 51)

Thus, the period of youth has, from the start, been linked with a particular need for socially necessary learning and personal development. In German-Austrian-American Charlotte Bühler's (1893–1974) first work on lifespan psychology in 1933, she placed youth in an age interval from the age of about 15 to about 25, as the last half of the human period of growing up (Bühler 1933). And with Erik Erikson's book, mentioned earlier, *Identity, Youth and Crises*, the conception of youth took the direction typical for the interpretation today, which is that youth is primarily a period for a more or less crisis-determined development of a personal identity or self-comprehension (Erikson 1968).

Historically, the development of the concept of youth has thus occurred in relation to the emphasis which, in the middle classes, was placed on the independent individual from the 1700s onwards. However, with the development of late-modernity, recent decades have seen a further expansion of the period of youth, so today it may often last up to 20 years. In addition, youth has become very much idealised – and commercialised – as the age of freedom, no responsibilities, and happiness, while, at the same time, the personal and societal problems that attach to youth seem to be steadily increasing.

The essence of this development, particularly as seen from a learning perspective, is that the demands on the formation of identity have undergone an explosive growth in line with cultural liberation – it is definitely not by chance that in Danish we often talk of 'identity work', which young people have to do, as well as getting through their education, form relationships with a partner and find their place in society.

Previously there was family affiliation, a gender role, class attachment and usually also an attachment to a particular profession, as well as a mass of given values and norms that the young person was expected to take on, perhaps through a somewhat rebellious process; now all this is disintegrating or becoming redundant, and young people must find their own way through their own choices. It is not only about education, career, partner and home; also lifestyle and personal identity and much more must be chosen. Development in these areas has been overwhelming, and young people and society currently have to struggle with new, untried processes, the conditions of which change almost from day to day – new educational opportunities, new consumer opportunities, new communications systems and new lifestyle offers make themselves felt in an almost chaotic confusion, everything seems possible, and yet young people perceive countless limitations, for many opportunities are completely inaccessible for the vast majority – only very few can become actors, television hosts, designers or sporting heroes, even though many secretly wish for it and do what they can in the hope of achieving it.

According to Piaget at least, human beings are cognitively fully developed from puberty, i.e. they have reached the formal operational stage and are equipped to think logically and deductively. But, more recently, several education researchers have pointed out that, on the one hand, far from all adults master this form of thought (see Shayer and Adey 1981), and, on the other hand, throughout the period of youth new possibilities can be developed for thinking dialectically, making use of practical logic, recognising how one can know, what one knows (meta-cognition), and mastering critical reflection (Brookfield 2000b). Modern brain research has most recently shown that the working memory – the brain centre that precisely stands for such advanced cognitive functions, is only fully developed at the end of the teenage years (see Gogtay *et al.* 2004). It is, thus, only during the period of youth that, together with all the other changes that take place during these years, we acquire our full cognitive capacity.

In terms of learning, the first part of the youth period is still subject to compulsory education, and later – at any rate according to society's target – one should go through some youth education and, as a rule, also some further education of a more vocational nature. However, although this would appear to be education with a specific subject content, all learning in the youth period from the age of about 12 or 13 onwards is very much oriented towards the formation of identity and can only be understood in this light.

This contradictory relationship leads to a number of problems, because the school and education system developed primarily to deal with subject learning, while matters of identity in its broadest sense are what young people are concerned about. Therefore, young people react more or less reluctantly to the academic subject requirements, which for the most part are forced upon them, and which they often find outdated, while the representatives of the system attempt to keep the pupils' concentration on the academic work, which they themselves are trained in, are committed to, and are under an obligation to uphold.

Upper secondary school (gymnasium) can be seen as a typical battlefield for this conflict. An increasing number of young people go on to attend upper secondary school, for academic education is more and more becoming a sine qua non if you want to get on in life. However, upper secondary school subjects and their content, and many of the teachers' qualifications and ways of thinking, are firmly rooted in a time that no longer exists.

Pupils go on to upper secondary school because it is their only option, and because here they can meet other young people with the same needs and problems, while the subjects, teaching and marks are, for many, a kind of necessary evil, which do not seem to be of much use to anyone. The teachers try to maintain in themselves and in others an understanding that, despite all, what is happening is both meaningful and important, and there are fervent hopes that pupils will 'take responsibility for their own learning'. However, who wants to take responsibility for something they do not feel they have any great influence on?

One of the most striking effects of these factors is considerable problems to do with enrolment in technical and scientific courses in a number of countries. Even though these courses bring employment opportunities with high status in society, high priority and good salaries, most young people go in other directions, typically towards humanistic, social, pedagogical and societal subjects, for these provide far better opportunities for establishing an interaction between the academic content and the formation of identity.

The identity process is, for most young people today, far more immediately important and far more urgent than career orientation, and in one way it is also a precondition for the choice of career, or part of it. So from the perspective of young people, there is good reason for the many searching activities, shifts and years out that the system views as expensive delays in the education of young people.

The most important things for young people to learn today are to be able to orient themselves, to be able to make choices that can be answered for, to keep up with everything, not to waste their lives on the wrong thing, to be able to decline in the many situations where a choice has to be made. Society and employers also demand maturity, independence, responsibility etc. – and as far as academic qualifications are concerned, there is always something to be got out of it if you do what you are interested in. Yet, nobody can say which academic qualifications will be relevant in five or ten years' time, so everyone must be prepared to go on to further education throughout most of life. The best security for the future is not to learn a subject on what are perceived as traditional premises, but to be ready to change and take hold of what is relevant in many different situations. Uncertainty cannot be countered by stability, but only by being open, flexible and constantly oriented to learning (see Simonsen 2000).

Youth is also the period in which to learn how to deal with gender and sexual relations. For both genders this is closely linked with the personal identity process – and here, as in education, it is most often the formation of identity that is given priority: young people today are often more absorbed in reflecting themselves in their partners than they are in the partners themselves. Typically, then, things start with great dreams of the ideal partnership, but the reality turns out to be a rocky road with turbulent ups and downs or obstructions, vulnerability and hurt over many years with unsettled relationships.

There is so much to be learnt in the period of youth: academically, emotionally, socially, societally – and, most of all, in terms of identity. Whereas childhood is a time for constructive assimilative learning, youth is a period for major accommodations and transformations in which, one by one, profound changes and reconstructions are made to the knowledge structures and the emotional patterns with regard to identity in a broad sense and to educational and social relationships etc. And the reflexivity that is so characteristic of late-modernity (see section 5.6), where it is always the individual's relationship to him- or herself that is the focal point of learning, unfolds without doubt most dramatically in the years of youth as an essential yet enormously taxing tool for the identity process.

11.4 Adults pursue their life goals

The beginning of the adult period might typically be marked by external events such as starting a family or finishing education. There are no decisively new cognitive opportunities; what happens in terms of learning and consciousness is that the person fully takes on the management of, and responsibility for, his or her own life, with this normally occurring gradually as a long process throughout the years of youth and into adulthood. All models in lifespan psychology include a phase called adulthood, perhaps with a distinction between a first and second adulthood. This phase is typically characterised by the following:

- the person has moved from his or her childhood home and has taken responsibility for his or her own life project;
- basic education is completed, perhaps including the gaining of a specific professional competence;
- the person is in a family situation or similar with a partner, and very often with children;
- the person is aiming for, and in many cases gains, a more or less permanent position in the labour market;
- there may be changes in the family situation and/or the work situation.

Naturally, not everyone realises, or wishes to realise, all of these things, but to a great extent they comprise a general societal norm, and surveys of youth show that this is also what the great majority of young people imagine for themselves, although they are not prepared to go that far before they have tried out a great number of options (for example, Simonsen 1994) – and they perhaps stop off at some of the areas, or all of them, before they get there.

In general, adulthood has traditionally been marked by a kind of ambition that implies a striving to realise more or less clear life aims relating to family, career, interests or something else – but in late-modernity this representation is also on its way to being overlaid by the continual societal changes, the unpredictability of the future, the conditioning of the market mechanism and the unending succession of apparent choices.

Many factors that were, in earlier times, for good or ill, already marked out for the individual, have now become things to be decided on again and again. It is no longer possible to make your choice of life course once and for all when young, and then expect to spend the rest of your life accomplishing it. Whereas once a large number of factors were given, based on gender, for example, or class affiliations, all now appears to be redundant. The fact that this is only how it appears can be seen from statistics showing that the large majority of people, now just as previously, live their lives in the way that their gender and social background has prepared them for – this is what is called 'social heredity' (see section 10.5). However, this does not influence the perception that now this is something people choose themselves, something for which they are responsible, and thus have only themselves to blame if it turns out to be unsatisfactory.

Just a generation ago, there were still relatively firm learning and consciousness patterns that were taken as given based on gender, class and degree of urbanisation during upbringing. There was, as a typical basis for the general conception, the authoritarian, patriarchal, middle-class man, a pillar of society and an idealised norm – this could, and still can, be indirectly seen in a great deal of law, history, sociology and psychology. There was also his wife with her solicitous, modest and ambivalent function of housewife. There was a working class with a close-knit worker culture and consciousness, based on the experience of being the oppressed who carried out the toil of society; there were the women with their double burden of family and work and its attendant ambivalence; and there were also the industrious and often narrow-minded independent lower middle classes and country dwellers. There was a merging of societal position, learning, education and forms of consciousness, which were limited and often repressive, but which also created a pattern the individual could follow (Simonsen and Illeris 1989).

Just some 20 years ago, Danish life-mode researchers Thomas Højrup and Lone Rahbek Christensen were able to mark out and differentiate by gender three main life modes – the self-employed life mode, the wage-worker life mode and the success-oriented life mode – as guidelines for the structuring of life and consciousness that applied to most of the population (Højrup 1983; Christensen 1987). However, a large survey of trade union members in the 1990s showed that the traditional working class now covered four very different patterns of attitudes (Jørgensen *et al.* 1992), late-modern sociologists relativised the traditional concept of class long ago (e.g. Giddens 1993), and social constructionists and postmodernists question the very concept of identity (see section 7.8).

With these developments, learning in adulthood has taken on a completely new perspective. With the earlier, firmer structures, the individual could use his or her years of youth to develop an identity, or at least a sort of draft identity, that would be of help in governing future learning. In career terms, school and education would have provided for the acquisition of a groundwork that was regarded as feasible for the rest of that person's life, so that whatever was needed later could generally be gained through practice learning at work and maybe a few additional courses. In life, also, it was necessary to keep up with any developments, but this did not go too fast for people to manage to get the requisite learning as they went along. Thus, for the vast majority of people, learning in adulthood was fairly manageable and predominantly assimilative in nature, with its most characteristic aspect probably being the development of a system of defence mechanisms that could screen out any new impulses that were too insistent, thus ensuring stability and self-respect.

Becoming an adult formally in our society means coming of age and so taking responsibility for one's own life and actions. This happens legally (in Denmark) on the eighteenth birthday, but from a psychological perspective it is actually a process, as has been mentioned earlier in the text, and it is characteristic that this process has become longer and longer, to such an extent that today it is most often accomplished well into a person's twenties or perhaps never. Late-modern society's promotion of youth makes it difficult to let it go.

In the field of education the prolongation of this process goes hand in hand with the continual extension of the average time spent in education. It is not so very long ago that the majority of Denmark's population received only seven years' schooling, but today there are nine years of compulsory education and a clear state target that everyone should have at least 12 years' education; and a majority go on to a further course of education of a longer or shorter length before the end of the preliminary period of education. In addition to this the adult education programmes have been greatly developed and vocationally related, although there has been a considerable decline in participation, probably only temporary, in recent years. Young people's expectations today are for recurrent or lifelong education, and they find it difficult to imagine that they 'could be stuck' in the same job all their lives.

However, it is basically characteristic that adults learn what they want, and have very little inclination to acquire something they do not want, i.e. something they do not perceive as meaningful for their own life goals, of which they are aware in varying degrees of clarity. A rule of thumb for understanding adults' learning would state that:

- adults learn what they want to learn and what is meaningful for them to learn;
- adults draw on the resources they already have in their learning;
- adults take as much responsibility for their learning as they want to take (if they are allowed to); and
- adults are not very inclined to engage in learning of which they cannot see the meaning or have any interest in (see Illeris 2004).

As a consequence of this, rather than having various more or less unconnected motives as the foundation for their educational and learning activities, adults have more coherent strategies relating to goals that are normally fairly clear and known to the individual (Ahrenkiel and Illeris 2000).

In the previous section I looked at how the conflict between the respective interests of the system and the participants dominates youth education today, creating major problems. In adult education these problems are traditionally different because adult education is nearly always voluntary in principle. Nevertheless, very many participants in adult education today have been indirectly forced to take part in the education programmes, and many even feel they have been 'placed' by different counselling bodies. It is experienced as particularly contradictory when one feels that one is an adult and would like to manage one's own life. Therefore, adult education programmes are, at present, a strange mixture of old ideals concerning public enlightenment and modern vocational orientation and economically oriented direction (see Ahrenkiel and Illeris 2000; Illeris 2004).

With the pace of change and need for reorganisation in the late-modern period, the phrase lifelong learning primarily implies a need to be constantly prepared for reorganisation (see Jarvis 2002; Coffield 2003). This can be hard enough for young people, but for those who first got caught up in this development as adults, the challenge of reorganisation is even harder. The stability, self-assurance and professional pride that were crucial qualifications for many a few years ago, now seem like burdensome encumbrances. Where before there was stability, there now has to be flexibility, and if there is to be any hope of survival in the job market, the defence mechanisms of stability must very quickly be replaced with service-mindedness and readiness for change – regardless of whether the defence has been developed in the form of middle-class values or a limiting wage-worker consciousness.

Societal demands that adults must learn on a far greater scale and in a totally different way than previously, are inescapable on every level. It is primarily a demand for a mental reorganisation and personal development, but there might also be technical or academic demands, e.g. typically in connection with information technology developments. In other words, these are demands for profound accommodative processes of a reflexive nature – and that is something many adults will not spontaneously accept.

At the same time, however, there are still many participants in adult education who are there of their own free will because they wish to, or need to, learn something specific – and in some cases for more social reasons also. On this basis it might be expected that these adults would, themselves, take responsibility for the learning the course is providing. However, ordinary conceptions and experiences of education often get in the way of this. Even though the institutions, the teachers and the participants might say and believe otherwise, everyone in the education situation obstinately expects that the responsibility will lie with the teacher. It is, after all, the teacher who knows what has got to be learnt.

The situation is paradoxical, for while these adult participants have a tendency to behave like pupils, they have a very hard time accepting the lack of authority the traditional pupil role entails. They get bored and become resistant in a more or less conscious way – but, nevertheless, they will not themselves take on the responsibility, for that is actually far more demanding. The conflict can only be resolved by effectively making a conscious break with the prevailing roles as pupils and teachers at school. And as a rule it is the teacher who has to take the initiative and insist on it. It is normally only when the participants realise that they truly can take responsibility and use the teacher as a support for their own learning that the picture alters, and after that the way is clear for the learning to become goal-directed, effective, transcendent and libidinal, as is characteristic of a learning process actually chosen by the individual (Illeris 1998).

However, there is much to suggest that the conditions described here stand in the way of complete changes. The 'new youth' of late-modernity, who have in recent years turned youth education upside down, are well on their way to making their entry into adult education as the 'new adults'. In 1998, Birgitte Simonsen made the following remark about this development:

> In a few years' time, these young people will really come into adult education, and then we will need all the flexibility we can get. In the field of adult education we in Denmark have an extremely well founded tradition for heterogeneity, which makes us hopeful. If, on the other hand, current trends towards homogeneity in large inflexible systems get the upper hand, major problems should be anticipated.
>
> (Simonsen 1998, p. 213)

Today this prediction is well on the way to being fulfilled, but at the same time it is mixed with the trends towards pressure and compulsion which have really gathered strength in the intervening years, and with tendencies towards savings, because there is a lack of political will to pay the bill for the lifelong learning for all, which is otherwise the professed creed.

11.5 Mature adults seek meaning and harmony

'The age of maturity', 'the third age' or 'second adulthood' are all terms for the phase of life that for most people in modern society lies between the so-called life turn and actual old age, and can well last a period of 20 years or more.

The life turn is a psychological phenomenon concerning the perception and acknowledgement that the remaining time in your life is not unlimited. It is, however, most often external events that bring about and mark the life turn – typical examples are the children leaving home, losing a job, taking early retirement or being given reduced hours; it can also be a divorce or the death of a near one, and for women the menopause may play a part in the situation (see Jensen 1993).

In contrast to the first age of adulthood, the mature age is characteristically not dominated by the same form of purposefulness – the goals being reached for do not have the same existential nature as having a family, raising children, or work and career. As far as they are able – and the mature age is for many today a period with a certain personal and financial ability – people spend their time on things they perceive as quality activities, such as cultural or social activities, helping others, their partner, if they have one, their children, grandchildren, or disadvantaged groups they are involved with.

In this context there may often be important elements of learning, both formal education and less formal processes of development and change, characterised by being something absolutely chosen by the persons themselves, because it is something they want to do, something they consider important for themselves or for other people. It can also be that the persons need to prove to themselves and to others that there are things they are well capable of, that they simply have not had the opportunity to do previously.

Learning in mature adulthood can thus be characterised by a personal libidinal motivation, without that aura of necessity or external incentive that often forms the basis for learning in earlier adulthood. This could apply to things one would like to study, things one would like to understand, or experience, or learn and use in specific contexts.

However, it must be remembered that this only applies to relatively privileged mature adults. Many people have more than enough to do just getting by practically and financially, and have neither the opportunity nor the reserves to look towards the self-actualisation or learning in which those in more favourable positions increasingly become involved. The new wave of learning and education for mature adults is, for the time being, a middle-class phenomenon mainly.

Cognitively there might be a trend towards learning beginning to go more slowly if it concerns new areas the person is not very committed to, but this does not normally apply when it concerns things he or she is interested in, and for which he or she has good presuppositions and experiences. The usual popular notion that elderly people are worse at learning things can thus be seen to relate only to the fact that they can be slower in learning something new – which they are often not particularly interested in acquiring. They are satisfied with their own interests and experiences, and if the new matter is not connected to that, it can make it more difficult to mobilise psychological energy.

It is something else, of course, if it is a case of dementia or other diseases – this is not within the scope of the present book – but it is still worth noting that even when such disability occurs there would seem to be a tendency for it not to directly affect the areas where one has special competence and which one has maintained, and where the brain, therefore, has been 'kept in good condition' (Goldberg 2005).

More generally it can be said that learning in mature adulthood that exceeds the here and now is often concerned with creating an overall picture or a holistic understanding of life's experience and contexts. Many researchers and authors have used the concept of 'wisdom' in this connection (see Merriam and Caffarella 1999, pp. 161ff.; Stuart-Hamilton 2000) – among others also some of the learning theoreticians who have been referred to in the above, e.g. David Kolb, Erik Erikson and Peter Jarvis (Kolb 1984; Erikson *et al.* 1986; Jarvis 2001a).

However, it seems to be difficult to pin down what wisdom actually is. There are very many different definitions of the concept, and a number of American researchers have, as usual, tried to divide wisdom up into elements or dimensions so that it takes on the character of a special form of intelligence that comes with age.

As I see it, wisdom is mainly a popular concept – something many others have also stated. What is understood by wisdom in myths and ordinary everyday language is fundamentally characterised by being something strongly subjective and person related. It is precisely the whole that a person can create of his or her total experience and understandings and which, if it is weighty and important, can be regarded by others as practical common sense of a more immediate nature than the expert knowledge with which we are constantly confronted in the modern world. It is not everyone who can achieve what others acknowledge as wisdom. But it may nevertheless be a good expression for the type of learning many strive for in mature adulthood.

11.6 Learning through the life ages

In the previous sections I have looked at some typical current background attitudes to learning in various life ages. It is important to stress that these are current attitudes, for life ages are only rooted in biology to a certain extent. The details of the various life ages are, to a great extent, determined by history and society, and can alter rapidly. It has become clear, for example, how late-modernity has influenced learning today, particularly in childhood and youth, but also increasingly in adulthood.

A large-scale Finnish study of life and learning courses can further throw these attitudes into relief (Antikainen *et al.* 1996; Antikainen 1998; Antikainen and Kauppila 2000). Certain clear differences were found between the attitudes of three generations to education and learning: the oldest generation's life histories take the form of survival accounts, in which education figures as a limited benefit which provided the opportunity for a learning that could positively contribute to their struggles in life. In the middle generation, the life histories of the men, in particular, take the form of career accounts, and education and learning play a part as a means to career development. In the young generation the life histories are characterised by reflexivity and individuality, and education is perceived as a consumer item to be made use of when there is a need for it or an interest in it. It is clear that the very different perspectives on education imply correspondingly large differences in the nature of the learning that takes place.

Thus, very different frames of reference for society and consciousness determine the learning conditions in the various life ages, and these frames of reference change rapidly in step with developments in society and consciousness. Nevertheless, there are also a number of important common links running through the life ages which are more general and which, to a certain extent, run across changing circumstances. From the descriptions previously given, three closely linked long lines of this kind can be pointed out.

First, a gradual *liberation* occurs throughout the life ages for the individual in relation to the external determination of learning. Whereas learning in childhood is framed in an interaction between biological maturing and external influences, in youth it is characterised to a great extent by young people's fight to have a say in things and, partly through this, construct their identity. In first adulthood people move towards learning what they themselves think is important, but to a great extent this is determined by their external conditions. It is only in mature adulthood that external determinations move into the background for those people who have the opportunities and the resources to liberate themselves.

In close interaction with this gradual liberation of learning from its external bondage there also typically occurs an *individuation*, i.e. learning increasingly directs itself towards the development of an individual person and is determined by personal needs and interests. Again it is a development which first takes off properly in the period of youth, but which only has a full impact in mature adulthood.

Finally, there also occurs a gradual development of *responsibility* for learning that is closely connected with the two other developments and so follows the same pattern.

In our society, it seems very clear that it should be both a condition and a goal for society to strive to organise itself on the lines of these developments and to support them. However, the earlier sections on social learning (Chapter 7) can also serve as a reminder that learning is not only an individual process, and that education can also have other perspectives than supporting personal development and the provision of qualifications for individuals, which the late-modern individualisation trend so clearly puts in central position. Society wants something from us, and individualisation goes hand in hand with equally strong measures that seek to control our learning.

11.7 Summary

Learning in the different life ages – childhood, youth, adulthood and mature adulthood – is qualitatively different, not just because the learning capacity of the brain gradually matures throughout the years of childhood and youth, but also because our life situations are essentially different, and this makes its mark on learning motivation to a high degree.

In childhood, learning is typically uncensored and trusting: the child seeks to acquire as much as possible and must trust the adults to present it with what it needs to know. From the beginning of puberty, however, there is growing interest in co-determining what is to be learned. The identity development of the years of youth concerns, among other things, being able to create some targets and frames for these choices, and, therefore, the identity process is very central to learning in this period. In adulthood, learning is fundamentally selective – it is not possible to learn everything – and there exist particular various life projects and life orientations, for example, concerning work, family and interests, which control the learning. In mature adulthood there is a tendency to seek to create a coherent understanding of one's values and experience, and motivation for learning more than this is limited to what one needs.

Up through the life ages there is constant development in the direction of learning becoming more self-directed and selective, as one gradually frees oneself from external ties. In spite of great differences in individual life processes, the development in learning orientation throughout the life ages seems to be characterised by a gradual liberation from societal ties, individuation in learning interest, and increased personal responsibility for learning.

Chapter 12

Learning in different learning spaces

This chapter deals with learning in relation to the most important of contexts or learning spaces in which it takes place. The first is 'everyday learning', i.e. the learning that takes place more generally as a function of being part of a society with certain norms, forms of practice, modes of thought etc. The next in line is learning in schools and education programmes and then learning in working life, where there is both more targeted training and more non-systematised learning in the process of doing the work. In recent years a new net-based or 'virtual' learning space has been added, and finally the chapter turns to interest-driven learning and learning that cuts across the learning spaces, in particular between education and work.

12.1 Learning spaces

It was firmly established earlier in this book that all learning is 'situated', i.e. that it takes place in a certain outer context and that this context is part of learning and influences both the learning process and its result (see section 7.1). This naturally applies to the individual specific situation, but one can also examine different types or categories of situations with some significant common features of importance for learning.

The type of society involved is the most general and fundamental element. It is, for example, clear that there is a difference between the learning opportunities in a late-modern market and knowledge society and in Stone Age or medieval society, and differences also exist between various contemporary societies. However, I will not enter this general level but instead examine the most important types of general learning contexts or learning spaces existing in modern societies such as in Denmark and similar countries, the general frames for learning situations each of them offers, and thus also the way in which the general societal conditions mark these spaces.

The first type of learning space I will take up is the everyday learning occurring in the many daily contexts where we are seldom oriented towards learning but, nevertheless, learn quite a lot. I then continue to the learning that takes place in school and educational contexts and in working life as modern society's two most important organised learning spaces. To these may be added the new 'virtual' space for what is called 'e-learning' or net-based learning, and finally what I will refer to as the 'interest-driven learning space' for voluntary activities. At the end of the chapter, I will discuss the possibilities for cutting across the different types of learning spaces and especially learning approaches that include both educational institutions and workplaces.

12.2 Everyday learning

Today, in connection with learning possibilities it seems quite natural to deal with various types of learning spaces. This is because there is a link with the fact that life in modern society is divided up into a number of different spaces or spheres that are directed by different rationales and do not have any immediately obvious connection – as has already been discussed in section 9.3 on everyday consciousness.

As a parallel to everyday consciousness, a concept of 'everyday learning' can be proposed, as that learning which occurs informally and apparently by chance in everyday life as one moves around the spaces of one's life without consciously intending to learn anything, but often busily absorbed in getting everything to function, and more or less understanding it.

In everyday learning one comes across a flood of impulses and impressions, and has a need for ways to relate to, navigate and make a selection between all these impulses so that one can manage one's life more or less smoothly. There is, naturally, a surface in all this jumble to which one relates consciously. As a rule, one makes more or less conscious decisions about what one by and large will spend time on, but it is only a surface, and beneath it are a multitude of impulses that influence us, also in the form of learning, without any conscious processing taking place (see section 2.5).

Another concept in this sphere is 'informal learning', which originally had to do with the more goal-directed form of everyday learning that occurs in non-industrialised societies, where learning has not yet gained its own institutionalised space. Before the concept of situated learning was developed, Jean Lave referred to informal learning of this type in her anthropological studies, characterised in these eight points by herself and Patricia Greenfield:

1   Embedded in daily life activities.
2   Learner is responsible for obtaining knowledge and skill.

3   Personal; relatives are appropriate teachers.
4   Little or no explicit pedagogy or curriculum.
5   Maintenance of continuity and tradition are valued.
6   Learning by observation and imitation.
7   Teaching by demonstration.
8   Motivated by social contribution of novices and their participation in adult sphere.

(Greenfield and Lave 1982, p. 183)

Naturally there are substantial differences between informal learning of this kind in a pre-industrial society that is more or less static in nature, and the learning opportunities in a modern society. In the current educational debate as it is conducted at international level, 'informal learning' is now spoken of when it has not been planned in the form of one type or other of education or schooling, and attempts have also been made to introduce the term 'non-formal learning' for the learning that takes place without having been planned but nonetheless in organised contexts such as at workplaces or in associations and the like (for example, EU Commission 2000, p. 8). However, British Helen Colley *et al.* have shown that these terms – and especially the distinction between informal and non-formal learning – are untenable professionally, are applied very differently and describe a distinction that cannot be maintained in practice (Colley *et al.* 2003; see section 4.1).

Thus I prefer to use the term everyday learning. On the one hand, this term is more qualitative in nature and, thereby, precisely underlines the unintended, yet omnipresent, element in this learning. On the other hand, it refers directly to the fact that it concerns the context in which the learning takes place.

12.3 School learning and educational learning

In our modern world, however, learning has become a key societal function that cannot be left to the chance of everyday learning to any great extent. It is, therefore, unavoidable that a great part of learning must be organised by society, and this takes place almost exclusively in schools and other educational institutions.

Historically this is linked to the fact that when society is organised capitalistically, on the one hand, a general interest arises in societal socialisation to accept the consequences of this form of society, and, on the other hand, procuring qualified labour is made a public matter in line with other matters that do not concern the individual enterprise (such as the system of justice, the health system, the military etc.). The private sector only takes on educational activities that are directly related to the special needs of the enterprises – even though the borderline between what is public and what is private in this area can vary somewhat from one country to another.

There are numerous descriptions of how the school and education system in Denmark have developed in close connection with the development of our industrialised capitalistic society and its qualification requirements (e.g. Simonsen 1976), and Norwegian sociologist Nils Christie has described in a more illustrative fashion how the necessity for a school developed in conjunction with the modernisation of society in a French village throughout the 1800s (Christie 1971). It has also been clearly enough shown how the fundamental function of school was, and basically still is, to discipline the growing generation to function in the context of wage work and also to accept and extend the existing society (e.g. Knudsen 1980).

The societal sorting function, and through this the reproduction of the social inequality of society, have also been carefully documented in Denmark and in other countries (see section 10.5 on 'social heredity') and, on a more general level, the French sociologist Pierre Bourdieu has addressed himself keenly to how schools' qualification and sorting functions are closely tied up with a legitimising function that justifies and continues both the prevailing ideology of that society and the sorting that takes place, so that social differences and societal grading are passed on from generation to generation (Bourdieu and Passeron 1977 [1970]). Since then Bourdieu has developed a comprehensive theory in which a highly significant function of school is that of being society's – i.e. the state's – most important institution for legitimising the current structures and ideological conditions, and socialising children to them: 'One of the major powers of the state is to produce and impose (especially through the school system) categories of thought that we spontaneously apply to all things of the world – including the state itself.' (Bourdieu 1998 [1994], p. 35).

Bourdieu's description is clearly influenced by the French circumstances, where the school system does not embrace the same degree of freedom as in Denmark, and where nationalism takes on a slightly different nature. However, the basic function of school and education is the same, and this is characterised by Bourdieu not simply as 'disciplining for wage work' (Knudsen 1980), but as 'symbolic violence', which is to say that it makes sure that society's dominance and power structures are accepted and internalised by the individual.

Nevertheless, it must be noted that Bourdieu's very radical statement is, to a certain extent, contradicted, or at any rate modified by the current very strong trends towards societal individualisation and globalisation. Today in both the individual and in the societal structures there are some very far-reaching expectations to the effect that through one's many personal choices one gives an individual mark to the common socialisation, and through this takes a higher degree of responsibility for one's own trajectory – with the attendant success or failure. And with globalisation the ties to the state and nation are also by now superimposed with a consciousness of the border-transcending nature of markets and of communication. English sociologist Anthony Giddens, for example, summarises this as follows: 'One of the distinctive features of modernity, in fact, is an increasing interconnection between the two 'extremes' of extensionality and intentionality: globalising influences on the one hand and personal dispositions on the other' (Giddens 1991, p. 1).

However, regardless of these important development trends, in order to understand the nature of the learning that takes place at school and is carried further in other parts of the education system, it is still crucial to realise that the act of going to school is basically a societal compulsion. This compulsion can be more or less direct; it can be a school obligation, as in most countries, or a teaching obligation, as it is in Denmark – but under all circumstances it is an obligation.

In terms of learning, it is crucial that from day one all the directly involved teachers, parents and pupils realise deep down that going to school, or receiving another form of teaching, is something that you have to do. There is no getting out of it – the constitution dictates it – and this knowledge is fundamental legally as well as in terms of consciousness. This permeates all the learning that takes place, precisely because it is so fundamental that it does not need to be said. And it carries on working after the teaching obligation has ended, most strongly in youth training, which, in our modern society, is so essential for the individual's societal opportunities that it is almost an indirect compulsion. And it is also very often continued further in adult education, because the participants more or less automatically continue to view the teacher and pupil/student roles in the way they have become accustomed to.

Some of the ways this influencing of learning actually functions is maintained in the concept of 'the hidden curriculum', which encompasses a number of the daily school routines that are not laid down in the curriculum or anywhere else, but which nevertheless play a strong part in socialisation through their constant daily repetition, year in, year out. American Philip Jackson has pointed out that pupils thus become accustomed to waiting, to rejections, interruptions and social seclusion (Jackson 1990 [1968]) – and British Peter Mortimore has been one of several to go further with this, stressing the vast amount of time wasted at school, although he has been more concerned with efficiency than with what this means for the participants in terms of socialisation (Rutter *et al.* 1979; Mortimore *et al.* 1988). In connection with a Danish survey Bauer and Borg have summarised the demands of the hidden curriculum on pupils as follows:

> The role of the pupil involves the pupil having to have motor and verbal control. This means that the pupil must be able to sit still for reasonably long periods, be quiet, and preferably speak only when

encouraged to by the teacher . . . the pupil must have the self-discipline to be able to work on projects alone for lengthy periods in spite of the close presence of classmates and various interruptions – . . . must be able to adapt to changing forms of authority and changing pedagogical strategies within short periods of time. At the same time the pupil must be able to endure a high degree of conformity, . . . must be able to give a good performance in competition with other pupils – . . . be attentive, and this attention must be directed towards the teacher and the subject activities, which are to a great extent completely foreign to the pupil's own life context . . . be ready to ignore his or her own needs and experiences from family and leisure time.

(Bauer and Borg 1986 [1976], p. 29)

Even though recent years have seen a certain softening of these patterns, it is still basically the case that school socialises children to accept the performance of externally determined activities according to the bell. This is also precisely the fundamental socialisation to wage labour and, as a whole, to accept capitalist society structures as a kind of 'second nature', i.e. as the framework conditions for the kind of life one can live.

In this connection it is also important to be aware of the strong effect of schools' assessments of pupils, considering the significance this assessment has for each individual's later education and job opportunities. In Denmark formal assessment is now postponed until the final year of ordinary school, but informal assessment starts on the first day of a child's school career. This subject has been thoroughly documented in Denmark by means of Steinar Kvale's survey of 'grading behaviour', which shows how upper secondary school pupils' attitude towards the giving of grades permeates all their activities, and how the teachers tend to undertake a kind of collective repression of these factors that is in conflict with their self-perception and professional identity. Kvale concludes that:

There is a huge gap between the behaviour that is officially desired of pupils as a result of education, and the behaviour which is promoted in a school based on grading choices. Giving grades promotes discipline, not independence, it promotes competition at the cost of co-operation, it promotes a tendency to loneliness at the cost of a libidinal attitude to learning, and a superficial form of adaptive learning as opposed to a creative form of learning.

(Kvale 1980, p. 189)

From the point of view of learning, what is important in all these well known matters is that the learning that takes place obtains its special mark of being 'school learning'. This can be difficult to see, especially because the whole thing is so much a matter of course, but even though Lave and

Wenger prefer to employ the concept of situated learning in connection with work experience (Lave and Wenger 1991), school learning is precisely just as situated, namely, as the type of learning that takes place in the school situation. Danish psychologist Kirsten Grønbæk Hansen reports as follows, for example, from a study of mathematics teaching in a vocational training school:

> School is just as much a context as other practices, and the skills the participants develop are attached to the school and cannot just be transferred to other communities of practice. . . . In viewing school as one community of practice among others, where what one is qualifying oneself for is ever more central participation, I was able to understand why most of my pupils thought that maths was a wonderfully concrete subject, with no need to consider its relevance – despite the fact that very few of them would have to use maths at the current level in their later career. Maths did not gain its significance through future work or anything else external to school; maths gained its significance in school and through school, as a part of school's community of practice. . . . School as a community of practice is already assigned a discursive interpretation [author's note: a commonly-held unspoken understanding], and if these powerful discourses are not taken into account in an analysis, ideas of this kind will only be seen as produced by the community.
>
> (Hansen 1998, pp. 10–11 and 12)

'Not for school, but for life!' was the motto that used to be found, in either Danish or Latin, over the entrance to many school buildings. And this classical formulation can still stand as an incantation that expresses with great precision what the school would very much like to be in its own understanding, but nevertheless *cannot* be because its raison d'être is that it is institutionalised as a differently situated world, isolated from the rest of life. Therefore, pupils, of course, also regard school learning as precisely 'learning for school', and this is also why the whole transfer issue exists (this was dealt with in more detail in section 4.7) – and, therefore, as a rule there is a 'practice shock' when one goes out to use one's education in practice.

School learning is obsessed and structured in such a way that in most cases there must be a demanding re-structuring both emotionally and in terms of content, before it can be applied outside the institutional context. But in modern society this entire situation is well on the way to becoming so inappropriate that it is no longer societally acceptable.

This is part of the background for the great current interest in concepts such as practice learning and competence. The gulf between institutionalised qualification in education programmes and modern societal competence requirements is becoming so great, and the readjustment processes and turn around time before the competence requirements come through so demanding and long-drawn-out, that there is a constant need to implement burdensome changes and reforms in education programmes in a continued chain of attempts to achieve balance. Society can neither do without the education programmes nor control them so that they are in step with its development. In general, development of society, of necessity, leads to a steadily increasing lack of simultaneity between the education programmes and the world they are supposed to educate for – a delay, which will also form a space for the unforeseen and the transcendent, which, paradoxically, society cannot do without either (see Illeris 1981, pp. 53ff.).

12.4 Learning in working life

During the past 10 to 15 years there has been an explosion of interest in the learning that can take place at, or in direct association with, a workplace. Part of the background for this is to be found in the general problems for learning in the institutionalised education programmes, which were discussed above. However, other general conditions that are very important can also be identified.

First, there has been a shift away from the idea that education and qualification were something that essentially belonged to childhood and youth, something that could be concluded when a certain vocational competence had been acquired, on which one could then base one's 40- to 50-year career with occasional supplementary training. It was an idea that was well matched by a school and education system that could provide such vocational competences and which could be developed and differentiated in step with developments. But it is quite obvious that this is no longer the case. Everybody must accept that their work functions change constantly and radically throughout the whole of working life, and it would seem to be appropriate that such continued competence development can take place in direct association with work.

Second, 'what has to be learned' has changed character (see section 5.1). Learning targets were formerly described in categories such as knowledge, skills and qualifications but, as already mentioned, it is the concept of competence that has come to the fore (see section 8.4) – and the degree and manner to which institutionalised education programmes can 'produce' a contingency system to function appropriately in new and unknown problem situations is an open question. It would seem more likely that such competences can be developed in step with the development at the workplaces where they are to be used.

Third, many adults, not least the low-skilled, are somewhat reluctant to 'go back to school', i.e. to return to the subordinate and child-like pupil role that can easily come to mark institutionalised learning if something is not deliberately done to organise the situation in a different way.

Fourth and finally, it should be mentioned that by placing a large part of the necessary learning out in the workplaces the public system may be able to achieve some savings in education costs, which seem to just grow and grow (this aspiration seems to be quite naive, however – I return to this issue in section 12.7).

But there are also some quite fundamental problems in connection with learning in working life that are not very much in focus right now. First and foremost, the overall aim of the workplaces is to produce goods and services and not to produce learning. And even though in many cases it would make good economic sense to invest in upgrading the employees' qualifications, there is an unmistakable tendency that when a pressed situation arises – and this seems to frequently be the case in late-modern market society – learning measures will often be downgraded in prioritisation in relation to current short-term needs.

This is why there is so much focus on the learning that can take place more or less 'by chance' in direct connection with the performance of the work and which thus in principle neither costs anything nor must be prioritised – the learning that, in a manner of speaking, comes 'by itself' (see Marsick and Watkins 1990; Garrick 1998). The problem is, however, that precisely this kind of learning, to a far greater extent than learning in working life that is structured and planned, tends to be narrow and lacking in theory. When it takes place in direct connection with the work, one can easily focus on what can create improvements here and now, while the broad lines and the wider contexts are omitted and, with them, the possibility of the learning having a wider application value in new situations and in connection with a more general understanding and an overview, which is decisive for what we call competence. (See Billett 2001; Beckett and Hager 2002; Illeris *et al.* 2004 for a broader discussion of these matters.)

The great current interest in learning in working life, cultivated not least in the supranational organisations that advise the countries' governments (for example, EU Commission 2000; OECD 2000, 2001) – although there is also a tendency to pursue an independent interest policy – is thus not as unambiguous as it often purports to be. But, on the other hand, there are clearly also some current matters pulling the picture in this direction, and there is good reason to expect learning in working life to play a greater role in the educational scene in the future.

What is it, then, that especially characterises working life as a learning space? In Denmark, Christian Helms Jørgensen and Niels Warring have worked with analyses of working life as learning space (Jørgensen and Warring 2003; Illeris *et al.* 2004). Like the present book they work with three dimensions of learning, but specifically in relation to working life:

1   The technical-organisational learning environment, the qualification requirements that the workplace as a technical and organisational system

has of the employees, and includes matters such as work content and division of labour, the opportunities for autonomy and using qualifications, the possibilities of social interaction, and the extent to which the work is a strain on the employees.

2   The social-cultural learning environment, which concerns social groupings and processes at the workplace and matters such as traditions, norms and values, and covers communities of work, cultural communities and political communities.

3   The employees' learning processes that concern the employees' consciousness and socialisation background, situation and future perspectives and covers work experience, education and social background.

In the book entitled *Learning in Working Life* (Illeris *et al.* 2004), these dimensions are merged with the learning triangle, an account of which is given in Chapter 3 of the present book, into what was termed 'a double perspective on learning in working life', and the 'holistic model' shown in Figure 12.1.

It should be noted that in contrast to the 'complex learning model' in Figure 7.1, section 7.1 in this book, this model does not concern learning in general but only learning in working life. At the level at the bottom of the figure, in Figure 7.1 'the environment' was polarised between the

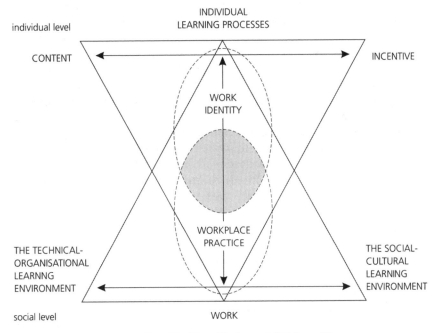

Figure 12.1 Learning in working life (after Illeris *et al.* 2004, p. 69)

immediate social situation and the underlying general societal situation, while in the working life model it is stretched out between the technical-organisational learning environment and the social-cultural learning environment, both of which concern the social situation at the workplace.

In addition, this model shows that the important general learning in working life takes place in interaction between workplace practice and the learner's work identity, but that there also is space for more limited learning processes that more or less circumvent these core fields, such as the acquisition of certain technical skills that can take place in a more limited interaction anchored between the workplace's technical-organisational learning environment and the learner's cognition, but naturally also can be related to the model's other elements to a greater or lesser extent.

On the more concrete level, there are a number of approaches to what is central in connection with the understanding of the learning that takes place in working life. In line with a classic learning understanding, most of these approaches place the main emphasis on the individual acquisition process, corresponding to the horizontal double arrow at the top of the model in Figure 12.1. This applies, in the first place, to the so-called industrial sociological approach which, in particular, has interested itself in the qualification requirements the work demands of the employees and how the qualifications are developed, now also including to a high degree what have been termed the 'process independent' or, more recently, the 'general qualifications' (for example, Braverman 1974; Andersen et al. 1994, 1996). Next, it applies as point of reference to the management-anchored approach also, which is termed 'organisational learning'. Americans Chris Argyris and Donald Schön have been key figures here for a generation, and they have emphasised, among other things, that the employees' learning is crucial to the development of the enterprises and that a distinction must be made between single-loop learning, which remains within, and double-loop learning, which exceeds, the existing frames of understanding (see Argyris and Schön 1978, 1996; Argyris 1992; Elkjær 1999; see section 8.6). Finally, it also refers to the approach that has roots in general adult education, mostly to individual learning when it, typically on a humanistic basis, interests itself in the employees' experience and interest in learning (for example, Weil and McGill 1989a; Marsick and Watkins 1990; Boud and Garrick 1999; Billett 2001; Ellström 2001; Evans et al. 2002; Rainbird et al. 2004).

In contrast are the approaches that very largely focus on the workplace as learning environment and the development or 'learning' of the workplace, i.e. on the bottom horizontal double arrow in Figure 12.1. This primarily concerns the approach that goes under the name of 'the learning organisation'. This is really a branching out of the organisational understanding of learning, but with the decisive difference that here the focus is on what is understood as the organisation's 'learning' that is made independent as something different and more than the sum of the employees' learning. A key work here is American Peter Senge's book about 'the fifth discipline' (Senge 1990). It must be clear, however, that with the learning concept I have developed here one cannot say that the organisation can learn – and much of what is marketed under the term 'the learning organisation' in my opinion has more to do with management and, sometimes, smart formulations than with learning.

But the approach that was launched with the book by Jean Lave and Etienne Wenger on 'situated learning' (Lave and Wenger 1991), mentioned several times previously, and later continued by Wenger in *Communities of Practice* (Wenger 1998), must also be said to mainly be oriented towards the workplace as the focal point of learning. This is the case despite the fact that to a large extent it has its roots in the Russian cultural-historical tradition and Vygotsky's understanding of learning, which is quite classically oriented towards the individual acquisition process. In Lave and Wenger it seems almost to be the case that when the individual has first entered the community of practice, by means of a learning process he or she will automatically move from 'legitimate peripheral participation' towards a more central and competent position. A more individual-oriented formulation of Vygotsky's approach can, however, be found in Finnish Yrjö Engeström, who, though he may work with learning in organisations, does so with a high degree of focus on the employees (for example, Engeström 1993, 1994, 1996).

I am thus on the way towards the third major approach to learning in working life, namely the approach that primarily focuses on the interaction between the social and the individual levels, i.e. on the vertical double arrow in the middle of the model in Figure 12.1. Here, there is reason to note the approach that has its roots in 'critical theory' (see section 7.4). Earlier it was the interaction between social conditions and their significance for the consciousness formation of the individual and the collective organisations that stood at the centre, in particular with Oskar Negt's work concerning 'sociological imagination and exemplary learning' (Negt 1971 [1968]; see section 8.2). But an important contribution is also to be found in the work of Ute Volmerg concerning the significance of the employees' opportunities for organising their own work, for communication with others at work and for applying the qualifications they have acquired as the three decisive focal points for their learning possibilities in working life (Volmerg 1976). Finally, there should be mention of Birgit Volmerg et al.'s study of 'the life world of private enterprises' ('*Betriebliches Lebenswelt*'), i.e. the way in which the employees seek and utilise the possibilities of the workplace for a free space to set their own agenda (Volmerg et al. 1986; Leithäuser 2000).

In addition, Danish Bente Elkjær has launched an approach that takes its point of departure in John Dewey's understanding of pragmatism (see section 8.2) and explicitly addresses the relation between the workplace and the employee as the key focus of learning in working life, but does not relate to societal learning outside of working life (Elkjær 2002, 2005).

It should, finally, be noted that on the basis of the learning model presented in Chapter 3, the present book seeks to establish an approach that combines focus on the relation or interaction between the individual and the environment – i.e. in working life, between the employee and the workplace – but simultaneously includes the individual acquisition process to a high degree.

If one tries to cut across all these approaches, it is possible in general to extract a number of possibilities and problems that especially characterise the learning that takes place in working life. Quite fundamentally, a huge amount of learning takes place in direct connection with the performance of the work, and the employees typically experience that this learning is of greater importance for them than learning in institutionalised education (CEDEFOP 2003). Viewed from the outside, it must, however, be maintained that fundamentally this learning is accidental in nature and that it is usually narrow and without theoretical foundation.

However, by systematically building up a learning-oriented environment this learning can be strengthened considerably – this is the main idea behind the approaches called 'organisational learning' and 'the learning organisation', although they do not agree when it comes to the relation between the individual and the organisation. Nonetheless, the risk will still remain of the learning obtaining a certain accidental flavour and an inadequate structure and systematics. Moreover, there is a tendency for the employees who are already best qualified to profit more from this procedure – but this may eventually be counteracted by introducing self-directed groups, projects or action learning programmes for all employees (see Illeris et al. 2004, chapter 8).

Another possibility – which can very well be combined with organisational learning – is to aim at targeted learning measures in close connection with the work. This can take place by means of personal backing for the individual employee in the form of instruction, guided learning, partner guidance, mentor schemes or coaching, through broadly based support from so-called 'ambassadors', 'super users' or 'gardeners', who are especially used in the ICT field, or through access to consultant assistance, and it can take place through teaching activities in close connection with the work. All of this can be backed up by means of regular staff development interviews or the like (see Illeris et al. 2004, Chapters 6 and 7).

Finally, there can be emphasis on more general measures such as internal or external networks and experience groups or job exchange and job rotation schemes where there also is a possibility for involving all staff organisationally (see Illeris et al. 2004, Chapters 6 and 8).

Under all circumstances there are three important issues that exist to one extent or another. The first is that learning in working life, to an even higher degree than learning by means of institutionalised education, has a tendency to especially favour those who already have the best education (the so-called 'Matthew effect'; see section 10.5). The second is that the necessary work will always receive higher priority than learning-oriented measures. The third is that learning measures can have a disturbing effect on the targeted work which is the purpose of the workplace.

These issues can be dealt with to a certain degree by learning in working life being combined with courses and education programmes, for example, such as those that take place in the so-called alternating education programmes in the apprentice and professional fields, where there is alternation between school and work experience periods. I return to this in section 12.7.

12.5 Net-based learning

Right from the time when 'programmed learning' started appearing in the 1960s, many quarters have attached great interest and great expectations for a high volume of learning activity to be mediated through ICT (information and communication technology, for example, Dirckinck-Holmfeld and Fibiger 2002).

When these possibilities emerged, learning was still predominantly perceived in the traditional sense of transfer of facts and information on a given subject, and it was believed that doing so through computer programmes would partly save considerable expenditures for instructors and schools, and partly enable the system to secure high and uniform quality.

Nevertheless, it did not become the big hit that some had expected. For even though the software programs were eventually developed and refined, they remained subject to the conditions of impersonal one-way communication, while at the same time development and updating of such programs turned out to be a task of considerable magnitude, also in financial terms. The impact was, in practice, rather limited, but for concrete information, instruction, etc., there were at least some obvious possibilities in the new medium, and even today the greater part of the computer-mediated learning activities in Denmark assume this form (Elkjær 2002).

With the emergence of the new demands for competence development it is, however, clear that such a learning approach will only be able to solve very limited tasks; development of personal skills cannot take place through impersonal instruction. Meanwhile, there has been quite considerable technological development, and today there is extensive development work concentrated on the so-called CSCL paradigm (computer-supported collaborative learning – see section 7.9), i.e. project work in groups where computer conferences are used in running academic cooperation between the participants and an instructor and among the participants themselves, to various degrees combined with group meetings in which participants get acquainted, receive academic input and can conduct the overall planning and coordination of the work of the group.

The specific future perspectives reach further forward towards proper 'virtual learning environments' (*inter alia* with reference to Etienne Wenger's aforementioned concept of communities of practice, Wenger 1998), in which also audio-visual media are used, i.e. the possibility of having a conversation and seeing the interlocutor even in distance learning.

These advances open possibilities for virtual learning that might, as concerns personal communication, be impeded by the computer mediation, but on the other hand offers some clear advantages compared to traditional institutionalised education programmes.

First, the independence of time and place offers enormous flexibility which, not least to many adults, is of key importance; participants are able to take part in the work irrespective of physical location and residence without leaving home and at the times when it is most convenient. In this way a lot of waste of time and transport costs are avoided at the same time as educational activities can be fitted into an everyday life in which there must also be room for work and family.

Second, there is a possibility of participating in education over long distances. This can be of great importance both in remote, thinly populated districts and for enterprises and organisations with staff posted in many destinations all over the world.

Third, the fact that the communication is written and staggered in time implies considerable learning advantages. On the one hand, through the personal contributions, the individual participant becomes more 'visible' as a person to both the teachers and the other participants, at the same time as skills in expressing oneself in writing briefly and coherently are strengthened to a far higher extent than in ordinary teaching, and today this is a very valuable qualification. On the other hand, the written communication requirement leads, to a higher degree than direct dialogue, to academic and partly also personal reflections of great significance for competence development.

Finally, it should be mentioned that even though the participants are not together, nonetheless a high degree of social and interactive qualifications can be developed through the written communication.

In this connection it must, however, at the same time be pointed out that the virtual communication requires a considerable measure of motivation and determination to participate, to a degree which is far from always present. For less motivated participants it is apparently easier to turn up at a school and take part in the direct dialogue than having to muster the self-discipline to work on the computer in the solitude of one's home.

In general, on the one hand, net-based learning provides some special opportunities, not least of which is considerable flexibility in relation to traditional teaching. On the other hand, however, some limitations exist with respect to the communicative and social aspects, which first and foremost require the participants to be strongly motivated.

It is therefore important that the net-based activities are supported by direct meetings as far as possible, where the participants can get to know each other as whole people and not just by name, written expression and pictures. This cannot always be done, but in general a lot of experience points to a combination of a net-based and a direct interaction being a form of learning that functions satisfactorily and efficiently for well-motivated participants, while it is less suitable if the participants are ambivalent or struggle against it, and/or the socialising element is central to the intended learning.

It should also be mentioned that net-based learning activities are not only a possibility within institutionalised education programmes, but to a high degree also in working life and in connection with interest-driven learning needs (see Dirckinck-Holmfeld *et al.* 2002; Illeris *et al.* 2004).

12.6 Leisure time interests and grassroots activity

An important learning space in modern society which has earlier been beyond the purview of education research includes all the forms of interest-based activities that people voluntarily participate in, often with great personal engagement and use of time. It can take the form of locally or globally oriented charitable work, politically oriented work in local branches of political parties, organisations, grassroots movements etc., spiritual and religious movements, work in associations within a range of activity areas from sport to music and art to historical or local interests, or it can be outdoor life and travel (for example, Wildemeersch *et al.* 2005).

The possibilities are almost limitless and the learning is, first and foremost, influenced by the fact that the activities are based on strong personal interest and motivation – i.e. precisely what is increasingly lacking in the more immediately learning-oriented courses in which many participate because of societal pressure and personal necessity rather than desire and engagement.

While public enlightenment, study circles and folk high schools took care of such movements, today it is characteristic that these possibilities for education are under increasing political pressure to become qualifying and vocationally oriented activities that can receive public support, while the interest-determined activities must go it alone and thus are more and more left up to those who can muster the resources necessary.

On the other hand, neither society nor its members can do without these activities. We cannot stand for everything being made subordinate to the dominant economic rationality, and the extensive development of engagement and creativity – and thus learning also – that can be observed in all these areas is also important fertile soil and a recruitment basis for the education sector, working life and the democratic functions of society. It is, therefore, also something that is acknowledged to a high degree in connection with the great international interest of recent years in 'education for citizenship' (for example, Jansen *et al.* 1998; Lockyer *et al.* 2003; van der Veen 2003) and also in connection with evaluation and recognition of prior learning (for example, Zucker *et al.* 1999; Harris 2000) as important elements in the competence society that is aimed at.

The great, open, interest-driven field of voluntary activities is thus at one and the same time a learning space that is important to society and yet relatively marginalised in relation to the education sector and working life. From the point of view of learning it is characterised by a high degree of participant motivation and, thus, also the strength and efficiency in learning that increasingly seems to be a problem in the institutionalised education programmes.

12.7 Transversal learning and alternating education

In the above I have dealt with five of society's most important general learning spaces. In practice each of them is typically divided into a number of sub-spaces such as the different divided contexts of everyday life, the subjects of the education programmes and the disciplines of the subjects, the different jobs and work functions of working life, the computers' programs, and all the various associations and fora of the voluntary activities.

Modern life is, similarly, split up into a mass of different activities each of which has its own arenas and perspectives. Learning naturally has a similar tendency to be split up into a number of themes (which is the term used in connection with the concept of everyday consciousness – see section 9.3) or a series of disjointed, assimilatively built up schemes (the term employed when it concerns the mental organisation of what is learned – see section 4.2).

From the point of view of learning, however, it is of decisive importance, not least if competence development is to take place, that the schemes are linked together through accommodative processes, i.e. that one understands and can obtain a general view of the connections between all the different kinds of experience and understandings one develops. It is, therefore, also important that connections can be created between the various learning spaces on a more practical level.

This is, of course, something we all work with in one form or another; we simply cannot avoid doing so. But today life is so complicated and split up and there are so many structuring matters lying outside of the reach of the individual that our overview and contextual understanding easily become more or less haphazard fractions of a pattern – a jigsaw puzzle which is missing a number of pieces and where some of those we do have have been wrongly put together while others have faded and are unclear. This is why it is so important that targeted learning efforts aim at creating firm connections between the different learning spaces and sub-spaces.

Schools and education programmes have always had difficulty with this. At school there are a great number of subjects with different teachers, different teaching materials and, sometimes, also different teaching rooms, placed anyhow on a school timetable that structures everything that takes place. Moreover, many education programmes are also split up in other ways, for example between teaching and work experience. One, naturally, cannot occupy oneself with everything at the same time, but it is inherent in the structure that if contexts are to be created, a special effort has to be made, and as a rule this only takes place to a very modest extent.

Most of all, it seems to be important to create better cohesion between the two main learning spaces to which societally determined learning and education are linked; in particular, the education system and working life. Therefore, I will discuss this field here as a key example of the difficulties that are encountered when one tries to create a connection between the learning spaces.

Precisely in this area, especially in Denmark and a number of other northern European countries, a solid tradition exists for the so-called alternating education programmes. These programmes are, in different ways, structured as interaction between school learning and work experience – and as we know it today this applies to the vocationally oriented youth education programmes and the medium-cycle further education professional programmes.

But it is not necessary to have occupied oneself with these education programmes for very long before it becomes clear that it is a great problem for the students to link what they learn in school with what they learn during work experience. One hears this complaint repeatedly, and education planners, institutions and teachers have, time and again, tried to do something about it without any great success.

At the same time, these education programmes also have the problem that it is difficult, and in many cases impossible, to obtain enough places for work experience, and that there is a tendency for students in work experience to be used as cheap labour and for the counselling to be inadequate. This problem has also been taken up repeatedly without any satisfactory general solutions having been found.

That this is constantly the case is, naturally, because there is an underlying cause that there is a refusal or inability to do something about – and it is not so difficult to identify. It is quite simply the case that having trainees places a considerable practical and financial strain on the workplaces. As pointed out in section 12.3, the workplaces do not exist to create learning but to create competitive goods and services – and they or their representatives are, of necessity, basically interested in the existence of sufficient well-qualified potential employees on the labour market who can perform the work without, or with a minimum of, on-the-job training.

On the other hand, it is clear enough – at any rate on the basis of the learning understanding in this book – that the best learning and competence development precisely presupposes that part of the learning takes place where the competences are to be used, i.e. at the workplaces. Nobody really denies this, and the past decade has seen a considerable amount of interest in these matters on the part of international bodies such as OECD and the EU and also in pedagogical research and discussion. From the point of view of learning, it is especially with a background in Jean Lave and Etienne Wenger's work on 'situated learning' and 'communities of practice' (already mentioned several times in this book, in particular in sections 7.6 and 12.3), that an argument has been made for what has been called 'rehabilitation of the apprenticeship system' – and this would also be valuable for both society and learning, that is if there were enough trainee places, and they were good enough, and the interaction between work experience and school learning also was adequate.

But this is not the case, and it will not be the case either if it is not made sufficiently attractive for the workplaces, public as well as private, to make trainee places available and become engaged in qualified training, and at the same time funds are made available, for the relevant staff of the schools and the trainee enterprises to engage in building up cooperation that is so good and close that the situation is made coherent for the participants.

This is not say that the existing work experience schemes are not valuable in various areas, but, on the other hand, it is merely propaganda when so-called responsible politicians and partly also employers constantly talk about how important it is to do something about the education programmes without making a serious attempt to find a solution to this key problem.

In our modern split-up society it is not easy to make learning and learning spaces cohere, even though this is decisively important for the learning. But precisely in connection with alternating education programmes, it is actually possible to do something effective to ease the cohesion, and it is also clear what has to be done. Nevertheless, our so-called 'learning society' is apparently not yet sufficiently mature for this to take place.

12.8 Summary

In practice, our learning takes place in a number of different contexts or learning spaces. In the above, five superior or general learning spaces were discussed: everyday life, the school and education system, working life, the net-based learning space, and the voluntary, interest-driven learning space. Each of these learning spaces is composed of a number of different sub-spaces.

Each of the learning spaces also places some special learning opportunities at disposal and, at the same time, influences the learning that takes place. Learning in everyday life is fundamental, but in our modern complex society it tends to be incoherent. The school and education system offers systematised, targeted learning possibilities, but this is, of necessity, 'school learning' that is not always immediately applicable outside of school and the education system. While learning in working life is more directly applicable, it tends to be narrow and lacking in theory without including wider contexts. Net-based learning or e-learning can constitute an appropriate supplement in many contexts, but it presupposes that the relevant multi-aspect programs are available and – to an even greater extent than other learning – that the participants have considerable motivation. Voluntary, interest-driven learning typically has great strength and quality precisely due to the participants' engagement and motivation, but it follows its own route and would therefore not be capable of meeting society's needs on its own.

In modern society it is of key importance that learning contexts are created across the learning spaces, but this is not immediately in agreement with the structure and mode of function of the societies, and attempts to move across the different learning spaces create great organisational and learning problems.

Chapter 13

Learning, education and society

In this chapter, I will discuss on a general level how the learning-oriented deliberations in the previous chapters can be utilised in connection with education programmes and their societal function. I start by identifying four typical misunderstandings about learning that often appear in pedagogical and educational contexts. I then examine more closely some key issues concerning the structure of the education programmes, especially with respect to choice of content and direction. Finally, I make some proposals concerning what could be appropriate and necessary paths to follow on the societal level from the perspective of learning, and on the general level.

13.1 Four misunderstandings about learning and education

This chapter deals with the relationship between learning and practical pedagogy and concludes with some considerations about present-day education policy in the perspective of learning. I will, however, begin by pointing out some very widespread misunderstandings or simplifications about learning in which we all are more or less socialised and which one repeatedly meets in discussions about learning, pedagogy, teaching and education policy with students, parents, teachers, administrators, politicians and, unfortunately, also oneself, at least if one does not very consciously and carefully try to avoid them.

They are popular understandings that are so widespread that we all have a part in them because we have met them right from the first day of school or earlier. At some level or other, most teachers and educators know that these are misunderstandings, but nevertheless often they embrace them, perhaps because it would be far too complicated to set oneself up against them on a daily basis. In the case of politicians, planners, administrators and others who take important decisions about education programmes without functioning within them every day, the misunderstandings frequently form such an unproblematic element that they take on the character of a kind of common sense.

It is, however, the case that when one takes these misunderstandings up in a more systematic form in professional contexts, one meets a typical double reaction: on the one hand that 'we knew that', and on the other hand that it is liberating to get it out into the open so that one can better relate to it.

In the first place, there is what I call *the ideological misunderstanding*. In essence it is that one immediately assumes that there is agreement between the objectives formulated for the education programme and the design of these programmes. This would, after all, be natural, because the objectives and the general organisational provisions are, as a rule, laid down by the same bodies. But these connections are by no means always present. When, for example, the Basic School Act is being debated, politicians throw themselves into discussions about every word in the statement of aims. But this is an ideological battle and it is rather distant from negotiations about the school's practical framework, which typically is about matters such as subjects, grading, tests and streamed or un-streamed classes. There are rarely any systematic attempts to find out how best to design a school or an education programme on the basis of the objectives that have been adopted – for example, whether a school where the teaching is divided into subjects and is curriculum oriented is the best suited to satisfying the objectives adopted.

In the context of adult education all parties support broad competence development centred on personal competences such as independence, responsibility, flexibility and creativity. But at the same time it can be enormously difficult to make a break with the educational traditions that limit the possibilities of the adult participants to practise such characteristics. For the education programmes typically function within some frames which, first and foremost, satisfy the traditions of the schools and administrative needs, and it is, for example, both complicated and difficult if co-determination by the participants is also to influence the frames themselves.

Public education programmes are, and have always been, a combination of qualifying and disciplining measures, but in the formulations of objectives the disciplining side is omitted, or it is expressed in ambiguous terms, for instance about strengthening the children's character or the current formulations about being in agreement with the needs of the labour market. But there are also some more or less hidden considerations that can play a role, sometimes without the decision-makers themselves being aware of it.

The ideological misunderstanding thus consists in a mixture of ideologically influenced markings and the targets that are actually at the base of the design and functions of the education programmes. There is thereby a cover up that stands in the way of targeted educational planning and creates uncertainty about the frames that apply to the daily practice in the programmes.

Second, there is what I call *the technological misunderstanding*. This is about regarding education as a production process, and it has therefore been most widespread in connection with the vocational education programmes that are closest to production. But technological thinking has also had considerable influence on the other parts of the education system.

To put it briefly, the thinking is that some qualifications or competences are to be produced and that this is best done by establishing some precise objectives and, on this basis, selecting the most effective and rational teaching activities. This typically results in some syllabi that lay down in more or less detail what is to take place and when – thus also setting some limits for the participants' co-determination. In the most extreme cases, the ideal has actually been that exactly the same is taking place for all participants at the same time all over the country, namely that which the experts have devised as being most appropriate and effective, for which reason any deviation from it must, by definition, be negative.

This technological approach oversees the fact that education is about living people who arrive with some capacities that are not restricted to knowledge and skills. They also include personal dispositions, good and bad experience, certain modes of understanding, interests, motivations, preferences, resistance, blocks, aversions and much more besides.

This is why the same influences work quite differently on the different participants. This has also been recognised in many areas, and for several years differentiation has been the topic of a great deal of speaking and writing. Nevertheless there is a tendency to hang on to the technological thinking, especially in connection with administrative decisions. This may be because the irrational human features are so impractical and unmanageable when it comes to economy and efficiency. But living people are not rational in this sense and, therefore, to put it bluntly, it is not at all rational to employ such a rational approach. It is, in fact, far more rational to ensure that there is space and room for the development of irrational human diversity.

In sum, the technological misunderstanding consists in regarding people as things, and learning as the external provision of competences. But people are living beings who themselves develop their competences, and education is about creating the best possible conditions and materials for this development in relation to the participants in question with the capacities they may have.

Third, there is what I call *the psychological misunderstanding*. This is, without doubt, the most widespread, and what is paradoxical about it is that at the same time as we all have a part in it to a greater or smaller degree, we are also very well aware that it is a misunderstanding. But we hang onto it because it is so convenient.

The misunderstanding is about us pretending that there is correspondence between what is taught and what is learned, even though we have known that this is not the case right back from our earliest school experiences. It is only some of what is taught that is learned, what each individual learns is different, there is a great deal of mislearning, and we also learn something other than what is taught.

In the day-to-day teaching this misunderstanding has a tendency to function in the way that the teacher can be satisfied and covered against criticism if he or she has taught the prescribed content, irrespective of how and what the participants have got out of it. It would also be formally difficult to demand more, but the angle of approach itself is wrong. A teacher's work should not fundamentally be understood as teaching, but as helping and supporting the participants' learning processes.

Another important matter in this connection has to do with the learning that takes place alongside the acquisition of academic content and which can be very inappropriate from the point of view of the objective of the education programme. A classic example is that many pupils learn that they are not good at mathematics or foreign languages or physical exercises. But it can also be about a great deal else – for example, that if there is something one does not understand it is better to keep one's mouth shut than to ask.

Much of this is closely connected with the fact that the education programmes also have a sorting function. There may not be anything written about it in the statements of objectives, but in a society with wide-ranging division of labour a selection has to take place at some stage or other. This function is, today, placed primarily in the education system where, as often shown, it largely makes itself felt as a reflection of the participants' social background, which thus seems to play a more decisive role for learning than what is taught and how (see section 10.5). In a study carried out some years ago in relation to the Danish primary school, it was a striking result that even very great differences in the pedagogical approach do not appreciably influence this sorting process, but on the other hand pedagogy can influence the pupils' learning and formation of opinion to a high degree (Illeris 1992).

To sum up, the psychological misunderstanding thus consists in focusing on teaching rather than learning, and the consequence is that masses of resources are used on activities that are inappropriate, have no effect, or in some cases work directly contrary to the intentions.

Fourth, there is what could be called *the utopian misunderstanding*. It is not as tangible as the others, but many years ago I heard a business manager express it very precisely. During a discussion he said, 'What we need is some independent young people who do as they are told'.

More generally it concerns the fact that one sometimes speaks and acts as if education can solve all problems, also those that are self-contradictory or are up against other and stronger societal forces that we do not want to interfere with. But education cannot magically produce both dependence and independence, just as it cannot, for example, cancel out social heredity.

All in all it is important to realise that there are strong tendencies in education policy and planning towards fundamental misunderstandings that are both well known and generally accepted and which most people know are wrong, but which, nevertheless, we are inclined to cling to because they are so convenient.

It is not least when we speak of learning in the form of competence development that some of the traditions of the education system have to be turned upside down. The key function of the misunderstandings has precisely been to veil the adaptation, disciplining and selection that suited the old industrial society. But if education is to be targeted and play a part in developing independence, responsibility, creativity, flexibility and all the other 'soft qualifications', we must take seriously that this requires education programmes where such characteristics are practised and related to the academic content one is working with – and that conditions will be bad for them if the participants are more or less forced to attend the courses, or if the programmes are not designed to include activity and reflection and the individual participant being able to see his or her interests in what is taking place.

On the basis of the learning understanding described in the previous chapters, in the following I will look more closely at what would be appropriate on the general level, taking my starting point in a number of key general pedagogical questions or problem areas.

13.2 Participation in organised learning

As already stated in the introduction to this book, learning is something that can take place in all possible different contexts and take many different, more or less constructive or defensive forms. In modern societies it is a key feature that a great deal of learning must be organised on a societal basis, because the complex social structures make it necessary for the members of society to have certain competences and a certain degree of common orientation in many areas. Such societally managed learning measures primarily take place within the education system and working life.

But such institutionalised learning can easily run into opposition and defence on the part of the participants, because fundamentally it takes place on the basis of the needs of society which are not always identical with what the individual members of society regard as their own needs. A quite fundamental question arises – actually preceding what we normally understand by pedagogy – concerning who can participate in institutionalised learning in a societally appropriate and personally acceptable manner, and how the society reacts when it runs into opposition with potential participants.

With the transition to a late-modern knowledge society, where learning has a key role and is defined as a societal issue from the perspective of basic national economy, this question would seem to have taken on new dimensions. In Denmark at any rate, within adult and youth education in particular, as early as the first years of puberty, one meets a considerable number of participants in schools and education who come more or less of necessity and not of their own free will, and who therefore do not benefit from their participation to any great extent – or even have negative benefit from the societal perspective – while, at the same time, they cause great problems for the teachers and institutions and create less favourable learning conditions for other participants (Illeris 2002). This is an enormous waste of societal and individual resources that could have been expended on something better.

From the point of view of learning, the questions concerning participants' motivation or the motive forces for, and barriers to, learning have thus become quite central and precede the more traditional pedagogical questions about the content and structure of the teaching. For these people it is not primarily a matter of motivation in relation to a certain learning content or certain work patterns, but of motivation for simply participating and becoming engaged in the types of education measures on offer.

In the case of the age when schooling is obligatory, participation is compulsory and the question can only be posed as a question of how – but it can, of course, be discussed when compulsory education should begin and how long it should last.

As pointed out in section 11.2, it is also the case that up to the ages of 11 to 13 children basically accept adults controlling and organising the conditions for their learning, although in modern society they also meet with influences that make this problematic. But in the last years of compulsory education there can be more fundamental problems concerning participation itself – these must, however, be solved without abandoning the participation requirement and therefore will not be discussed any further here.

The problem is, however, different, in the youth education programmes, i.e. for the approximately 16–20-year-olds. On the one hand, education is no longer compulsory and the participants also reach the age of majority during the period. On the other hand, society has a broadly formulated policy, which enjoys widespread support, that as many as possible should complete a qualifying youth education programme, and the target in Denmark is to come up to 95 per cent of a youth cohort (see section 11.3).

But a very large share of young people find it difficult to complete these education programmes, both the upper secondary and the vocationally oriented, which can be seen both within the programmes themselves and from the high drop-out rate. This is a central problem for society and there are no indications that it can be solved without fundamental political new orientations. From the point of view of learning, it is basically the case that young people are taken up with their identity process – working out how to create themselves, who they want to be and who they can be – while the education programmes and the extensive counselling are concerned with guiding them and providing them with the right competences in relation to the needs of society and working life.

The lack of engagement, the more or less well-articulated protests, and the high drop-out rate show clearly that something quite different must take place than what is on offer now for a significant number of the young people if the large societal resources that are spent on them now are to lead to anything other than conflicts and defeats. These young people are unhappy with their position as pupils. They already have at least nine years' experience of not being particularly good at it, and this is not the way for them to develop a sustainable identity – not even if they are offered work experience, production schools and all sorts of exciting projects. (Production schools are non-residential schools for young people aged between 18 and 25 years in which practical, creative and artistic production take up most of the time, but some elementary school subjects are taught.)

What these young people need, first and foremost, is access to real working life. It is this and only this that counts because it is the path to an adult identity they can accept, and more directly education-oriented measures must take their point of departure in this. But, unfortunately, working life is not especially willing to receive them. In spite of all the campaigns, there are still far too few real trainee places, because today for the workplaces trainees generally mean difficulty and disturbance to a degree that clearly exceeds the advantages of being able to exploit the trainees' cheap labour.

Therefore, the problem can only be solved in a societally sustainable way if the workplaces, both private and public, are in one form or other obliged, or undertake, to take on these young people. This would be the necessary and decisive contribution to securing a competitive level of education for these 'vulnerable youngsters', and it would lead to large-scale savings in both the education and the social sectors. This could then be used to give the workplaces compensation that would balance the costs of their societally necessary contribution.

Such a reform in the youth area would also be a good contribution to solving the similar problem in the adult area, because a large number of the adults who are not motivated for educational learning and feel that they have been forced to 'go to school again' are precisely the low-skilled who never had their negative relation to school learning improved (see Illeris et al. 2004; Illeris 2006).

In addition, some of the same problems are to be found here, apart from the fact that we are now talking about adults who, in a different way from youngsters, feel humiliated and treated like children when the 'system' –

whether represented by an employment service, a local authority, an employer or others – forces them into educational measures with the threat of financial and social marginalisation. In this area also there is colossal economic waste and human devaluation.

But in contrast to the young, these are adults who already have an identity, however split and worn down it might be, and the problem is somewhat different. Typically here, and in a far more tangible manner than in the case of young people, there is a clear ambivalence, as discussed in section 9.4. This means that the great majority of the adults who feel bad about having to educate themselves know deep down that they will have to do so if they wish to maintain a reasonable existence. Therefore, in the case of adults one can achieve a great deal by appealing to the positive side of their ambivalence and remaining open and straight about the negative side.

But also, here, access to working life is a crucial point. Learning clearly takes place more quickly and better if one experiences that the activities are not only about achieving a competence but also, with a reasonable degree of certainty, an acceptable job.

On the whole, the clear conclusion concerning the question about participation in organised learning is that while in the case of children whose participation is compulsory it is a matter of offering learning opportunities they can experience as relevant and engaging, in the case of young people and adults sustainable learning presupposes sustainable motivation, and ways must be found to meet the motivational preconditions that apply.

13.3 Learning and curriculum

The more classic pedagogical questions concerning the structure of the education programmes are traditionally dealt with within the pedagogical discipline called curriculum theory. In a classically narrow sense this has to do with the selection of the content of the teaching and teaching forms, but today is also used more broadly about everything from the grounding and legitimacy of the teaching, its societal function, objectives, planning, management and evaluation, and the participants' qualifications and interests, to its practical implementation and different teaching methods (for example, Doll 1993; Pinar *et al.* 1995). In addition, a distinction must be made between subject-based curriculum theory, relating to teaching in the individual subject – thereby presupposing that the teaching is subject divided – and the overall or general curriculum theory that cuts across the subjects and deals with more general issues.

Four general curriculum guidelines can be deduced from the theories about learning and non-learning in the above.

First, the understanding that all learning includes a content, an incentive and an interactive dimension (see Chapters 3, 5, 6 and 7) must basically imply that all educational planning and analysis also includes these three dimensions. To some extent this is an expansion of the usual view in the area of curriculum theory where the selection of material or content corresponds to the content dimension of learning, and the selection of teaching forms or work patterns corresponds to the interactive dimension, but the incentive dimension is not taken up as an independent and important area in the same manner. In connection with the planning and structuring of teaching, the incentive dimension of learning concerns, in particular, relating to the participants' motivation, the background for their participation (apart from their academic pre-qualifications), and the conclusions that can be drawn from this. In continuation of this, there might be a need for reflection about how the teaching can contribute to furthering and strengthening positive elements in the motivation.

Second, there is the question of types of learning (see Chapter 4), where it is a matter of the need for appropriate and up-to-date learning, meaning that, in general, education planning must pave the way for interaction between assimilative and accommodative processes. It will be relevant to aim at cumulative processes such as learning by heart and the like in special cases only. With respect to the transformative processes, this is something that increasingly takes place during the years of youth in connection with identity development, and in adult education programmes when it comes to participants who are in profound processes of realignment. But because these processes are so very individually conditioned, as a rule it is only if the measures have a clear and open main emphasis on personality development that the possibility for transformative learning becomes a direct part of the planning.

Third, it is important, but rather unusual, in connection with educational planning to take a targeted interest in the types of defence against learning that could possibly occur in participants in relation to the topic of the education programme (see sections 9.3 and 9.4). When it comes to young people, and especially adult participants, there will always exist some degree or other of everyday consciousness here, i.e. that the participants come with a semi-automatic defence against learning that transcends their acquired pre-understandings. If it is a course that the participants have enrolled in voluntarily on the basis of their own needs and interests, one can generally reckon with the will to overcome the everyday consciousness in the area in question. But in all cases where participation is more or less forced or against the person's will, typically the defence of everyday consciousness against new understandings will fully apply. And if learning is planned that requires demanding readjustment on the part of some participants, for example in the form of transformative processes, an identity defence can also play a role, even though the person in question wishes for it and is prepared to accept that the readjustments are necessary.

Fourth and finally, there can be resistance to learning (see section 9.5). When planning educational measures, it can sometimes be appropriate to consider whether there will be something in the course being planned that will give rise to serious resistance on the part of the participants and how one is going to relate to it. As pointed out earlier, resistance is an excellent point of departure for important learning, and therefore it can also be a good idea to have thought about it in advance. In some cases one can even incorporate it in the planning in order to strengthen and qualify the learning.

13.4 Learning content and forms of activity

In the above I have taken my point of departure in the understanding of learning and on this basis I have identified some matters of importance for planning and structuring educational activities on a general level. I will proceed in the opposite direction in the following, taking my starting point in some of the key areas and issues of curriculum theory, and examine how one can relate to them from a learning perspective.

I will start by examining the absolutely classic key field of curriculum theory concerning the content of education – what the participants are intended to learn. Naturally I will not enter into the numerous specific subject areas in the different education programmes. But, on the other hand, there are some very important general matters to do with the nature of teaching content that I will take up here in close relation to the content dimension of learning, which I discussed in Chapter 5.

Here it was emphasised as a key point that, today, what is to be learned does not merely have to do with knowledge and skills, but also with attitudes, understanding, insight, general cultural orientation, acquisition of methodology and personal characteristics such as independence, responsibility, cooperation and flexibility, everything that is collected under the modern concept of competence.

Naturally, this can all be acquired in many different ways, and many different forms of activity can be appropriate according to the topic of the learning and where one is placed in the education system. There is, however, a key crosscutting question concerning the extent to which, and where, the teaching or dissemination should be subject oriented (including interdisciplinary, where appropriate), problem oriented or, perhaps, experience or practice oriented, because such a distinction is of vital importance for the character of what is learned.

Subject-oriented procedures are mainly suited to dissemination and aim at leading to learning results concerning knowledge, skills, understanding and meaning as well as general culture and/or methodology orientation and understanding.

By subject orientation is meant that the activity is centred around a certain material lying within the frames of a specific subject or subject area. But there are also 'subject-oriented' areas of material that are not clearly related to a specific subject because the subjects and areas of material are constantly developing. There is, in addition, material that is included in two or more different subject areas where the perspectives typically are different. Finally, it may be a case of interdisciplinarity in the sense that one moves across two or more subjects or subject areas.

Problem-oriented procedures are mainly suited to dissemination and aim at leading to learning results covering both the above-mentioned categories and the development of personal characteristics.

By problem orientation is meant that the activity takes a point of departure in a problem or an issue that may be precisely formulated in a problem statement. The material or academic content is thus selected on the basis of what is relevant for illustrating a problem or problems, that the material appears in some context as well as proposals for a solution, if applicable. This has the advantage that the material appears in a context that provides a certain relevance and perspective and requires that one does something with the material, takes a position, thereby causing one to become a player in relation to the material. Problem orientation is often, but not necessarily, connected with project work as the form of organisation (for example, Illeris 1999, 2004).

Experience-oriented procedures are mainly suited to dissemination and aim at leading to learning results that are in the nature of the development of personal characteristics.

By experience orientation is meant that the activity itself, and the participants' personal attitude to it, are at the centre. Although the materials or academic content of the activity can also be of significant importance, the activity is built up around the experience and the personal relationship. This can be play and games in many different forms, for example, typically role play, computer play, simulation, drama, competitions or transaction analysis, or it can go over into a more individual-oriented direction such as personality development, survival trips or, in the most extreme form, in encounter groups, sensitivity training and the like.

Practice-oriented procedures, like the problem-oriented procedures, are broadly suited to disseminating learning results that are both more traditional and personality-developing in nature, although they do not immediately lead to an overview and theoretically based understanding. These are, first and foremost, trainee programmes of different kinds, see sections 12.4 and 12.7.

The definitions in the above are, of course, not precise and this is clear from the use of the words 'mainly' and 'broadly' – because there will often be gliding transitions between the different categories. But the categorisation serves to point to some key pedagogical matters in connection with the development from more traditional teaching and dissemination in the direction of competence development. In most forms of education this has mainly to do with the relation between traditional subject orientation and the more broadly based problem orientation, while most of the experience-based forms are, to a greater extent, mainly relevant when it has immediately to do with personality development with a view to inter-action and leadership, and the practice-oriented forms have, as mentioned, first to do with trainee programmes.

13.5 Learning, direction and participation

From the point of view of learning, another very important mistake in connection with structuring education programmes is the question of the participants' co-determination in directing what is to take place. Tradition-ally this is, unfortunately, not an area of great weight in curriculum theory, first and foremost probably because curriculum theory has traditionally been oriented towards the primary school in particular. While the question can also be relevant in the elementary classes, it becomes an urgent issue from about the age of 12–13, and in the youth and adult education programmes it is a field of quite decisive importance for the nature of what is learned.

It is a fact that young people and adults are far more prepared to mobilise the mental energy necessary for accommodative and transformative learning processes if they, themselves, can play a part in deciding what the learning is about and the forms of activity that are utilised. It is also inherent here that their attitudes will typically be less defensive and that the chances of new impulses being halted by everyday consciousness are fewer. It is also important that the motivational and emotional matters associated with learning, to a large extent, influence the quality of the learning with respect to attitudes, permanence and application possibilities (see Chapter 6), and these matters will typically be more positive when participants have an influence on what is taking place.

There are two main levels for the direction of educational activities. The general level concerns the frames that have already been established politically and administratively. What is of key importance here is the degree or 'density' of the framework provisions. This can vary from a very high degree of openness, which is for example the tradition at folk high schools and day high schools (similar to folk high schools but non-residential), to elaborate detailed management, seen especially within the vocationally oriented education programmes in connection with the education and teaching technology approach (for example, Skinner 1968; Tyler 1950). But this approach has now been abandoned in several places, in particular, because it tends to have a negative effect on the motivation of both teachers and students and thus leads to poor learning results.

It is obvious that if the participants are to play a part in deciding how the education programme and the teaching are directed, the framework conditions must be relatively open in nature. The framework conditions can also directly open the way for such co-determination.

The second level in connection with teaching direction and participants' co-determination concerns daily practice. Three forms of direction can basically be distinguished.

Teacher direction is the traditional form where it is the teachers who more or less autocratically decide what is to take place and how. This must, of necessity, be the case during the first years of primary school, preferably in cooperation with parents on the overall guidelines. But when the children get older, and in the youth and adult education programmes, it need not continue in this way, even though both teachers and pupils tend to continue what is experienced as the immediately obvious way of directing the activities.

Participant direction means that all participants – teachers, pupils/students and any others that may be involved – direct together and thus make direction an important matter, which means a lot for the motivation and the quality of the learning. There will typically be a certain division of roles between the parties, fundamentally in that the teachers are responsible for compliance with the framework conditions while pupils or students are responsible for what takes place being experienced as important, relevant and instructive. And even though it is rarely concretely expressed, it is an important underlying premise that if agreement cannot be negotiated, it is the pupils or students who must take responsibility for the final decision because it is their learning that is at stake (see Illeris 1999).

Self-direction is a key concept within adult education, in the USA in particular, and partly also in other English-speaking countries. 'Self-directed learning' is about the adult students themselves organising and taking responsibility for their own learning (for example, Tough 1967, 1971; Knowles 1970, 1973, 1975; Brockett and Hiemstra 1991; Candy 1991; Tennant 1997; Merriam and Caffarella 1999). In practice, however, there is no clear borderline in relation to participant direction, partly because in participant direction, as mentioned, it is the learners who have the final responsibility, and partly because, in practice, self-direction very often means that teachers, supervisors and others are involved in the direction. The difference is perhaps rather on the cultural level where the Nordic countries have a very firm tradition of participant direction in the field of public enlightenment, while the English-speaking countries do not have this tradition but are, on the other hand, more individualistically oriented by tradition.

On the whole, in this context, it is important to be aware that these three levels of direction can very well be practised side by side or in a process of interaction, and in practice very often are. For example, in a participant-directed course it is eminently possible to agree to include sequences where it is a teacher who takes over the direction and the responsibility. Nevertheless, the question of direction is important and central, because awareness of who has, and takes, responsibility in the final analysis is of great importance for the attitude and responsibility of the participants.

In general, and in parallel with other matters of direction in democratic societies, it would be most reasonable and appropriate for schools and education up to the age of about 14 years to be wholly or mainly teacher directed, and for this to then be followed by a period up to about the age of 20 years where it is a conscious and systematic aim that the students gradually take over more and more of the direction, and subsequently in principle for there to be participant direction within the frames of the education programme and general self-direction for the individual's education as a whole.

The latter also applies to the position of political and administrative bodies in relation to adults' education. One can plan for, and encourage, adults to involve themselves in education and lifelong learning, one can create incentives in many ways, but in the final analysis the decision is up to the adults themselves, and it is not appropriate from the point of view of economy, democracy or learning to make use of financial pressure as an incentive in this connection (see Illeris 2004).

13.6 Content, direction, forms of knowledge and patterns of work

On the basis of the two previous sections, it is now possible to introduce an overview model (Figure 13.1) that I developed earlier as a continuation of Kolb's learning model (Kolb 1984; see section 5.2; Illeris 1995, 2004).

The model is built up around two axes designating the two conditions concerning the organisation of the education programmes which I have identified in the above as being central to learning, namely, selection of content and direction of the activities.

The direction is the vertical axis stretched out between the poles of *teacher direction* and *participant direction*, self-direction either lying outside of the education programmes or taking on the character of participant direction. Correspondingly, selection of content is the horizontal axis stretched out between *subject orientation* and *problem orientation*, as experience orientation and practice orientation only enter the educational activities in special cases.

From the point of view of learning, the poles of the two axes point out to the form of learning or knowledge that is typically furthered in extension of the weighting of these four poles, referring to the forms of knowledge in Kolb's model (section 5.2). By means of teacher direction, what is particularly promoted is *assimilative knowledge*, subject orientation

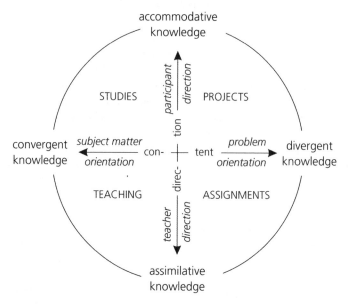

Figure 13.1 A didactic model (after Illeris 1995, p. 131)

especially promotes *convergent knowledge*, participant direction favours *accommodative knowledge*, and by means of problem orientation *divergent knowledge*, in particular, is furthered.

The four spaces between the axes of the model show on this basis four typical educational work patterns that are staked out by means of the chosen forms of direction and content selection, and promote (but do not determine) certain forms of knowledge.

1   A combination of teacher direction and subject orientation produces the pattern of work we generally term *teaching*, promoting assimilative and convergent knowledge, in particular.

2   A combination of teacher direction and problem orientation results in *assignments* set by the teacher or other bodies which can range from simple sums to large-scale, complex tasks. This promotes, in particular, assimilative and divergent knowledge.

3   A combination of participant direction and subject orientation results in *studies*, i.e. the pupils or students themselves work on acquiring a given material, thus promoting accommodative and convergent knowledge.

4   And, finally, a combination of participant direction and problem orientation results in *projects*, where it is the participants' own problems that form the starting point for investigation, elaboration and proposals

for a resolution. This promotes accommodative and divergent knowledge especially.

It is not the point of the model, in general, to emphasise certain pedagogical work patterns, but to point out that fundamentally different pedagogical procedures have certain characteristics influencing the nature of the knowledge that is acquired and the learning that takes place. The pedagogical structuring must, therefore, be weighted on the basis of considerations of the objective of the educational course in question. It will/should as a rule – except, perhaps, for very brief courses – be a combination of more or all types of work patterns, but in a carefully considered balance corresponding to the overall objective of the course.

If the primary objective, for example, concerns the acquisition of a certain subject matter, it will usually be appropriate for teaching and assignments to have considerable weight, while there may be room for a minor project towards the conclusion of the course. But if the objective implies a higher degree of competence development, it would be in order for project work to play a more central role.

The question of the weighting of different work patterns with the associated forms of content selection and direction of activities is thus the key general didactic concern when it comes to the practical organisation of a given educational course within the framework conditions that are laid down in advance. In some cases, however, this weighting will form part of the framework conditions, wholly or partially, and unfortunately often in a way that does not harmonise with the given objective. In this case it would be relevant to point out this contradiction to those who have established the frames, and those who are to fulfil them.

13.7 Learning and current educational policy

This is a book about learning. I have now gradually moved from matters directly to do with learning over to the question of the basis for participation in educational programmes and the direction of learning and framework conditions within the education system.

Today, every country openly acknowledges that there is a great need for more and more members of society to obtain more and better education. It is, first and foremost, necessary in order to secure continued economic growth and international competitiveness, but also for reasons of social cohesion and the welfare of members of society, as in our part of the world these three objectives are always formulated in this order, thus indicating indirectly their order of prioritisation (for example, OECD 1996; EU Commission 2000).

However, almost all of these countries are experiencing increasing problems with education programmes. Since the start of the millennium, in Denmark we have, among other things, experienced an increase in the group of young people who do not complete a qualifying education and a radical decline in participation in adult education. If one views this issue from the perspective of learning as it has been developed in this book, and this is very reasonable when it concerns more and better learning, the following picture emerges, however.

The point of departure is primarily taken in the content dimension of learning, i.e. in society's need for up-to-date qualifications and competences, both vocationally because of stepped up international competition and, more generally, for people to be able to manage their lives in our increasingly more complex and changeable society. There are, in addition, some more recent tendencies towards national cultural rearmament that is to serve to strengthen the internal cohesion of society.

The next step is to consider the interactive dimension, i.e. the way in which the education programmes are structured. In parts of the education system there has been growing interest in project work and similar forms of work which could be appropriate in relation to modern competence requirements – but traditional subject-divided class teaching still dominates. There is also a tendency to give the individual institutions greater freedom to organise the activities themselves while simultaneously investing in increased market orientation, for example, in the form of free choice of school, ranking of schools and educational institutions, more tests, evaluations and reports as well as increased user payments.

The third dimension of learning, the incentive dimension, is approached especially by developing the counselling options, even though this seldom functions satisfactorily for those who are most in need of it. In addition there is increased use of negative economic incentives, i.e. financial penalties for those who will not take part in educational activities in situations where society judges it to be necessary.

In general, it is clear enough that education policy is fundamentally directed on economic rather than learning premises. As a very striking example it can be mentioned that the overall policy in relation to adult education in Denmark since the turn of the twenty-first century has become a matter that is largely managed by the Ministry of Finance.

The net result of all this, as clearly demonstrated, is steadily increasing problems and tendencies towards less and worse learning. There are, naturally, many reasons for this, and much of it is inherent in general trends in the development of society that do not specifically have to do with education and learning but which, nonetheless, affect the area to a high degree. But the question is the degree to which the measures initiated on the basis of economically dominated thinking of a neo-liberal nature are the right way to tackle these problems.

There are, of course, many financial considerations, and it cannot be excluded that the result could be better if the will existed to devote more resources to the area. But this might not even be necessary. One could also choose to attempt to resolve an issue that fundamentally concerns learning, on a learning basis.

One would then have to put the three dimensions of learning on an equal footing as a point of departure because each of them has its significance in all forms of learning. But in the present situation it would probably be wise to try to turn the whole approach to the area upside down by taking up the dimensions in the opposite order to that which is practised now and outlined in the above.

Taking a point of departure in the incentive dimension of learning, one would have to start by establishing that good learning – including, among other things, understanding and overview, activating affirmative, flexible and creative feelings, and which is durable and applicable in a broad range of known and new situations – basically presupposes positive motivation and personal engagement.

This means that we would have to listen much more to what the potential participants are motivated for engaging themselves in – and in order to avoid any misunderstanding: motivation is not necessarily the same as desire. To a high degree it can also be insight into what is appropriate and necessary. In Chapter 11, I briefly sketched what the most important drives for learning are in the different life ages – childhood, youth, adulthood and mature adulthood – and one could try to take this seriously as a point of departure, instead of economic considerations.

It would then be found that up to puberty children are actually highly motivated to learn what the adults whom they trust present to them. Therefore, this is the time for a great deal of fundamental learning, which should naturally be organised with relatively fixed frames in accord with the ages and development of the children, and the content of which should probably be adjusted in relation to current social conditions so that, for example, computers and other electronic media, foreign languages, corporality and health and general orientation about society receive a more prominent position. Other areas must, correspondingly, be left out or, at least, cut down. But there is hardly any reason why the learning cannot be increased if it is understood broadly, the needs of the children are met and supported, there is alternation between targeted activities and free play, and there are sufficient qualified adults to take care of it.

In the case of young people, it must be understood that in a way that has not previously been known, identity formation today is quite central in the consciousness and behaviour of young people and directs their motivation and engagement. This by no means runs counter to learning – on the contrary, identity formation is a learning process of a breadth and depth that goes much further than 'learning as syllabus acquisition'. But it implies that one must be more oriented towards the problems as they are experienced by the young, with all the differences inherent in this, and it implies, of necessity – as pointed out in section 13.4 – that something quite radical must be done to ensure acceptable routes of access for these young people to real working life.

With respect to the adults, what is most important is that their motivation requires them to be treated as adult persons and not just as potential labour. There can be some preliminary problems in this regard, also for the adults themselves, and these must be solved by means of conscious and targeted transfer of more and more responsibility for learning to the adult participants themselves. The paradox here is that economic thinking and the need on the part of the authorities to decide in far too much detail gets in the way of the great social economic potential inherent in offering qualifying adult education programmes on the adults' own terms. In this area also, access to working life is quite central for the low-skilled especially and something that must be made simpler for both economic and educational reasons.

Finally, in the case of mature adults one should be aware that interest-based adult education can, to a high degree, play a part in keeping them going so that they can obtain more from this life stage and will also tend to remain on the labour market for longer.

It is such considerations, with a point of departure in the incentive dimension of learning, which I have outlined here that need to be brought to the fore if the present contradiction between the aims of the politicians and the education policy that is pursued is to be solved constructively. Naturally, as in the above, there must be considerations based on the interactive and content dimensions of learning linked to this, but what is absolutely central is to seek to cover society's learning needs with a starting point in the persons concerned.

This is a large-scale, ambitious project but, on the other hand, it could contribute to solving a number of current social problems in a way that is progressive and profitable from the points of view of both learning and the economy.

13.8 Summary

Educational measures cannot, of course, be planned solely with a point of departure in learning issues. But at present there are some types of misunderstandings about learning that are widespread in connection with the organisation of education programmes and, to a much too large extent, the point of departure is taken in economic considerations when the frames are being established.

Therefore, there is good reason for learning considerations to be more involved and centred around the needs of different groups of participants when education is planned and, at the same time, for emphasising the character of the programmes' content and direction, so that there is better agreement between the objectives of the education programmes and their daily practice.

Chapter 14

Overview

This final chapter starts by summing up the learning understanding developed in the preceding chapters. I then look at the way in which the many different learning theoreticians and others whose contributions I have drawn on are placed in relation to the tension field for learning illustrated in the learning triangle developed. I conclude with some brief reflections and perspectives in relation to my view of the position and message of the book.

14.1 Summary of the learning theory developed

In the following I will strive to provide a brief crosscutting summary of the main elements in the learning understanding developed in this book. The summary will not follow the line of progression that the presentation has been based on. However, in a concentrated form I try to retain the most important aspects of the conclusions I have reached.

The learning conception presented is fundamentally based on the understanding that human ability to learn is an integrated part of the human life and survival potential and, as such, is libidinous in nature at the outset. However, during the pre-school years a resistance potential is split off as a separate potential that can be activated when the life potential meets serious obstacles.

As to the process of learning, I see it as an entity uniting both a direct or media-disseminated interaction process between the individual and his/her material and social environment and an inner mental process of acquisition. As this acquisition process has both a content and an incentive element, three dimensions form part of all learning: content, incentive and interaction. This also means that learning is always played out on an individual and a social and societal level at the same time, and the learning result has the character of an individual phenomenon that is always socially and societally marked.

The main categories of the interaction processes that make up the 'raw material' or input of the learning processes may be characterised as perception, transmission, experience, imitation, activity or participation. However, these categories should not be regarded as separate, but rather as characteristics that can be combined in the single learning event, each of them being more or less present or prominent in a pattern unique to the specific situation.

The interaction starts with the 'mother-child-dyad' between the baby and its primary care person. Already in this interaction, the mother or other primary care person is the carrier of current societal markings and structures, and at the same time the interaction always takes place in a societally structured space. Later, the interactions will gradually take on the form of a direct or mediated relation to societal totality.

Through the internal psychological processes of acquisition, cognitive structures of knowledge, understanding and abilities and dynamic patterns of emotions, motivations and volition are developed in an integrated way. This integration means that content structures are always emotionally obsessed, and incentive patterns include content features. Together, content and incentives are conducive to the development of personality.

The internal psychological processes can be of a predominantly cumulative (mechanical), assimilative (additive), accommodative (transcendent) or transformative (personality changing) character. Through cumulative processes new structures and patterns are established, while new elements are added to already existing structures and patterns through assimilative processes. Through accommodative processes existing structures and patterns are dissociated and reconstructed so that new assimilative constructions can take place. And through transformative processes, there is simultaneous reconstruction of several structures and patterns across the learning dimensions.

Accommodative and transformative processes are activated when the individual meets impulses or situations it cannot manage on the basis of existing structures and patterns. While memory and applicability of the learning results of cumulative and assimilative processes to some degree presuppose a subjective connection to the original learning situation, in principle the results of accommodative and transformative processes are freely accessible. Further, the learning results can be predominantly convergent (unambiguous) or divergent (ambiguous), and accommodative and transformative reconstruction can be more or less offensive or defensive.

A special form of accommodation is reflection, which typically comprehends material from different structures and takes place without any direct input of new stimuli from the environment. The basis of reflection is a more or less conscious experience of a subjectively important challenge or contradiction. Self-reflection or reflexivity is a special kind of reflection that can lead to increased self-consciousness and, therefore, is an important element of personality. In late-modern society biographicity is developed as a junction of reflexivity and personality.

Learning processes can vary from limited events in a specific area of learning to broad and comprehensive developments comprising the whole personality and identity. They can be of a predominantly content, incentive or interactive character, but always include all of these dimensions to some extent, and they may also be integrated with biologically conditioned maturing or ageing processes. Learning typically takes place in phases or stages that change between 'plateaus' with a relatively level and predominantly assimilative development, and steps or 'jumps' of a predominantly accommodative nature.

Some learning processes involve active resistance or defensive rejection, blocking or distortion. Typically impulses that are at odds with existing structures and patterns, and, therefore, potentially might provoke accommodative processes, may be distorted so that the discrepancy is repressed and the distorted impulse, accordingly, can be managed by assimilation. In modern society it is necessary for the individual to develop such defence mechanisms that are part of a more general everyday consciousness that seeks to accommodate the overwhelming number of influences by avoiding linking of the different structures, and thus tend to split the consciousness into a series of more or less distinct spaces. There may, in addition, be more far-reaching identity defence that seeks to protect the identity of the individual in the face of demands and challenges that lead the way to, or necessitate changes of, identity.

As a whole, the totality of these interaction processes and internal processes of acquisition and elaboration form a lifelong process of experience. Learning takes on this character to the extent that it is related to a subjectively relevant social context in which the learner is actively involved and relates impulses to previous experience and future perspectives. Learning of this kind will typically concern problems that are subjectively important and are dealt with in relation to relevant possibilities of forward-pointing action on the basis of already established experiential patterns.

People typically have different life situations and life perspectives in the various life ages, and these conditions influence the character of learning generally. In childhood and up to puberty, the child will very largely seek to acquire as many of the influences it meets as possible, trustingly and without censorship. In the years of youth and up to the establishment of a more or less stable personal identity – in our society a process that easily can last until well into the twenties or the thirties and is frequently more or less incomplete in nature – learning is basically influenced by precisely this identity process, and all learning impulses are typically filtered through a question that is something like: What does this mean for me and my identity? In adulthood, learning is typically fundamentally selective and sceptical. It is impossible to learn everything and one must therefore make selections; it is necessary for this selection mechanism to be more or less automated in everyday life. Large-scale learning choices are usually made more consciously on the basis of criteria that concern the individual's life situation and life projects. In mature adulthood, where the individual realises that his/her lifetime is limited, learning becomes even more selective.

Both the general character of the learning situation – for instance, everyday life, school or education, working life, leisure-time interests or net-based activities – and its specific content and emotional appeal will always leave a mark on the learning that takes place. Correspondingly, the situation of the learner both as to general features such as age, gender and societal background and, more specifically, in relation to interests, background and preconditions in the situation, will also always mark the learning.

From the point of view of education it is important that all aspects of learning-related matters – including each of the three learning dimensions, each of the four learning types and important types of barriers to learning, as well as the participants' age, gender, background and life situation – receive specific emphasis in the planning, structuring and implementation of the educational course. In our present society there is a tendency for economically based considerations to overshadow learning-oriented matters to such an extent that it leads to considerable individual and societal waste of resources.

14.2 Positions in the tension field of learning

In Figure 3.2, I presented the learning field as a triangle stretched over the three learning dimensions. It is my basic assumption that these dimensions are always represented in learning processes and that a comprehensive learning theory consequently must include all three dimensions and how they are related to each other.

In the intervening chapters I have, accordingly, involved a number of theories about, or of relevance for, learning. I will now try to take a general view of these theoretical positions by approximately fitting them into the learning triangle (Figure 14.1). This may simultaneously contribute to concretisation of the character of the learning field.

The upper line of the learning field connects the content and incentive poles, and along this line most of what is normally labelled *developmental psychology* is situated, as it usually comprises both the content and the incentive dimensions of individual development, whereas interactive conditions are usually only briefly considered here.

At the pole of content, I have placed Piaget as an important and typical representative of the content approach, with strong emphasis on cognition. Close to this pole I shall also place Kolb, whose theory and model also mainly relate to the content dimension of learning. I also place Nissen here although his considerations of the specific demand of psychological energy

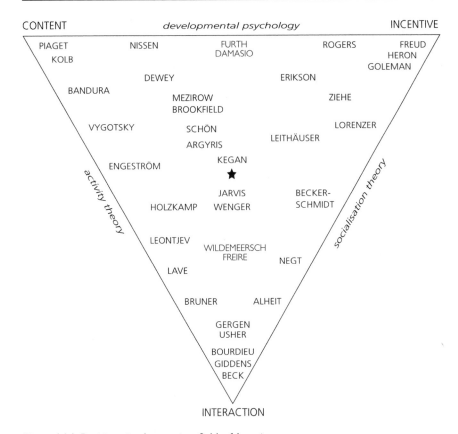

CONTENT   *developmental psychology*   INCENTIVE

Figure 14.1 Positions in the tension field of learning

in connection with accommodative processes place him one step further out of the line towards the incentive pole.

I have placed Freud at the incentive pole as the most important and typical representative, even though he only indirectly discussed learning. Heron and Goleman must also be placed right beside Freud. Both have specifically dealt with the emotional or motivational side of learning, although they also have insight into the other dimensions. Close to Freud I shall also place Rogers with his interest in the development of the self and learning in this context. However, it must be observed that Rogers conceives of the self as both a content and incentive structure, and therefore his position is not close to the incentive pole but one step in the direction of the content pole.

Right in the middle between these two poles is the position of Furth, who is deliberately trying to find an equal balance between Piaget and Freud. I place Damasio in the same position, as the representative of brain research who has most emphatically pointed to the inseparable interaction between emotions and reason.

In addition, some other contributing positions mainly relate to the developmental psychological understanding, although they are not positioned right up to the upper borderline of the field because, to some extent, they involve societal conditions. In the direction of the content pole I place Dewey and, slightly towards the incentive pole, Erikson with his psycho-analytical orientation. To these may be added two adult education specialists, Mezirow and Brookfield, who with their broad orientation can be placed between Dewey and the middle of the figure.

The left-hand line of the learning triangle goes from the content pole down towards the interaction pole. Along this line I primarily place the *activity theory* approach of the Russian cultural historical school, which is precisely characterised by its intention of relating cognitive learning to its societal conditions.

At this line I, therefore, first of all place Vygotsky and Leontjev, the former somewhat in the direction of the content and the latter somewhat in the direction of the interaction pole – and between the two I place Engeström as their contemporary Finnish heir.

Furthermore, there are three other contributors to be placed in the area along this line. First, Bandura, whose theory of 'social learning' I find so cognitively oriented that, in spite of the fact that he launched this concept, I place him close to the content pole. Second, Lave, who with her anthropological starting point must be placed towards the interaction pole. And finally, Bruner, who started his career right up in the content corner but, through a remarkable development over several decades, has moved down along this sideline, so that I now find it correct to place him close to the interaction pole.

One certain position is that of Holzkamp (and also Holzkamp-Osterkamp) who, while being closely attached to the cultural historical tradition, in his later years deliberately tried to reach out towards the incentive domain and therefore must be placed a step towards the centre of the field. And, also in this area are Argyris and Schön, who are a little difficult to fit in. With their single- and double-loop model, they have apparently an individual psychological approach, which should place them in the upper part of the field, but, on the other hand, they relate themselves to the domain of organisational learning, which is a social area. Moreover, they primarily deal with the content side of learning but do not avoid emotional references. Thus they must be placed rather close to the centre of the field, but somewhat in the direction of the cognitive pole.

The right sideline of the learning triangle goes from the incentive pole down towards the interaction pole. Along this line, the main contribution is the critical theory of the Frankfurt School and its extension in various approaches relating more or less to *socialisation theory*.

Nearest to the incentive pole here I place Lorenzer, nearest to the interaction pole it must be Negt, and in between the two is the position of Becker-Schmidt with her focus on the ambivalences. In addition, there are two more contributors that I have involved to a significant extent, namely Ziehe – whose position must be a little up towards the developmental psychological area, and Leithäuser, who, at least in his earlier works about everyday consciousness, includes elements that reach out towards the content pole. Finally, I will place yet another German here, namely Alheit, who, with his interest in biography, I place quite far down near the interaction pole.

At the bottom of the figure and in the middle between the two sidelines, there are, finally, a number of positions that are clearly or predominantly socially or societally oriented and only in a general way relate to the psychological dimensions of learning.

Close to the interaction pole I will place the positions of the sociologists Beck, Giddens and Bourdieu with their contributions concerning the conditions of late-modern society for learning, and slightly higher up towards the middle Gergen, as a representative of the social constructionist approach, which is essentially of a psychological nature but very much directed towards the social interaction processes, and Usher, who with his postmodern orientation also belongs in this area.

Another step towards the centre of the field, and still halfway between the two sidelines, I place Wildemeersch with his special interest in social movements, and Freire with his orientation towards elementary and simultaneously political learning for oppressed peoples in developing countries.

Finally, there are the three theoreticians whom I have dealt with in particular in Chapter 8 on holistic learning and who must, therefore, be placed close to the centre of the figure. These are Kegan, who I place at the individual-oriented side of the centre because of his largely psychological approach, Jarvis, who seeks to range broadly and in a balanced way but who with his sociological starting point I must place just under the centre, and Wenger, who with his key concept concerning communities of practice comes a little further down towards the interaction pole.

Concerning the figure, in conclusion I would like to establish that the learning approach presented in this book argues as its crucial point that the whole learning field must be taken into account in any dealing with learning in theory or practice, and thus seeks to place itself with the focal point close to the centre of the figure.

I would also like to mention that I find it remarkable and disturbing that almost all the theoreticians I have discussed are men. Only three women are mentioned in connection with the figure: Jean Lave, Ute Holzkamp-Osterkamp and Regina Becker-Schmidt. In contrast to this in Western cultural circles there are probably at least as many women as men occupied with learning and teaching in practice in schools and institutions and in other contexts.

The type of theory development I have been dealing with here is thus clearly something that appeals to men to a higher degree than to women, and this can be related to Baron-Cohen's theory about men's stronger system orientation and women's stronger empathy orientation (see section 10.4). It may be hoped that one day a book will appear about learning in an empathetic perspective that is more general in character than Belenky *et al.*'s study *Women's Ways of Knowing* (Belenky *et al.* 1986; see section 10.4).

14.3 Conclusion and perspective

In the above I have tried to show how the understanding of learning that I have presented has drawn on contributions from many different positions, which together cover the whole of the learning field between content, incentives and interaction. However, this does not mean that the conception is merely a juxtaposition of a number of different contributions with their various scientific and theoretical bases and attitudes.

On the contrary, the understanding is built up from the fundamentally constructivist position which was developed by Piaget – generally acknowledged to be one of the founders of constructivism. I consider the linkage to the Freudian theory universe as relatively unproblematic in this connection. It has been made with a close reference to Furth's pointing out of fundamental similarities between the theory constructions of Freud and Piaget, which makes it possible to see Freud's theories in a constructionist perspective. From this point of view, Freud's conception of human drives becomes a parallel to Piaget's conception of the function of equilibration between assimilative and accommodative processes – as a connecting link between the biologically and genetically developed fundamentals of the human species and the individual human being's construction of him- or herself as a subject, i.e. as a societal individual.

Furthermore, when learning is conceived of as an integration of the internal psychological processes that Piaget and Freud have dealt with and the social interaction processes between the individual and its environment, it also becomes possible in this frame of understanding to include sociality as a constructive force, such as it is conceived of in social constructionism. Thus the contradiction between constructivism and social constructionism, which Gergen has paid much attention to, in my understanding takes on the character of an integrated interaction between two types of construction processes which are both essential to, and necessary for, learning.

Parallel to the close connections of internal psychological processes to the biological and genetic basis of the human species, the social processes have a basic connection to the societally developed environment. In the social processes, societally developed individuals are involved in situations that are framed by existing societal structures. In our modern society – and to a rising extent in societies the world over – this means, within the globalised, market-oriented, late capitalist form of society with its dominating multinational capital, high technology, economic thinking and power policies, the colossal tensions between rich and poor countries and population groups and the untenable over-consumption of the Earth's resources.

Thus, fundamentally learning is a process mediating between man as a biologically and genetically developed species and the societal structures developed by man. Learning develops knowledge, abilities, understandings, emotions, attitudes and sociality, which are important elements of the conditions and raw material of society. But societal circumstances also develop into independent structures with a character of given frames that set the conditions of the knowledge, the abilities, the understandings, the emotions, the attitudes and the sociality that can be displayed.

In this perspective, learning is an important mediating connection in a most topical question about whether human qualities are able to match and cope with current societal structures which the very same human capacities have been the incentives for developing – or whether societal development has taken over the last bit of power from the human basis that has created it and is about to destroy its own existence.

Learning, in this connection, is not just a neutral process. Learning might contribute to the strengthening both of human forces and of blind societal developments – and societally institutionalised learning efforts in education and other places are, consequently, not just value-neutral technical or economic matters. Therefore, the study of the nature of learning and understanding of its mode of functioning and significance is not only a scholarly and hugely complex matter, it is also input for the societal development that can make a contribution to maintaining a central and specifically human perspective in a world in which economic and technological lines of approach seem to be on the way to making mankind an object of its own fantastic creations.

References

Adorno, Theodor W. (1972 [1951]): Freudian Theory and the Pattern of Fascist Propaganda. In Theodor W. Adorno: *Soziologische Schriften I, Gesammelte Schriften, Band 8*. Frankfurt a.M.: Suhrkamp.

——, Frenkel-Brunswik, Else, Levinson, Daniel J. and Sanford, R. Nevitt (1950): *The Authoritarian Personality*. New York: Harper & Brothers.

Ahrenkiel, Annegrethe and Illeris, Knud (2000): *Adult Education between Emancipation and Control*. Paper. The Adult Education Research Project, Roskilde University.

Alheit, Peter (1994): The Biographical Question as a Challenge to Adult Education. *International Review of Education*, 40.

—— (1995): Biographical Learning. In Peter Alheit *et al.* (eds): *The Biographical Approach in European Adult Education*. Vienna: ESREA/Verband Wiener Volksbildung.

Allport, Gordon W. (1967): *Pattern and Growth in Personality*. New York: Holt, Rineholt and Winston.

Andersen, Anders Siig, Olesen, Henning Salling, Sommer, Finn M. and Weber, Kirsten (1993): *En oplevelse for livet*. Roskilde: The Adult Education Research Group, Roskilde University. [An experience for life].

Andersen, Vibeke, Illeris, Knud, Kjærsgaard, Christian, Larsen, Kirsten, Olesen, Henning Salling and Ulriksen, Lars (1994): *Qualifications and Living People*. Roskilde: The Adult Education Research Group, Roskilde University.

——, ——, ——, ——, —— and —— (1996): *General Qualification*. Roskilde: The Adult Education Research Group, Roskilde University.

Anderson, John R. (1988): Cognitive Style and Multicultural Populations. *Journal of Teacher Education*, 1 (39), pp. 2–9.

Andreasen, Nancy C. (2005): *The Creating Brain: The Neuroscience of Genius*. New York: Dana Press.

Antikainen, Ari (1998): In Search of Meaning and Practice of Life-long Learning. In Knud Illeris (ed.): *Adult Education in a Transforming Society*. Copenhagen: Roskilde University Press.

—— and Kauppila, Juha (2000): The Story of a Learner: Educational Generations and the Future of Liberal Adult Education (Folksbildning) in Finland. In Knud Illeris (ed.): *Adult Education in the Perspective of the Learners*. Copenhagen: Roskilde University Press.

——, Houtsonen, Jarmo, Kauppila, Juha and Turunen, A. (1996): *Living in a Learning Society: Life-Histories, Identities and Education*. London: Falmer.

Argyris, Chris (1992): *On Organizational Learning.* Cambridge, MA: Blackwell.
—— (2000): *The Next Challenge in Organizational Learning: Leadership and Change.* Paper presented at the Learning Lab Denmark Opening Conference. Copenhagen, November 6.
—— and Schön, Donald (1978): *Organizational Learning: A Theory of Action Perspective.* Reading, MA: Addison-Wesley.
—— and —— (1996): *Organizational Learning II – Theory, Method, Practice.* Reading, MA: Addison-Wesley.
Aronowitz, Stanley and Giroux, Henry A. (1985): *Education under Siege: The Conservative, Liberal and Radical Debate over Schooling.* South Hadley, MA: Bergin and Garvey.
—— and —— (1991): *Postmodern Education: Politics, Culture, and Social Criticism.* Minneapolis, MN: University of Minnesota Press.
Ausubel, David P. (1968): *Educational Psychology: A Cognitive View.* New York: Holt, Rinehart and Winston.
Baltes, Paul B. and Schaie, K. Warner (eds) (1973): *Life-Span Developmental Psychology: Personality and Socialization.* New York: Academic Press.
Bandura, Albert (1977): *Social Learning Theory.* Englewood Cliffs, NJ: Prentice-Hall.
—— and Walters, Richard H. (1963): *Social Learning and Personality Development.* New York: Holt, Rinehart and Winston.
Baron-Cohen, Simon (2003): *The Essential Difference.* London: Penguin.
Bateson, Gregory (1972): *Steps to an Ecology of Mind.* San Francisco, CA: Chandler.
Bauer, Mette and Borg, Karin (1986 [1976]): *Den skjulte læreplan.* Copenhagen: Unge Pædagoger. [The hidden curriculum].
Bauman, Zygmunt (1998): *Globalization: The Human Consequences.* Cambridge, UK: Polity Press.
Beck, Ulrich (1992 [1986]): *Risk Society: Towards a New Modernity.* London: Sage.
—— and Beck-Gernsheim, Elizabeth (2002): *Individualization: Institutionalized Individualism and its Social and Political Consequences.* London: Sage.
Becker-Schmidt, Regina (1987): Dynamik sozialen Lernens: Geschlechterdifferenz und Konflikte aus der Perspektive von Frauen. In Regina Becker-Schmidt and Gudrun-Axeli Knapp: *Geschlechtertrennung – Geschlechterdifferenz – Suchbewegungen sozialen Lernens.* Bonn: J.H.W. Dietz Nachf. [The dynamics of social learning: gender difference and conflicts as viewed from a female perspective].
Beckett, David and Hager, Paul (2002): *Life, Work and Learning: Practice in Postmodernity.* London: Routledge.
Belenky, Mary Field, Clinchy, Blythe McVicker, Goldberger, Nancy Rule and Tarule, Jill Mattuck (1986): *Women's Ways of Knowing: The Development of Self, Voice, and Mind.* New York: Basic Books.
Berliner, Peter and Berthelsen, Jens (1989): Passiv aggression. *Nordisk psykologi,* 4, pp. 301–315. [Passive aggression].
Berlyne, Daniel E. (1960): *Conflict, Arousal, and Curiosity.* New York: McGraw-Hill.
Bernstein, Basil (1971): *Class, Codes and Control.* London: Routledge & Kegan Paul.
Berthelsen, Jens (2001): *Dilemmaet som lærer – om undervisning med læring gennem dilemmaer.* Copenhagen: Samfundslitteratur. [The dilemma as teacher: about teaching by learning from dilemmas].

Billett, Stephen (2001): *Learning in the Workplace: Strategies for Effective Practice*. Crows Nest, NSW: Allen & Unwin.

Bjerg, Jens (1972): *Pædagogisk udviklingsarbejde i folkeskolen*. Roskilde: Roskilde University. [Educational developmental work in primary and lower secondary school].

—— (ed.) (1976): *Pædagogisk udviklingsarbejde – principper og vilkår belyst ved Brovst-projektet 1970–74*. Copenhagen: Munksgaard. [Education developmental work: principles and conditions illustrated by the Brovst-project 1970–74].

Borg, Vilhelm (1971): *Industriarbejde og arbejderbevidsthed*. Copenhagen: Røde Hane. [Industrial work and worker consciousness].

Botkin, Jams W., Elmandjra, Mahdi and Malitza, Mircea (1979): *No Limits to Learning – Bridging the Human Gap: A Report to the Club of Rome*. Oxford: Pergamon.

Boud, David (1989): Some Competing Traditions in Experiential Learning. In Susan Warner Weil and Ian McGill (eds): *Making Sense of Experiential Learning: Diversity in Theory and Practice*. Buckingham: Open University Press.

—— and Garrick, John (eds) (1999): *Understanding Learning at Work*. London: Routledge.

—— and Walker, David (1990): Making the Most of Experience. *Studies in Continuing Education*, 2, pp. 61–80.

——, Cohen, Ruth and Walker, David (eds) (1993): *Using Experience for Learning*. Buckingham: Open University Press.

——, Keogh, Rosemary and Walker, David (1985) (eds): *Reflection: Turning Experience into Learning*. London: Kogan Page.

Bourdieu, Pierre (1998 [1994]): *Practical Reason: On the Theory of Action*. Cambridge, UK: Polity Press.

—— and Passéron, Jean-Claude (1977 [1970]): *Reproduction in Education, Society and Culture*. London: Sage.

Bowles, Samuel and Gintis, Herbert (1976): *Schooling in Capitalist America*. New York: Basic Books.

Brah, Avtar and Hoy, Jane (1989): Experiential Learning: A New Orthodoxy. In Susan Warner Weil and Ian McGill (eds): *Making Sense of Experiential Learning: Diversity in Theory and Practice*. Buckingham: Open University Press.

Braverman, Harry (1974): *Labor and Monopoly Capital*. New York: Monthly Review Press.

Brockett, Ralph D. and Hiemstra, Roger (1991): *Self-Direction in Adult Learning: Perspectives on Theory, Research, and Practice*. New York: Routledge.

Brookfield, Stephen D. (1987): *Developing Critical Thinkers – Challenging Adults to Explore Alternative Ways of Thinking and Acting*. Milton Keynes: Open University Press.

—— (1990a): *The Skillful Teacher: On Technique, Trust, and Responsiveness in the Classroom*. San Francisco, CA: Jossey-Bass.

—— (1990b): Using Critical Incidents to Explore Learners' Assumptions. In Jack Mezirow and Associates (eds): *Fostering Critical Reflection in Adulthood*. San Francisco, CA: Jossey-Bass.

—— (1995): *Becoming a Critically Reflective Teacher*. San Francisco, CA: Jossey-Bass.

—— (2000a): Transformative Learning as Ideology Critique. In Jack Mezirow and Associates (eds): *Learning as Transformation: Critical Perspectives on a Theory in Progress*. San Francisco, CA: Jossey-Bass.

—— (2000b): Adult Cognition as a Dimension of Lifelong Learning. In John Field and Mal Leicester (eds): *Lifelong Learning: Education Across the Lifespan*. London: Routledge-Falmer.

—— (2005): *The Power of Critical Theory: Liberating Adult Learning and Teaching*. San Francisco, CA: Jossey-Bass.

Brostrøm, Stig (1977): *Struktureret pædagogik*. Copenhagen: Pædagogisk Landsforbund. [Structured pedagogy].

Bruner, Jerome S. (1960): *The Process of Education*. Cambridge, MA: Harvard University Press.

—— (1966): *Toward a Theory of Instruction*. Cambridge, MA: Harvard University Press.

—— (1971): *The Relevance of Education*. New York: Norton.

—— (1986): *Actual Minds, Possible Worlds*. Cambridge, MA: Harvard University Press.

—— (1990): *Acts of Meaning*. Cambridge, MA: Harvard University Press.

—— (1996): *The Culture of Education*. Cambridge, MA: Harvard University Press.

—— (2002): *Making Stories: Law, Literature, Life*. Cambridge, MA: Harvard University Press.

——, Goodnow, Jacqueline J. and Austin, George A. (1956): *A Study of Thinking*. New York: Wiley.

——, Olver, Rose, R., Greenfield, Patricia M. and Hornsby, Joan Rigley (1966): *Studies in Cognitive Growth*. New York: Wiley.

Brückner, Peter (1972): *Zur Sozialpsychologie des Kapitalismus*. Frankfurt a.M.: Europäsche Verlagsanstalt. [The social psychology of capitalism].

Bühler, Charlotte (1933): *Der menschliche Lebenslauf als psychologisches Problem*. Leipzig: Hirzel. [The human life course as a psychological problem].

—— (1968): The General Structure of the Human Life Cycle. In Charlotte Bühler and Fred Massarik (eds): *The Course of Human Life*. New York: Springer.

Burr, Vivian (1995): *An Introduction to Social Constructionism*. London: Routledge.

Buss, David M. (1999): *Evolutionary Psychology: The New Science of the Mind*. Boston, MA: Allyn and Bacon.

Butler, Judith (1993): *Bodies that Matter: On the Discursive Limits of 'Sex'*. New York: Routledge.

—— (2004): *Undoing Gender*. New York: Routledge.

Campos, Joseph J., Barrett, Karen Caplovitz, Lamb, Michael E., Goldsmith, H. Hill and Stenberg, Craig (1983): Socioemotional Development. In Paul H. Mussen (ed.): *Handbook of Child Psychology*. New York: Wiley, 4th edition.

Candy, Philip C. (1991): *Self-Direction for Lifelong Learning: A Comprehensive Guide to Theory and Practice*. San Francisco, CA: Jossey-Bass.

Castells, Manuel (1996): *The Rise of the Network Society*. Cambridge, MA: Blackwell.

CEDEFOP (European Centre for the Development of Vocational Training) (2003): *Lifelong Learning: Citizens' Views*. Luxembourg: Office for Official Publications of the EU.

Chaiklin, Seth (ed.) (2001): *The Theory and Practice of Cultural-Historical Psychology*. Århus: Aarhus University Press.

——, Hedegaard, Mariane and Jensen, Uffe Juul (eds) (1999): *Activity Theory and Social Practice: Cultural-Historical Approaches*. Århus: Aarhus University Press.

Chodorow, Nancy (1978): *The Reproduction of Mothering: Psychoanalysis and the Psychology of Gender*. Berkeley, CA: University of California Press.

Christensen, Lone Rahbek (1987): *Hver vore veje*. Copenhagen: Etnologisk Forum. [Each our ways].

Christiansen, Frederik Voetmann (1999): Exemplarity and Educational Planning. In Henning Salling Olesen and Jens Højgaard Jensen (eds): *Project Studies*. Copenhagen: Roskilde University Press.

Christie, Nils (1971): *Hvis skolen ikke fantes*. Oslo/Copenhagen: Christian Ejlers. [If school did not exist].

Coffield, Frank (2003): The Hole in the Heart of Current Policies of Lifelong Learning. In CEDEFOP (European Centre for the Development of Vocational Training) (ed.): *Policy, Practice and Partnership: Getting to Work on Lifelong Learning*. Thessaloniki: CEDEFOP.

——, Moseley, David, Hall, Elaine and Ecclestone, Kathryn (2004): *Learning Styles and Pedagogy in post-16 Learning: A Systematic and Critical Review*. London: Learning and Skill Research Centre.

Cole, Michael (1996): *Cultural Psychology: A Once and Future Discipline*. Cambridge, MA: Harvard University Press.

Cole, Michael and Cole, Sheila R. (1989): *The Development of Children*. New York: Scientific American.

—— and Scribner, Sylvia (1978): Introduction. In Lev S. Vygotsky: *Mind in Society: The Development of Higher Psychological Processes*. Cambridge, MA: Harvard University Press.

—— and Wertsch, James V. (1996): *Contemporary Implications of Vygotsky and Luria*. Worcester, MA: Clark University Press.

Coleman, James S., Campbell, Ernest Q., Hobson, Carol J., McPartland, James, Mood, Alexander M. Weinfeld, Frederic D. and York, Robert L. (1966): *Equality of Educational Opportunity*. Washington, DC: National Center for Educational Statistics.

Colley, Helen, Hodkinson, Phil and Malcolm, Janice (2003): *Informality and Formality in Learning*. London: Learning and Skills Research Centre.

Cronbach, Lee J. and Snow, R. (1977): *Aptitudes and Instructional Methods*. New York: Irvington.

Damasio, Antonio R. (1994): *Descartes' Error: Emotion, Reason and the Human Brain*. New York: Grosset/Putnam.

—— (1999): *The Feeling of What Happens: Body, Emotion and the Making of Consciousness*. London: Vintage.

Darwin, Charles (1958 [1859]): *The Origin of Species by Means of Natural Selection or the Preservation of Favoured Races in the Struggle for Life*. London: Oxford University Press.

Descartes, René (1967 [1637]): *The Philosophical Works of Descartes*. Cambridge, UK: Cambridge University Press, 3rd reprint.

Dewey, John (1902): *The Child and the Curriculum*. Chicago, IL: Chicago University Press.

—— (1916): *Democracy and Education*. New York: Macmillan.

—— (1965 [1938]): *Experience and Education*. New York: Collier Books.

Dillenbourg, Pierre (1999): What do you Mean by Collaborative Learning? In Pierre Dillenbourg (ed.): *Collaborative Learning – Cognitive and Computational Approaches*. Oxford: Elsevier Science.

Dirckinck-Holmfeld, Lone (1990): *Kommunikation på trods og på tværs. Projektpædagogik og datamatkonferencer i fjernundervisning*. Ålborg: PICNIC-nyt nr. 9, Aalborg Universitet. [Communication in Defiance and Across Borders: Project Education and Computer Conferences in Distant Education].

―― (2000): Virtuelle læringsmiljøer på et projektpædagogisk grundlag. In Simon Hejlesen (ed.): *At undervise med IKT*. Copenhagen: Samfundslitteratur. [Virtual learning environments based on project education].

―― and Fibiger, Bo (eds) (2002): *Learning in Virtual Environments*. Copenhagen: Samfundslitteratur.

――, Tolsby, Håkon and Nyvang, Tom (2002): E-læring systemer i arbejdsrelateret projektpædagogik. In Knud Illeris (ed.): *Udspil om læring i arbejdslivet*. Copenhagen: Roskilde University Press. [E-learning systems in work related project education].

Doll, Willam E. (1993): *A Post-Modern Perspective on Curriculum*. New York: Teachers College Press.

Dominicé, Pierre (2000): *Learning from Our Lives*. San Francisco, CA: Jossey-Bass.

Donaldson, Margaret (1986): *Children's Minds*. London: Fontana, 2nd edition.

Dreyfus, Hubert and Dreyfus, Stuart (1986): *Mind over Machine*. New York: Free Press.

Duncker, Karl (1945 [1935]): *On Problem-Solving*. The American Psychological Association, Psychological Monographs, 5.

Dunn, Rita (1996): *How to Implement and Supervise a Learning Style Program*. Alexandria, VA: Association for Supervision and Curriculum Development.

―― and Dunn, Kenneth (1978): *Teaching Students Through their Individual Learning Styles: A Practical Approach*. Reston, VA: Prentice-Hall.

―― and ―― (1992): *Teaching Elementary Students Through their Individual Learning Styles: Practical Approaches for Grades 3–6*. Boston, MA: Allyn & Bacon.

―― and ―― (1993): *Teaching Secondary Students Through their Individual Learning Styles: Practical Approaches for Grades 7–12*. Boston, MA: Allyn & Bacon.

―― and Griggs, Shirley (eds) (2003): *Synthesis of the Dunn and Dunn Learning-Style Model Research*. New York: St John's University.

Ebbinghaus, Hermann (1964 [1885]): *Memory: A Contribution to Experimental Psychology*. New York: Dover.

Elger, Christian E., Friederici, Angela, Koch, Christof, Luhmann, Heiko, von der Malsburg, Christoph, Menzel, Randolf, Monyer, Hannah, Rösler, Frank, Roth, Gerhard, Scheich, Henning and Singer, Wolf (2004): Das Manifest – Elf führende Neurowissenschaftler über gegenwart und Zukunft der Hirnforschung. *Gehirn & Geist*, 6. [The manifest – eleven neuroscientists on the present situation and the future of brain research].

Elkjær, Bente (1999): In Search of a Social Learning Theory. In Mark Easterby-Smith, John Borgoyne and Luis Araujo (eds): *Organizational Learning and the Learning Organization*. London: Sage.

―― (2002): E-læring på arbejdspladsen. In Knud Illeris (ed.): *Udspil om læring i arbejdslivet*. Copenhagen: Roskilde University Press. [E-learning at the workplace].

——— (2005): *Når læring går på arbejde: et pragmatisk blik på læring i arbejdslivet.* Copenhagen: Samfundslitteratur. [When learning goes to work: a pragmatic view on learning in working life].

Ellström, Per-Erik (2001): Integrating Learning and Work: Conceptual Issues and Critical Conditions. *Human Resource Development Quarterly*, 4, pp. 421–436.

Engeström, Yrjö (1987): *Learning by Expanding: An Activity-Theoretical Approach to Developmental Research.* Helsinki: Orienta-Kunsultit.

——— (1993): Developmental Studies of Work as a Testbench of Activity Theory: The Case of Primary Care and Medical Practice. In Seth Chaiklin and Jean Lave (eds): *Understanding Practice: Perspectives on Activity and Context.* New York: Cambridge University Press.

——— (1994): *Training for Change: New Approach to Instruction and Learning in Working Life.* Geneva: ILO.

——— (1996): Developmental Work Research as Educational Research. *Nordisk Pedagogik*, 3, pp. 131–143.

———, Miettinen, Reijo and Punamäki, Raija-Leena (eds) (1999): *Perspectives on Activity Theory.* Cambridge, MA: Cambridge University Press.

Eraut, Michael (1994): *Developing Professional Knowledge and Competence.* London: Falmer.

Erikson, Erik H. (1968): *Identity, Youth and Crisis.* New York: Norton.

———, Erikson, Joan M. and Kivnick, H.O. (1986): *Vital Involvement in Old Age.* New York: Norton.

EU Commission (2000): *Memorandum on Lifelong Learning.* Brussels: EU.

Evans, Karen, Hodkinson, Phil and Unwin, Lorna (eds) (2002): *Working to Learn – Transforming Learning in the Workplace.* London: Kogan Page.

Festinger, Leon (1957): *A Theory of Cognitive Dissonance.* Stanford, CA: Stanford University Press.

Field, John (2002): *Lifelong Learning and the New Educational Order.* Stoke-on-Trent: Trentham Books, 2nd edition.

Finger, Matthias (1995): Adult Education and Society Today. *International Journal of Lifelong Education*, 2 (14), pp. 110–119.

——— and Asún, José Manuel (2001): *Adult Education at the Crossroads: Learning Our Way Out.* London: Zed.

Flavell, John H. (1963): *The Developmental Psychology of Jean Piaget.* New York: Van Nostrand.

Freire, Paulo (1970): *Pedagogy of the Oppressed.* New York: Seabury.

——— (1971): *Cultural Action for Freedom.* Cambridge, MA: Harvard Educational Review.

Freud, Anna (1942 [1936]): *The Ego and the Mechanisms of Defence.* London: Hogarth Press.

Freud, Sigmund (1940 [1915]): Triebe und Triebschicksale. In Sigmund Freud: *Gesammelte Werke I.* London: Imago.

——— (1940 [1894]): Die Abwehr-Neuropsychosen. In Sigmund Freud: *Gesammelte Werke I.* London: Imago.

——— (1959 [1921]): *Group Psychology and the Analysis of the Ego.* London: Pelican Freud Library.

——— (1962 [1927]): *The Future of an Illusion.* London: Hogarth Press.

—— and Breuer, Joseph (1956 [1895]): *Studies on Hysteria*. London: Pelican Freud Library.

Furth, Hans G. (1981 [1969]): *Piaget and Knowledge: Theoretical Foundations*. Chicago, IL: Chicago University Press, 2nd edition.

—— (1987): *Knowledge As Desire*. New York: Columbia University Press.

Gagné, Robert M. (1970 [1965]): *The Conditions of Learning*. New York: Holt, Rinehart and Winston, 2nd edition.

Gardner, Howard (1983): *Frames of Mind: The Theory of Multiple Intelligences*. New York: Basic Books.

—— (1991): *The Unschooled Mind: How Children Think and How Schools Should Teach*. New York: Basic Books.

—— (1993): *Multiple Intelligences: The Theory in Practice*. New York: Basic Books.

—— (1999): *Intelligence Reframed. Multiple Intelligences for the 21st Century*. New York: Basic Books.

Garrick, John (1998): *Informal Learning in the Workplace: Unmasking Human Resource Development*. London: Routledge.

Gaulin, Steven J.C. and McBurney, Donald H. (2001): *Psychology: An Evolutionary Approach*. Englewood Cliffs, NJ: Prentice Hall.

Gergen, Kenneth J. (1991): *The Saturated Self: Dilemmas of Identity in Contemporary Life*. New York: Basic Books.

—— (1994): *Realities and Relationships*. Cambridge, MA: Harvard University Press.

Gherardi, Silvia (2006): *Organizational Knowledge: The Texture of Workplace Learning*. Oxford: Blackwell.

Giddens, Anthony (1990): *The Consequences of Modernity*. Stanford, CA: Stanford University Press.

—— (1991): *Modernity and Self-Identity*. Cambridge, UK: Polity Press.

—— (1993): *Sociology*. Cambridge, UK: Polity Press.

Giroux, Henry A. (1981): *Ideology, Culture, and the Process of Schooling*. Philadelphia, PA: Temple University Press.

—— (1983): *Theory and Resistance in Education: Towards a Pedagogy for the Opposition*. London: Heinemann.

—— (1988): *Schooling and the Struggle for Public Life: Critical Pedagogy in the Modern Age*. Minneapolis, MN: University of Minnesota Press.

—— (ed.) (1997): *Pedagogy and the Politics of Hope: Theory, Culture and Schooling – A Critical Reader*. Boulder, CO: Westview Press.

Gogtay, Nitin – *et al.* (2004): Dynamic Mapping of Human Cortical Development during Childhood through Early Adulthood. *Proceedings of the National Academy of Sciences of the USA*, 101 (21), pp. 8174–8179.

Goldberg, Arnold (ed.) (1978): *The Psychology of the Self*. New York: International Universities Press.

Goldberg, Elkhonon (2001): *The Executive Brain: Frontal Lobes and the Civilized Mind*. New York: Oxford University Press.

—— (2005): *The Wisdom Paradox: How Your Mind can Grow Stronger as Your Brain gets Older*. New York: Gotham Books.

Goldberger, Nancy Rule, Tarule, Jill Mattuck, Clinchy, Blythe McVicker and Belenky, Mary Field (eds) (1996): *Knowledge, Difference, and Power: Essays Inspired by Women's Ways of Knowing*. New York: Basic Books.

Goleman, Daniel (1995): *Emotional Intelligence: Why it can Matter More than IQ*. London: Bloomsbury.

—— (1998): *Working with Emotional Intelligence*. London: Bloomsbury.

——, Boyatzis, Richard and McKee, Annie (2002): *Primal Leadership*. Boston, MA: Harvard Business School Press.

Greenfield, Patricia and Lave, Jean (1982): Cognitive Aspects of Informal Education. In Daniel A. Wagner and Harold W. Stevenson (eds): *Cultural Perspectives on Child Development*. San Francisco, CA: Freeman and Company.

Griffin, Peg and Cole, Michael (1984): Current Activity for the Future: The Zo-Ped. In Barbara Rogoff and James V. Wertsch (eds): *Children's Learning in the 'Zone of Proximal Development'*. San Francisco, CA: Jossey-Bass.

Guilford, Joy P. (1967): *The Nature of Human Intelligence*. New York: McGraw-Hill.

Habermas, Jürgen (1971): *Thesen zur Theorie der Sozialisation*. Frankfurt a.M.: Limit-Druck. [Theses on the theory of socialisation].

—— (1984–87 [1981]): *The Theory of Cummunicative Action*. Cambridge, UK: Polity Press.

—— (1988 [1963]): *Theory and Practice*. Cambridge, UK: Polity Press.

—— (1989a [1968]): *Knowledge and Human Interest*. Cambridge, UK: Polity Press.

—— (1989b [1962]): *The Structural Transformation of the Public Sphere*. Cambridge, UK: Polity Press.

Hansen, Erik Jørgen (1972): *Lighed gennem uddannelse*. Copenhagen: Socialforskningsinstituttet. [Equality through education].

Hansen, Kirsten Grønbæk (1998): Er læring mere end situeret praksis? *Dansk pædagogisk tidsskrift*, 2, pp. 6–16. [Is learning more than situated practice?].

Hansen, Mogens (2005): De mange intelligenser – mangfoldighedens pædagogik. In Mogens Hansen, Per Fibæk Laursen and Anne Maj Nielsen: *Perspektiver på de mange intelligenser*. Copenhagen: Roskilde University Press. [Multiple intelligences – a pedagogy of multitude].

——, Thomsen, Poul and Varming, Ole (1997): *Psykologisk-pædagogisk ordbog*. Copenhagen: Gyldendal, 11th edition. [Psychological-pedagogical dictionary].

Harris, Judy (2000): *The Recognition of Prior Learning: Power, Pedagogy, and Possibility – Conceptual and Implementation Guides*. Pretoria: Human Sciences Research Council.

Hedegaard, Mariane and Hansen, Vagn Rabøl (1992): *En virksom pædagogik: kritik og alternativ praksis*. Århus: Århus Universitetsforlag. [Activity pedagogy: critique and alternative practice].

Hegel, Georg Wilhelm Friedrich (1967 [1807]): *The Phenomenology of Mind*. New York: Harper.

Hermansen, Mads (1996): *Læringens univers*. Århus: Klim. [The universe of learning].

Heron, John (1992): *Feeling and Personhood: Psychology in Another Key*. London: Sage.

Hiemstra, Roger and Sisco, Burton (1990): *Individualizing Instruction: Making Learning Personal, Empowering, and Successful*. San Francisco, CA: Jossey-Bass.

Hilgard, Ernest R. (1980): The Trilogy of Mind: Cognition, Conation and Emotion. *Journal of the History of the Behavioral Sciences*, 16, pp. 107–117.

Hodkinson, Phil, Hodkinson, Heather, Evans, Karen, Kersh, Natasha, Fuller, Alison, Unwin, Lorna and Senker, Peter (2004): The Significance of Individual Biography in Workplace Learning. *Studies in the Education of Adults*, 1 (36), pp. 6–24.

Højrup, Thomas (1983): *The Concept of Life-Mode*. Lund: Ethnologia Scandinavica.

Holford, John, Jarvis, Peter and Griffin, Colin (eds) (1998): *International Perspectives on Lifelong Learning*. London: Kogan Page.

Holzkamp, Klaus (1972): *Kritische Psychologie – Vorbereitende Arbeiten*. Frankfurt a.M.: Fischer. [Critical psychology: preliminary drafts].

—— (1983): *Grundlegung der Psychologie*. Frankfurt a.M.: Campus. [Foundations of psychology].

—— (1995): *Lernen – Subjektwissenschaftliche Grundlegung*. Frankfurt a.M.: Campus. [Learning: the foundation of a science of the subject].

Holzkamp-Osterkamp, Ute (1978): Erkenntnis, Emotionalität, Handlungsfähigkeit. *Forum Kritische Psychologie*, 3. Argument Sonderband AS 28. Berlin: Argument-Verlag. [Recognition, emotionalism, action ability].

Horkheimer, Max and Adorno, Theodor W. (1944): *Dialectic of Enlightenment*. New York: Social Studies Association.

Horner, Matina S. (1974): The Measurement and Behavioral Implications of Fear and Success in Women. In John W. Atkinson and Joel O. Raynor (eds): *Motivation and Achievement*. New York: Wiley.

Illeris, Knud (1981): *Modkvalificeringens pædagogik*. Copenhagen: Unge Pædagoger. [The pedagogy of counter qualification].

—— (1984): Erfaringer med erfaringspædagogikken. *Unge Pædagoger*, 2, pp. 22–33. [Experiences of experiential pedagogy].

—— (1992): The Significance of Educational Strategies. *British Educational Research Journal*, 1, pp. 17–23.

—— (1995): *Læring, udvikling og kvalificering*. Roskilde: The Adult Education Research Group, Roskilde University. [Learning, development and qualification].

—— (1996): *Piaget and Education*. Paper for the Fifth International Conference on Experiential Learning, Cape Town. Roskilde University.

—— (1998): Adult Learning and Responsibility. In Knud Illeris (ed.): *Adult Education in a Transforming Society*. Copenhagen: Roskilde University Press.

—— (1999): Project Work in University Studies: Background and Current Issues. In Henning Salling Olesen and Jens Højgaard Jensen (eds): *Project Studies*. Copenhagen: Roskilde University Press.

—— (2002): *The Three Dimensions of Learning*. Copenhagen: Roskilde University Press/Leicester, UK: NIACE. (American issue 2004: Malabar, FL: Krieger Publishing).

—— (2003a): Learning, Identity and Self Orientation in Youth. *Young – Nordic Journal of Youth Research*, 4 (11), pp. 357–376.

—— (2003b): Adult Education as Experienced by the Learners. *International Journal of Lifelong Education*, 1 (22), pp. 13–23.

—— (2004): *Adult Education and Adult Learning*. Copenhagen: Roskilde University Press/Malabar, FL: Krieger Publishing.

—— (2006): Lifelong Learning and the Low-Skilled. *International Journal of Lifelong Education*, 1 (25), pp. 15–28.

——, Andersen, Vibeke, Kjærsgaard, Christian, Larsen, Kirsten, Olesen, Henning Salling and Ulriksen, Lars (1995): *Almenkvalificering*. Copenhagen: Roskilde University Press. [Generic Qualification].

—— et al. (2004): *Learning in Working Life*. Copenhagen: Roskilde University Press.

Jackson, Philip W. (1990 [1968]): *Life in Classrooms*. New York: Teachers College, Columbia University.

James, William (1890): *The Principles of Psychology I–II*. New York: Holt, Rinehart and Winston.

Jansen, Theo, Finger, Matthias and Wildemeersch, Danny (1998): Lifelong Learning for Responsibility: Exploring the Significance of Aesthetic Rationality for Adult Education. In John Holford, Peter Jarvis and Colin Griffin (eds): *International Perspectives on Lifelong Learning*. London: Kogan Page.

Jarvis, Peter (1987): *Adult Learning in the Social Context*. New York: Croom Helm.

—— (1992): *Paradoxes of Learning: On Becoming an Individual in Society*. San Francisco, CA: Jossey-Bass.

—— (1997): *Ethics and Education for Adults in a Late Modern Society*. Leicester, UK: NIACE.

—— (1999): *International Dictionary of Adult and Continuing Education*. London: Kogan Page, 2nd edition.

—— (2001a): *Learning in Later Life*. London: Kogan Page.

—— (2001b): *The Age of Learning: Education and the Knowledge Society*. London: Kogan Page.

—— (2002): *The Implications of Life-Wide Learning for Lifelong Learning*. Paper presented at the Danish EU Presidency Conference, Elsinore, 9 October.

—— (2004): *Adult Education and Lifelong Learning: Theory and Practice*. London: Routledge-Falmer, 3rd edition.

—— (2005a): Towards a Philosophy of Human Learning: An Existentialist Perspective. In Peter Jarvis and Stella Parker (eds): *Human Learning: An Holistic Approach*. London: Routledge.

—— (2005b): Human Learning: The Interrelationship of the Individual and the Social Structures. In Peter Jarvis and Stella Parker (eds): *Human Learning: An Holistic Approach*. London: Routledge.

—— (2006): *Towards a Comprehensive Understanding of Human Learning*. London: Routledge.

—— (2007): *Globalisation, Lifelong Learning and the Learning Society: Sociological Perspectives*. London: Routledge.

—— and Parker, Stella (eds) (2005): *Human Learning: An Holistic Approach*. London: Routledge.

——, Holford, John and Griffin, Colin (1998): *The Theory and Practice of Learning*. London: Kogan Page.

Jencks, Christopher, Smith, Marshall, Acland, Henry, Bane, Mary Jo, Cohen, David, Gintis, Herbert, Heyns, Barbara and Michelson, Stephan (1972): *Inequality: A Reassessment of the Effect of Family and Schooling in America*. New York: Basic Books.

Jensen, Johan Fjord (1993): *Livsbuen – voksenpsykologi og livsaldre*. Copenhagen: Gyldendal. [The Life Arch].

Joas, Hans (1996 [1992]): *The Creativity of Action*. Cambridge, UK: Polity Press.

Jonsson, Gustav (1969): *Det sociale arvet*. Stockholm: Folksam. [Social heredity].

Jørgensen, Christian Helms and Warring, Niels (2003): Learning in the Workplace: The Interplay between Learning Environments and Biographical Learning Trajectories. In Christian Helms Jørgensen and Niels Warring (eds): *Adult Education and the Labour Market VII B*. Copenhagen: Roskilde University Press.

Jørgensen, Henning, Lassen, Morten, Lind, Jens and Madsen, Morten (1992): *Medlemmer og meninger*. Aalborg: CARMA, Aalborg University. [Members and meanings].

Jørgensen, Per Schultz (1999): Hvad er kompetence? *Uddannelse*, 9, pp. 4–13. [What is competence?].

Judd, Charles H. (1908): The Relation of Special Training to General Intelligence. *Educational Review*, 36, pp. 28–42.

Kant, Immanuel (2002 [1781]): *The Critique of Pure Reason*. Cambridge, UK: Cambridge University Press.

Kegan, Robert (1982): *The Evolving Self*. Cambridge, MA: Harvard University Press.

—— (1994): *In Over Our Heads: The Mental Demands of Modern Life*. Cambridge, MA: Harvard University Press.

—— (2000): What Form Transforms? A Constructive-Developmental Approach to Transformative Learning. In Jack Mezirow *et al.*: *Learning as Transformation: Critical Perspectives on a Theory in Progress*. San Francisco, CA: Jossey-Bass.

Kernberg, Otto (1975): *Borderline Conditions and Pathological Narcissism*. New York: Jason Aronson.

Knowles, Malcolm S. (1970): *The Modern Practice of Adult Education: Andragogy versus Pedagogy*. New York: Associated Press.

—— (1973): *The Adult Learner: A Neglected Species*. Houston, TX: Gulf Publishing.

—— (1975): *Self-Directed Learning*. New York: Association Press.

Knudsen, Herman (1980): *Disciplinering til lønarbejde*. Ålborg: Aalborg Universitetsforlag. [Disciplining for wage labour].

Köhler, Wolfgang (1925 [1917]): *The Mentality of Apes*. Harmondsworth: Penguin.

Kohut, Heinz (1971): *The Analysis of the Self: A Systematic Approach to the Psychoanalytic Treatment of Narcissistic Personality Disorders*. New York: International Universities Press.

—— (1977): *The Restoration of the Self*. New York: International Universities Press.

Kolb, David A. (1984): *Experiential Learning: Experience as the Source of Learning and Development*. Englewood Cliffs, NJ: Prentice-Hall.

—— and Fry, Roger (1975): Toward an Applied Theory of Experiential Learning. In Cary L. Cooper (eds): *Theories of Group Processes*. London: Wiley.

Krech, David, Crutchfield, Richard S. and Bellachey, Egerton L. (1962): *Individual in Society*. New York: McGraw-Hill.

Kristensen, Jens Erik (2001): Citation from an interview by John Villy Olsen: Et begreb kom snigende. *Folkeskolen*, 15, pp. 6–8. [A concept came sneaking].

Krovoza, Alfred (1976): *Produktion und Sozialisation*. Frankfurt a.M.: Europäische Verlagsanstalt. [Production and socialisation].

Kupferberg, Feiwel (1996): *Kreativt kaos i projektarbejdet*. Ålborg: Aalborg Universitetsforlag. [Creative chaos in project studies].

Kvale, Steinar (1980): *Spillet om karakterer i gymnasiet*. Copenhagen: Munksgaard. [The grading game in upper secondary school].

Lasch, Christopher (1978): *The Culture of Narcissism: American Life in an Age of Diminishing Expectations*. New York: Norton.

Lave, Jean and Wenger, Etienne (1991): *Situated Learning: Legitimate Peripheral Participation*. New York: Cambridge University Press.

LeDoux, Joseph (1996): *The Emotional Brain: The Mysterious Underpinning of Emotional Life*. New York: Simon and Schuster.

—— (2002): *Synaptic Self: How Our Brains Become Who We Are*. New York: Penguin.

Leithäuser, Thomas (1976): *Formen des Alltagsbewusstseins*. Frankfurt a.M.: Campus. [The forms of everyday consciousness].

—— (1998): The Problem of Authoritarianism: Approaches to a Further Development of a Traditional Concept. In Knud Illeris (ed.): *Adult Education in a Transforming Society*. Copenhagen: Roskilde University Press.

—— (2000): Subjectivity, Lifeworld and Work Organization. In Knud Illeris (ed.): *Adult Education in the Perspective of the Learners*. Copenhagen: Roskilde University Press.

—— and Volmerg, Birgit (1977): Die Entwicklung einer empirischen Vorschungsperspektive aus der Theorie des Alltagsbewusstseins. In Thomas Leithäuser *et al.* (eds): *Entwurf zu einer Empirie des Alltagsbewusstseins*. Frankfurt a.M.: Suhrkamp. [The development of an empirical research perspective from the theory of everyday consciousness].

Leontjev, Aleksei N. (1981 [1959]): *Problems of the Development of the Mind*. Moscow: Progress. [Collected manuscripts from the 1930s].

Lindeman, Eduard C. (1926): *The Meaning of Adult Education*. Montreal: Harvest House.

Lockyer, Andrew, Crick, Bernard and Annette, John (eds) (2003): *Education for Democratic Citizenship: Issues of Theory and Practice*. Aldershot: Ashgate.

Lorenzer, Alfred (1972): *Zur Begründung einer materialistischen Sozialisationstheorie*. Frankfurt a.M.:Suhrkamp. [Foundations of a materialistic theory of socialisation].

Lowen, Alexander (1967): *The Betrayal of the Body*. New York: Collier Books.

—— and Lowen, Lesley (1977): *The Way to Vibrant Health*. London: Harper & Row.

Luhmann, Niklas (1995 [1984]): *Social Systems*. Stanford, CA: Stanford University Press.

Luria, Aleksander R. (1976 [1974]): *Cognitive Development*. Cambridge, MA: Harvard University Press. [Based on empirical research in the 1930s].

Lyotard, Jean-François (1984 [1979]): *The Postmodern Condition: A Report on Knowledge*. Manchester: Manchester University Press.

Lysgaard, Sverre (1967): *Arbeiderkollektivet*. Oslo: Universitetsforlaget. [The workers' community].

Madsen, K.B. (1966): *Almen Psykologi I*. Copenhagen: Gyldendal. [General psychology].

Mager, Robert F. (1961): On the Sequencing of Instructional Content. *Psychological Reports*, 9, pp. 405–413.

Mahler, Margaret S., Pine, Fred and Bergman, Anni (1975): *The Psychological Birth of the Human Infant*. New York: Basic Books.

Marcuse, Herbert (1955): *Eros and Civilization*. Boston, MA: Beacon.

—— (1964): *One Dimensional Man*. London: Routledge & Kegan Paul.

Marsick, Victoria J. and Watkins, Karen E. (1990): *Informal and Incidental Learning in the Workplace*. London: Routledge.

Maslow, Abraham (1954): *Motivation and Personality*. New York: Harper & Row.

—— (1971): *The Farther Reaches of Human Nature*. New York: Viking Press.

Maturana, Humberto R. and Varela, Francisco J. (1980): *Autopoiesis and Cognition: The Realization of the Living*. Dordrecht: Reidel.

McClelland, David C. (1961): *The Achieving Society*. Princeton, NJ: Van Nostrand.

—— and Winter, David G. (1969): *Motivating Economic Achievement*. New York: The Free Press.

——, Atkinson, John W., Clark, Russell A. and Lowell, Edgar L. (1953): *The Achievement Motive*. New York: Appleton-Century-Croft.

McDougall, William (1963 [1908]): *An Introduction to Social Psychology*. London: Methuen.

Merleau-Ponty, Maurice (1962 [1945]): *The Phenomenology of Perception*. London: Routledge & Kegan Paul.

Merriam, Sharan B. and Caffarella, Rosemary S. (1999): *Learning in Adulthood: A Comprehensive Guide*. San Francisco, CA: Jossey-Bass, 2nd edition.

Mezirow, Jack (1978): *Education for Perspective Transformation: Women's Re-entry Programs in Community Colleges*. New York: Teachers College, Columbia University.

—— (1990): How Critical Reflection Triggers Transformative Learning. In Jack Mezirow *et al.*: *Fostering Critical Reflection in Adulthood*. San Francisco, CA: Jossey-Bass.

—— (1991): *Transformative Dimensions of Adult Learning*. San Francisco, CA: Jossey-Bass.

—— (1998): On Critical Reflection. *Adult Education Quarterly*, 3, pp. 185–198.

—— (2000): Learning to Think Like an Adult: Core Conceptions of Transformation Theory. In Jack Mezirow and Associates (eds): *Learning as Transformation: Critical Perspectives on a Theory in Progress*. San Francisco, CA: Jossey-Bass.

Montola, Markus and Stenros, Jaakko (2004): *Beyond Role and Play: Tools, Toys and Theory for Harnessing the Imagination*. Helsinki: Ropecon.

Mortimore, Peter, Sammons, Pamela, Stoll, Louise, Lewis, David and Ecob, Russell (1988): *School Matters: The Junior Years*. Wells: Open Books.

Musgrove, Frank (1965): *Youth and the Social Order*. Bloomington, IN: Indiana University Press.

Myers, Isabel Briggs (1980): *Gifts Differing: Understanding Personality Type*. Palo Alto, CA: Davies-Black Publishing.

Negt, Oskar (1971 [1968]): *Soziologisches Phantasie und exemplarisches Lernen*. Frankfurt a.M.: Europäische Verlagsanstalt. [Sociological imagination and exemplary learning].

—— and Kluge, Alexander (1993 [1972]): *Public Sphere and Experience*. Minneapolis, MN: University of Minnesota Press.

Nicolini, Davide, Gherardi, Silvia and Yanow, Dvora (eds) (2003): *Knowing in Organizations*. New York: M.E. Sharpe.

Nielsen, Harriet Bjerrum and Rudberg, Monica (1994 [1991]): *Psychological Gender and Modernity*. Oslo: Scandinavian University Press.

Nissen, Thomas (1970): *Indlæring og pædagogik*. Copenhagen: Munksgaard. [Learning and pedagogy].

Næss, Arne (1963 [1962]): *Filosofiens Historie II – fra middelalder til nyere tid*. Copenhagen: Vintens Forlag. [The history of philosophy].

OECD (1996): *Lifelong Learning for All*. Paris: OECD.

—— (2000): *Knowledge Management in the Learning Society*. Paris: OECD. Centre for Educational Research and Innovation.

—— (2001): *Cities and Regions in the New Learning Economy*. Paris: OECD. Centre for Educational research and Innovation.

—— (2002): *Understanding the Brain: Towards a New Learning Science*. Paris: OECD Publications Service.

Olesen, Henning Salling (1981): *Eksemplariske læreprocesser og arbejderuddannelse.* Unge Pædagoger, 2, pp. 13–26. [Exemplary learning processes and the education of workers].

—— (1989 [1985]): *Adult Education and Everyday Life.* Roskilde: The Adult Education Research Group, Roskilde University.

Olsen, Ole Andkjær and Køppe, Simo (1981): *Freuds psykoanalyse.* Copenhagen: Gyldendal. [Freud's psychoanalysis].

Pavlov, Ivan P. (1927): *Conditioned Reflexes.* New York: Oxford University Press.

Piaget, Jean (1946): *La formation du symbole chez l'enfant.* Neuchâtel: Delachaux et Nestlé. [Children's formation of symbols].

—— (1951 [1945]): *Plays, Dreams and Imitation in Childhood.* New York: Norton.

—— (1952 [1936]): *The Origin of Intelligence in Children.* New York: International Universities Press.

—— (1959 [1926]): *The Psychology of Intelligence.* London: Routledge & Kegan Paul.

—— (1967 [1964]): *Six Psychological Studies.* New York: Random House.

—— (1980a [1974]): *Adaptation and Intelligence: Organic Selection and Phenocopy.* Chicago, IL: University of Chicago Press.

—— (1980b): *Recent Studies in Genetic Epistemology.* Cahiers de la foundation des archives Jean Piaget, 1.

—— (1981): *Intelligence and Affectivity: Their Relationship During Child Development.* Palo Alto, CA: Annual Reviews Inc.

Pinar, William F., Reynolds, William M., Slattery, Patrick and Taubman, Peter M. (1995): *Understanding Curriculum.* New York: Peter Lang.

Polanyi, Michael (1966): *The Tacit Dimension.* New York: Doubleday.

Rainbird, Helen, Fuller, Alison and Munro, Anne (eds) (2004): *Workplace Learning in Context.* London: Routledge.

Reich, Wilhelm (1969a [1933]): *Character Analysis.* London: Vision.

—— (1969b [1933]): *The Mass Psychology of Fascism.* New York: Farrer, Strauss & Giroux.

Rogers, Carl R. (1951): *Client-Centered Therapy.* Boston, MA: Houghton-Mifflin.

—— (1959): A Theory of Therapy, Personality, and Interpersonal Relationships, as Developed in the Client-Centered Framework. In Sigmund Koch (ed.): *Psychology: A Study of a Science, Vol. III.* New York: McGraw-Hill.

—— (1961): *On Becoming a Person.* Boston, MA: Houghton-Mifflin.

—— (1969): *Freedom to Learn.* Columbus, OH: Charles E. Merrill.

Rogoff, Barbara (2003): *The Cultural Nature of Human Development.* Oxford: Oxford University Press.

—— and Lave, Jean (eds) (1984): *Everyday Cognition: Its Development in Social Context.* Cambridge, MA: Harvard University Press.

—— and Wertsch, James W. (eds) (1984): *Children's Learning in the 'Zone of Proximate Development'.* San Francisco, CA: Jossey Bass.

Rutter, Michael, Maughan, Barbara, Mortimor, Peter and Ouston, Janet (1979): *Fifteen Thousand Hours.* London: Open Books.

Salovey, Peter and Mayer, John D. (1990): Emotional Intelligence. *Imagination, Cognition and Personality,* 3 (9), pp. 185–211.

Scheich, Henning (2002): *Lern- und Gedächtnisforschung.* http://leb.bildung-rp.de/info/veranstaltungen/bericht/2002-11-20_ggt_scheich.pdf [Research on learning and memory].

Schön, Donald A. (1983): *The Reflective Practitioner: How Professionals Think in Action*. New York: Basic Books.

—— (1987): *Educating the Reflective Practitioner*. San Francisco, CA: Jossey-Bass.

—— (1991): *The Reflective Turn: Case Studies in and on Educational Practice*. New York: Teachers College Press.

Schuller, Tom (1998): Age and Generation in Life Course Modelling. In Kirsten Weber (ed.): *Life History, Gender and Experience*. Roskilde: The Adult Education Research Group, Roskilde University.

Scribner, Sylvia and Cole, Michael (1974): *Culture and Thought: A Psychological Introduction*. New York: Wiley.

Senge, Peter (1990): *The Fifth Discipline: The Art and Practice of the Learning Organization*. New York: Doubleday.

Sennett, Richard (1998): *The Corrosion of Character*. New York: Norton.

Shayer, Michael and Adey, Philip (1981): *Towards a Science of Science Teaching*. London: Heinemann Educational.

Simonsen, Birgitte (1976): *Dansk uddannelsespolitik og planlægning*. Roskilde: RUC-forlag. [Danish educational politics and planning].

—— (1994): *Unges forhold til familieliv og kønsroller*. Roskilde: The Adult Education Research Group, Roskilde University. [Young people's relations to family life and sex roles].

—— (1998): Individualisering og demokrati i ungdomsuddannelser – teser om 'De nye unge – de nye voksne'. In Knud Illeris, Birgitte Simonsen and Annegrethe Ahrenkiel: *Udspil om læring og didaktik*. Copenhagen: Roskilde University Press. [Individualisation and democracy in youth education: thesis on 'the new young – the new adults'].

—— (2000): New Young People, New Forms of Consciousness, New Educational Methods. In Knud Illeris (ed.): *Adult Education in the Perspective of the Learners*. Copenhagen: Roskilde University Press.

—— and Illeris, Knud (1989): *De skæve køn, 1 and 2*. Copenhagen: Unge Pædagoger. [The unequal genders].

Skinner, Burrhus F. (1948): *Walden Two*. London: Macmillan.

—— (1968): *The Technology of Teaching*. New York: Appleton-Century-Crofts.

—— (1971). *Beyond Freedom and Dignity*. New York: Knopf.

Solms, Mark and Turnbull, Oliver (2002): *The Brain and the Inner World: An Introduction to the Neuroscience of Subjective Experience*. London: Karnac.

Spearman, Charles (1923): *The Nature of 'Intelligence' and the Principles of Cognition*. London: Macmillan.

Stern, Daniel N. (1985): *The Interpersonal World of the Infant: A View from Psychoanalysis and Developmental Psychology*. New York: Basic Books.

—— (1995): *The Motherhood Constellation: A Unified View of Parent-Infant Psychotherapy*. New York: Basic Books.

—— (2004): *The Present Moment in Psychotherapy and Everyday Life*. New York: Norton.

Sternberg, Robert J. (1996): Styles of Thinking. In Paul B. Baltes and Ursula M. Staudinger (eds): *Interactive Minds: Life-Span Perspectives on the Social Foundation of Cognition*. Cambridge, MA: Cambridge University Press.

Stuart-Hamilton, Ian (2000): *The Psychology of Aging: An Introduction*. London: Jessica Kingsley.

Sugarman, Leonie (2001): *Lifespan Development: Frameworks, Accounts, and Strategies.* Hove, UK: Psychology Press, 2nd edition.

Taba, Hilda (1962): *Curriculum Development: Theory and Practice.* New York: Harcourt, Brace and World.

Tennant, Mark (1997): *Psychology and Adult Learning.* London: Routledge, 2nd edition.

—— (1998): Adult Education as a Technology of the Self. *International Journal of Lifelong Education,* 4 (13), pp. 364–376.

Thorndike, Edward Lee (1931): *Human Learning.* New York: Appleton-Century-Crofts.

—— and Woodworth, Robert S. (1901): The Influence of Improvement in One Mental Function upon the Efficiency of Other Functions. *Psychological Review,* 3, pp. 247–261.

Tough, Allan M. (1967): *Learning without a Teacher: A Study of Tasks and Assistance during Adult Self-Teaching Projects.* Toronto: Ontario Institute for Studies in Education.

—— (1971): *The Adult's Learning Projects: A Fresh Approach to Theory and Practice in Adult Learning.* Toronto: Ontario Institute for Studies in Education.

Tyler, Ralph W. (1950): *Basic Principles of Curriculum and Instruction.* Chicago, IL: University of Chicago Press.

Usher, Robin (1993): Experiential Learning or Learning from Experience: Does it Make a Difference? In David Boud, Ruth Cohen and David Walker (eds): *Using Experience for Learning.* Buckingham: Open University.

—— (1998): Adult Education and Lifelong Learning in Postmodernity. In Knud Illeris (ed.): *Adult Education in a Transforming Society.* Copenhagen: Roskilde University Press.

—— (2000): Impossible Identities, Unstable Boundaries: Managing Experience Differently. In Knud Illeris (ed.): *Adult Education in the Perspective of the Learners.* Copenhagen: Roskilde University Press.

—— and Johnston, Rennie (1996): *Adult Learning and Critical Practices: Toward a Re-theorisation of Experience.* Paper presented at the 5th ICEL Conference, Cape Town. University of Southampton.

——, Bryant, Ian and Johnston, Rennie (1997): *Adult Education and the Postmodern Challenge: Learning Beyond the Limits.* London: Routledge.

Varela, Francisco J., Thompson, Evan and Rosch, Eleanor (1991): *The Embodied Mind: Cognitive Science and Human Experience.* Cambridge, MA: MIT Press.

Vedfelt, Ole (2002): *Ubevidst intelligens: Du ved mere end du tror.* Copenhagen: Gyldendal, 2nd edition. [Unconscious Intelligence: You know more than you believe].

Veen, Ruud van der (2003): Community Development as Citizen Education. *International Journal of Lifelong Education,* 6 (22), pp. 580–596.

Vester, Michael (1969): Solidarisierung als historische Möglichkeit. *Heidelberger Blätter,* 14–16. [Solidarity as a historical possibility].

Volmerg, Birgit, Senghaas-Knobloch, Eva and Leithäuser, Thomas (1986): *Betriebliche Lebenswelt: Einer Sozialpsychologie industrieller Arbeitsverhältnisse.* Opladen: Westdeutscher Verlag. [Life world at work: A social psychology of work conditions in industry].

Volmerg, Ute (1976): Zur Verhältnis von Produktion und Sozialisation am Beispiel industrieller Lohnarbeit. In Thomas Leithäuser and Walter Heinz (eds): *Produktion, Arbeit, Sozialisation*. Frankfurt a.M.: Suhrkamp. [Conditions of production and socialisation in industrial wage labour].

Vygotsky, Lev S. (1978): *Mind in Society: The Development of Higher Psychological Processes*. Cambridge, MA: Harvard University Press.

—— (1986 [1934]): *Thought and Language*. Cambridge, MA: MIT Press.

Watson, John B. and Raynor, R. (1920): Conditioned Emotional Reactions. *Journal of Experimental Psychology*, 3, pp. 1–14.

Webb, Thomas W. and Nielsen, Jørgen Lerche (1996): Experiential Pedagogy. In Henning Salling Olesen and Palle Rasmussen (eds): *Theoretical Issues in Adult Education*. Copenhagen: Roskilde University Press.

Weil, Susan Warner and McGill, Ian (eds) (1989a): *Making Sense of Experiential Learning: Diversity in Theory and Practice*. Buckingham: Open University Press.

—— and —— (1989b): A Framework for Making Sense of Experiential Learning. In Susan Warner Weil and Ian McGill (eds): *Making Sense of Experiential Learning: Diversity in Theory and Practice*. Buckingham: Open University Press.

——, Jansen, Theo and Wildemeersch, Danny (2004): *Unemployed Youth and Social Exclusion in Europe: Learning for Inclusion?* Aldershot: Ashgate.

Wenger, Etienne (1998): *Communities of Practice: Learning, Meaning and Identity*. Cambridge, MA: Cambridge University Press.

—— and Snyder, William (2001): *Harvard Business Review on Organizational Learning*. Boston, MA: Harvard Business School Press.

——, McDermott, Richard and Snyder, William M. (2002): *Cultivating Communities of Practice*. Boston, MA: Harvard Business School Press.

Wertsch, James V. (1981): *The Concept of Activity in Soviet Psychology*. Armont, NY: Sharpe.

—— (1985): *Culture, Communication, and Cognition: Vygotskian Perspectives*. Cambridge, MA: Cambridge University Press.

—— (1998): *Mind as Action*. Oxford: Oxford University Press.

Wildemeersch, Danny (1989): The Principal Meaning of Dialogue for the Construction and Transformation of Reality. In Susan Warner Weil and Ian McGill (eds): *Making Sense of Experiential Learning: Diversity in Theory and Practice*. Buckingham: Open University Press.

—— (1991): Learning from Regularity, Irregularity and Responsibility. *International Journal of Lifelong Education*, 2, pp. 151–158.

—— (1992): Ambiguities of Experiential Learning and Critical Pedagogy. In Danny Wildemeersch and Theo Jansen (eds): *Adult Education, Experiential Learning and Social Change: The Postmodern Challenge*. Haag: VUGA.

—— (1998): Social Learning as Social Change – Social Change as Social Learning. In Knud Illeris (ed.): *Adult Education in a Transforming Society*. Copenhagen: Roskilde University Press.

—— (1999): Paradoxes of Social Learning. In Henning Salling Olesen and Jens Højgaard Jensen (eds): *Project Studies*. Copenhagen: Roskilde University Press.

—— (2000): Lifelong Learning and the Significance of the Interpretive Professional. In Knud Illeris (ed.): *Adult Education in the Perspective of the Learners*. Copenhagen: Roskilde University Press.

—— and Jansen, Theo (eds) (1992): *Adult Education, Experiential Learning and Social Change: The Postmodern Challenge*. Haag: VUGA.

——, Finger, Matthias and Jansen, Theo (1998): *Adult Education for Social Responsibility: Reconciling the Irreconcilable?* Frankfurt a.M.: Peter Lang.

——, Strobants, Veerle and Bron, Michal (eds) (2005): *Active Citizenship and Multiple Identities in Europe: A Learning Outlook*. Frankfurt a.M.: Peter Lang.

Willis, Paul E. (1977): *Learning to Labour: How Working Class Kids get Working Class Jobs*. Farnborough: Saxon House.

Wolf, Alison (2004): Education and economic performance: Simplistic theories and their policy consequences. *Oxford Review of Economic Policy*, 2 (20), pp. 315–333.

Yorks, Lyle and Kasl, Elisabeth (2002): Toward a Theory and Practice for Whole-Person Learning: Reconceptualizing Experience and the Role of Affect. *Adult Education Quarterly*, 3 (52), pp. 176–192.

——, O'Neil, Judy and Marsick, Victoria J. (1999): *Action Learning: Successful Strategies for Individual, Team, and Organizational Development*. Baton Rouge, LA: Academy of Human Resource Development.

Ziehe, Thomas (1975): *Pubertät und Narzissmus*. Frankfurt a.M.: Europäische Verlagsanstalt. [Puberty and narcissism].

—— (1985): Vorwärts in die 50er Jahre? In Dieter Baacke and Wilhelm Heitmeyer (eds): *Neue Widersprüche: Jugendliche in den 80er Jahren*. Munich: Juventa. [Forward into the 1950s?].

—— (1989): *Ambivalenser og mangfoldighed*. Copenhagen: Politisk revy. [Ambivalences and multitude].

—— (1997): Om prisen på selv-relationel viden: Afmystificeringseffekter for pædagogik, skole og identitetsdannelse. In Jens Christian Jacobsen (ed.): *Refleksive læreprocesser*. Copenhagen: Politisk revy. [On the price of self-relational knowledge: De-mystification effects in education, school and identity formation].

—— (1998): Adieu til halvfjerdserne! In Jens Bjerg (eds): *Pædagogik – en grundbog til et fag*. Copenhagen: Reitzel. [Goodbye to the 1970s].

—— (2004): *Øer af intensitet i et hav af rutine: Nye tekster om ungdom, skole og kultur*. Copenhagen: Politisk revy. [Islands of intensity in sea of routine: New texts on youth, school and culture].

—— and Stubenrauch, Herbert (1982): *Plädoyer für ungewöhnliches Lernen*. Reinbek: Rowohlt. [Pleading for unusual learning].

Zucker, Brian J., Johnson, Chantell C. and Flint, Thomas A. (1999): *Prior Learning Assessment: A Guidebook to American Institutional Practices*. Chicago, IL: Council for Adult and Experiential Learning.

Index